"I can think of no better mentor from church history for pastors today than Charles Haddon Spurgeon. In his high view of ministry, love for God's Word, commitment to the church, and countless other areas, he is a model of zeal, faithfulness, and perseverance. In this book, Alex has collected some of Spurgeon's best teaching on pastoral ministry. Put it to work and introduce the next generation of pastors to a mentor they can learn from for the rest of their lives."

Geoff Chang
Assistant Professor of Historical Theology, and Curator of the Spurgeon Library, MBTS; Author, *Spurgeon, the Pastor: Recovering a Biblical and Theological Vision for Ministry*.

"Pastor and Spurgeon scholar Alex DiPrima has served pastors and seminary professors, by putting together ten choice lectures by Charles Haddon Spurgeon from his classic works, *Lectures to My Students* and *An All Around Ministry*. The new formatting, helpful footnotes, and introduction to each lecture, gives pastors, professors, and mentors a tool to train the next generation for faithful gospel ministry. DiPrima's introduction to the book will inspire pastors seeking to mentor men for ministry. I'll be recommending *Servants of Christ, Lovers of Men* as a go-to book for pastoral training."

Phil Newton
Director of Pastoral Care & Mentoring, Pillar Network; Visiting Professor of Pastoral Theology, SWBTS; Author, *40 Questions about Pastoral Ministry* and *Shepherding the Pastor*.

"A ring's setting does not enhance the beauty of a diamond. Rather, it ensures its beauty is visible. *Servants of Christ, Lovers of Men* does the same with selected works from Charles Spurgeon. This fresh look at some of the Prince of Preacher's most helpful pastoral training materials will bless generation to come."

Garrett Kell
Pastor of Del Ray Baptist Church, Alexandria, VA;
Author, *Pure in Heart: Sexual Sin and the Promises of God*

"DiPrima mines gold from the Spurgeon treasury and packages it uniquely in *Servants of Christ, Lovers of Men*. This book is unique because of its brilliant preface, "The Pastor's Pastor," the contextual essays leading each chapter, and numerous citations of sources that Spurgeon marshalled, many from the 19th century. The result? You will feel like you are beside Spurgeon in his study as he prepares these addresses and seated before him in his classroom as he delivers them. Excellent!"

Ray Rhodes
Pastor of Grace Community Church in Dawsonville, GA; Author, *Susie: The Life and Legacy of Susannah Spurgeon* and *Yours, Till Heaven: The Untold Love Story of Charles and Susie Spurgeon*

"With a judicious selection of Charles Spurgeon's counsels to his fellow-pastors and preachers, thoughtfully introduced, Alex DiPrima brings the wisdom and experience of that gifted minister within our reach. For those unaware of Spurgeon's output in this sphere, or daunted by its size and weight, this collection serves either as a taster or a refresher, offering to modern ministers the most widely-applicable and enduringly-relevant of Spurgeon's pastoral guidance. Reading these lectures will not bestow upon you Spurgeon's gifts, but should stir the same graces which he received and enjoyed, and help make your heart happy and your labour lively."

Jeremy Walker
Pastor of Maidenbower Baptist Church, Crawley;
Host, *From the Heart of Spurgeon* podcast

"Reading Charles Spurgeon is always enjoyable and always edifying. This selection of Spurgeon's addresses on pastoral ministry serves up both in heaps. Whether you're a pastor or aspire to be one, I heartily recommend that you let Spurgeon pastor you, and teach you something of how to train pastors, by reading this book. If you're anything like me, you'll have a hard time putting it down."

Bobby Jamieson
Associate Pastor, Capitol Hill Baptist Church, Washington, DC; Author, *The Path to Being a Pastor: A Guide for the Aspiring*

Servants of Christ, Lovers of Men

ALEX DIPRIMA

Servants of Christ, Lovers of Men

Spurgeon on Pastoral Ministry

Servants of God, Lovers of Men

Copyright © 2023 Alex DiPrima

All rights reserved. This book may not be reproduced, in whole or in part, without written permission from the publishers.

H&E Publishing, West Lorne, Ontario
www.hesedandemet.com

Cover and layout design by Chance Faulkner
Front cover image of C.H Spurgeon. Scanned, colourized, and provided from the private collection of Pastor T.D. Hale.

Paperback ISBN: 978-1-77484-124-2
eBook ISBN: 978-1-77484-125-9

Contents

The Pastor's Pastor	1
1. The Minister's Self-Watch	11
2. The Call to the Ministry	37
3 The Preacher's Private Prayer	69
4. Sermons—Their Matter	89
5. The Minister's Fainting Fits	111
6. The Minister's Ordinary Conversation	131
7. Earnestness	149
8. The Blind Eye and the Deaf Ear	177
9. Forward!	201
10. A New Departure	229
Scripture Index	259

The Pastor's Pastor

Charles Haddon Spurgeon (1834–92) loved pastoral ministry. He loved being a pastor himself, and he loved training, befriending, and supporting other pastors in their ministries. He taught regularly on pastoral theology and wrote books full of practical wisdom and guidance for pastors. His grandfather, his father, his brother, and his two sons were all pastors. His wife, Susie, founded a book fund for poor pastors. Simply put, pastoral work shaped Spurgeon's life, his thought, and his closest relationships.

In 1851, when he was only seventeen years old, Spurgeon took his first pastorate in the village of Waterbeach, just outside of Cambridge. Once he accepted this call to pastor, the course of his life was set. When faced with the prospect of pursuing a college degree that would've required him to leave his congregation, he declined, considering the idea of separation from his flock to be intolerable.[1] Only a call to shepherd another congregation in the heart of the world's largest city could induce him to remove. In 1854, he accepted the call to pastor one of London's most historic Baptist churches, then called New Park Street Chapel. It would later change its name under Spurgeon's ministry to the Metropolitan Tabernacle. Spurgeon shepherded this congregation for nearly four decades until his death in 1892. In that time, he would see the membership of the church grow from 232 to 5,311.[2]

In 1857, just a few years into his London ministry, Spurgeon founded what came to be known as the Pastors' College, which

---

[1] C. H. Spurgeon, *C. H. Spurgeon's Autobiography, compiled from His Diary, Letters, and Records by His Wife and his Private* Secretary, vol. 1 (London: Passmore and Alabaster, 1897), 242.

[2] Figures recorded in the annual membership roles in the archives of the Metropolitan Tabernacle in London.

was a two-year training institution for pastors. Spurgeon's work in training ministers through the College was profoundly fruitful by any measure. By 1871, graduates of the Pastors' College accounted for ten percent of all Baptist ministers in England and Wales. By Spurgeon's death in 1892, that number had risen to over twenty percent.[3] During his thirty-five years as College President, Spurgeon trained 863 men for the ministry and helped to plant nearly 200 new churches in Britain alone.[4] It has been estimated that between 1865 and 1887 Spurgeon and his students founded over half of the new Baptist churches in England.[5]

The Pastors' College had three main requirements for admission. First, Spurgeon expected all incoming students to show evidence of true piety and holiness before God. Second, they were required to demonstrate a proven track record in preaching and soul-winning. With only rare exceptions, Spurgeon expected applicants to have at least two years of preaching experience if they were to be admitted. The third requirement was instances of proven usefulness in Christian work. Spurgeon said, "We want soldiers, not fops, earnest labourers, not genteel loiterers. Men who have done nothing up to their time of application to the college, are told to earn their spurs before they are publicly dubbed as knights."[6]

But if these requirements seemed great, from another angle the College's admission standards were set rather low. To start, the College required no pre-requisites in terms of education, not even the ability to read. All were welcome regardless of one's

---

[3] Kenneth D. Brown, *A Social History of the Nonconformist Ministry in England and Wales 1800-1930* (Oxford, UK: Clarendon Press, 1988), 33-34, 98.

[4] D. W. Bebbington, "Spurgeon and British Evangelical Theological Education," in D. G. Hart and R. A. Mohler, Jr., eds., *Theological Education in the Evangelical Tradition* (Grand Rapids, MI: Baker, 1996), 221; Peter J. Morden, *C. H. Spurgeon: The People's Preacher* (Farnham, UK: CWR, 2009), 151.

[5] Morden, *C. H. Spurgeon: The People's Preacher*, 151.

[6] C. H. Spurgeon, *Lectures to My Students*, First Series (London: Passmore and Alabaster, 1881), 34.

educational background. Furthermore, with only rare exception, the education offered at the College was provided entirely free of charge. More than that, Spurgeon saw to it that basic needs like housing, clothing, books, basic health care, and even pocket money were provided for the students.[7] Spurgeon determined from the outset that educational and financial disadvantages would not hinder men from entering the College.[8]

All of these standards, taken together, attracted exactly the sort of men Spurgeon was after—common men from the ordinary ranks of society who were marked by godliness of character, evident preaching ability, and a readiness to give their all in service to Christ and his church. To such men, Spurgeon was utterly devoted. He gave his best energies to training, supporting, and sending them all over England and the world.

Spurgeon's classic work, *Lectures to My Students*,[9] stands as a lasting testament to his passion for training pastors. These lectures were delivered to the students of the Pastors' College and later compiled for publication. It was Spurgeon's custom, when able, to deliver an extemporaneous lecture on Friday afternoon to the assembled student body of the College. The focus of these lectures was on pastoral theology and practical pastoral issues. They embody Spurgeon's ideals for pastoral ministry, and focus on spiritual devotion, preaching, and practical leadership.

Spurgeon's love and care for the pastors he trained did not end once they graduated. He continued to keep in touch with them, pray for them, and provide counsel and support for them. He developed a robust network of pastors that convened annually at what was known as the College Conference, an invite-only

---

[7] Arnold Dallimore, *Spurgeon: A New Biography* (Carlisle, PA: Banner of Truth, 1985), 105.

[8] Bebbington, "Spurgeon and British Evangelical Theological Education," 224–228.

[9] C. H. Spurgeon, *Lectures to My Students*, 3 vols. (London: Passmore and Alabaster, 1881-1894).

gathering of current and former students of the Pastors' College. The conference usually spanned three or four days and included reports from men who had gone out from the College, addresses by various pastors and leaders within the group, and special times for prayer and fellowship among the men. It was Spurgeon's task as President of the College Conference to bring the annual President's address. He regarded these conferences as the highlight of the year, and he put considerable effort into preparation for his annual message. A few years after his death, some of his most memorable addresses were collected into a volume titled, *An All-Round Ministry*,[10] which is still in print today.

Spurgeon for today

My interest in preparing the volume in hand stems in no small part from my own background and experience with Charles Spurgeon. I grew up among Christians who revered and admired Spurgeon, and viewed themselves self-consciously as continuing in his theological tradition. Throughout my upbringing, Spurgeon was often quoted, his books were recommended, and his ministry was celebrated. When, in my teenage years, I first expressed my aspirations to pursue pastoral ministry, I was immediately encouraged to read *Lectures to My Students*, which I did several times.

While in seminary, I began to read Spurgeon's sermons and to study more of his biography. I found myself increasingly drawn to Spurgeon for his emphasis on the person and work of Christ, his understanding of the vital importance of doctrine, and his bright and joy-filled outlook on the Christian life, the mission of the church, and the hope of heaven. His vision for theology, ministry, and church life deeply resonated with me. I knew I had found my man.

---

[10] C. H. Spurgeon, *An All-Round Ministry: Addresses to Ministers and Students* (London: Passmore and Alabaster, 1900).

The Pastor's Pastor

When the idea of pursuing doctoral studies was first introduced to me, I was certain who I wanted to study. Spurgeon's influence on my life had already been massive, and I longed to know more about him and to understand him in greater depth. The next five years which I spent studying Spurgeon were a welcome delight and challenge that shaped me in manifold ways.

As part of my doctoral work, I gave considerable attention to Spurgeon's many benevolent institutions, including Spurgeon's work through the Pastors' College. I came to appreciate, as I hadn't before, how unique Spurgeon's perspectives on pastoral ministry were in his own day. He was self-consciously aware that he was pioneering an approach to theological training that, if it ever existed in England, had fallen out of fashion among the upper classes and educated elite. His distinctive approach to pastoral training would focus on Calvinist and Puritan theology, experimental piety, Christ-centered preaching, and energetic pastoral leadership.

As I eventually entered pastoral ministry myself, I found Spurgeon's perspectives uniquely helpful and tremendously relevant to my own ministry. I found his writings on the ministry unmatched for their flare, insight, and relevance. As a young pastor I felt understood, supported, and challenged by Spurgeon. Eagerly, I recommended *Lectures to My Students* to other pastors and men aspiring to the ministry. I quickly found that I was not alone in experiencing great personal benefit from Spurgeon's writings on the pastoral ministry.

As I was studying Spurgeon both as a scholar and a pastor, I began to see the potential value of compiling an edited volume of Spurgeon's best lectures and addresses on pastoral ministry. Such a volume, I believed, could accomplish two purposes. First, it could make Spurgeon's best thoughts on pastoral ministry more easily accessible and readable for a new generation of pastors. Second, such a volume could serve as an introduction to Spurgeon's perspectives and could provoke further study of his material on the ministry.

I am pleased that this project has now come to fruition in the present volume. Spurgeon's perspectives on the ministry, contained in this collection of lectures and addresses, are as relevant today as they were in the nineteenth century. Here is wisdom for the busy pastor navigating the diverse challenges of the ministry. Here is encouragement for the preacher seeking to proclaim Christ faithfully to his flock week by week. Here is comfort and support for the weary minister overwhelmed by the troubles and trials of pastoral work. Here is help for pastors.

The lectures and addresses
The first eight addresses in this collection are taken from *Lectures to My Students*, which has been a classic among pastors since it first appeared in the 1870s. *Lectures to My Students* was originally published in three volumes. The first two volumes include lectures on a variety of pastoral subjects. The third volume is almost entirely devoted to the use of illustrations and anecdotes in preaching. Most of the modern unabridged editions bundle the first three volumes together into one book, and sometimes include as a fourth volume Spurgeon's *Commenting and Commentaries*, which includes his thoughts about the utility of commentaries in general as well as a running catalogue of various commentaries with Spurgeon's comments on their relative quality (or lack thereof).

All of the lectures I have selected from *Lectures to My Students* are drawn from the first two volumes, as I consider these volumes to contain the content that is most timeless and relevant to pastors today. Choosing which lectures should be included in the present collection was exceedingly difficult. Several excellent lectures were left on the threshing floor. Chief among them were the lectures titled, "Attention," "The Holy Spirit in Connection with

The Pastor's Pastor

Our Ministry," and "On Conversion as Our Aim." I am resigned to content myself with the hope that what I have prepared in this edited collection will serve as an introduction to the unabridged edition of *Lectures to My Students*. This volume will have failed in its aim if it does not stimulate readers to explore that larger collection of Spurgeon's lectures.

The final two addresses of this book are taken from *An All-Round Ministry*, which contains twelve messages delivered by Spurgeon at the Annual College Conference. The various addresses that Spurgeon delivered at the College Conference took up a host of different topics, and usually came in the form of a pastoral charge, an impassioned exhortation, or a rallying cry of sorts for the men who gathered together for the conference. This tremendous resource is full of leadership lessons, pastoral insights, and timeless counsel that showcase Spurgeon's wisdom and breadth of perspective on the privileges and challenges of pastoral leadership. A mere two chapters in the book in hand can only serve as a sneak preview of what the full volume has to offer pastors today.

Lectures to My Students and *An All-Round Ministry* together represent the fullest collection of Spurgeon's pastoral wisdom. They provide a pastoral smorgasbord of practical counsel and insight for the hungry pastor. The present volume serves as an introduction and primer to those larger works and endeavors to capture, in more compact form, something of their force and brilliance.

Method of selection

My particular selection of the addresses that form the ten chapters of this book were based on three main factors. First, quite simply, I went for the best of Spurgeon's lectures and addresses. Even among those who have not read much of Spurgeon, many are nonetheless aware of his classic lectures, "The Call to the

Ministry" or "The Minister's Fainting Fits." Some addresses like these simply had to be included because they are among Spurgeon's best and most well-known material.

Second, I have selected addresses that I believe best represent the man himself and the central burdens that motivated him. My instincts in this respect have led me to select lectures and addresses that are taken up with matters of piety, preaching, and pastoral leadership. My own opinion is that these concerns dominated Spurgeon's thinking when it came to pastoral ministry. The ideal minister in Spurgeon's mind was a man who truly walked with God, evinced an evident preaching gift, and possessed the leadership qualities necessary to guide the people of God in their mission and ministry.

The third factor governing my selection was my sense of the relevance of the various addresses to pastors today. The reality is, not all of Spurgeon's material is still relevant. *Lectures to My Students*, for example, contains lectures such as "On the Voice," which assumes a context without modern audio amplification technology, and "The Workers with Slender Apparatus," which refers to pastors without access to quality books—hardly an issue for anyone today who has access to the internet. There are also chapters in the third volume on illustrations and anecdotes that may not connect as well with contemporary audiences. However, the lectures and addresses I have selected for this collection are evergreen, and will be relevant to pastors until Christ returns.

Alterations and expansions of the text
On the whole, I have endeavored to leave the text of the various lectures and addresses essentially unaltered. To my knowledge, I have not deleted a single word, and have only made minor alterations to the grammar of the original text in order to make it more readable for contemporary audiences. Spurgeon's writing sometimes includes what would today be regarded as run-on sentences,

as well as the overuse of semi-colons, colons, and exclamation points. These aspects of his style were commonplace in the writing of the Victorians, but would be considered somewhat cumbersome by today's standards.

In general, Spurgeon's writing was considered delightfully fresh and engaging by his readers, especially in comparison to the tiresome and pedantic style that prevailed among many ministers in his day. Even today, the lectures and addresses read quite well. Any who wish to speak and write in a manner that will be appreciated beyond one's lifetime would do well to imitate Spurgeon's simplicity and ease of expression, his muscular vocabulary, and his healthy use of illustrations, metaphors, and anecdotes.

I have included footnotes for all of Spurgeon's quotations in the various addresses, which are almost wholly lacking in the original text. I have endeavored to identify the author (with dates), the title of the work cited, and, when possible, bibliographical information from a nineteenth century edition of the work that perhaps Spurgeon himself may have used. I have also included footnotes for references to particular historical figures, events, and literary characters. Additionally, I have included my own section headings for greater ease in reading.

I introduce each address with a brief essay that either provides historical context, a summary of the address's main points, or my own personal and pastoral observations concerning the subject at hand. These short introductions are only given as an appetizer to the larger entree. If they do not accomplish that aim, feel free to skip them on your way to the main course!

An invitation to learn and grow

I close with a personal invitation. I invite you to take *your* seat in the Pastors' College and learn from this faithful and proven minister. I believe he has something to say that pastors today dearly need to hear. In these lectures and addresses, Spurgeon comes alongside us in the ministry, and pastors the pastors. He invites us to pursue progress in our ministries, and he shows us the way forward. He reminds us that there is always room to grow and improve in service to Christ, and that the Lord is worthy of our greatest efforts and our most zealous devotion. Spurgeon holds out the hope to us that we can experience more of Christ in our ministries and more of the Spirit's help in pastoral work. He holds forth a vision for pastoral ministry that is bright with holiness, strong in conviction, and full of spiritual power. There is something in these pages for pastors who wish to know better what it means to shepherd the flock, for ministers who long to be renewed in their service to Christ and his church, and for men who want to experience more of the Spirit's power in preaching. All of this and more you will find in these chapters.

1
The Minister's Self-Watch

Introduction

In this seminal lecture, Spurgeon addresses the vital importance of the minister's own self-examination with respect to his life and ministry. The first half of the lecture focuses on the need for ministers to ensure that they themselves are truly converted, and also enumerates some of the disastrous effects of an unconverted ministry. In Spurgeon's day, it was not uncommon for men to enter the ministry simply because it was seen as a respectable profession. This was particularly the case in the state church. Thus, it was not at all unusual to come across men in the ministry who had never experienced the new birth themselves. Of course, to Spurgeon, it was deplorable for any man to enter upon a pastoral call without having first been savingly united to Christ. In the first part of this address, he makes this point emphatically.

In the second half of the lecture, Spurgeon develops the importance of true piety and godly character among ministers. In the Pastors' College, the cultivation of vital godliness was one of the requirements for admission. Spurgeon would not accept students who reflected "a low state of piety, a want of enthusiasm, a failure in private devotion, a lack of consecration."[1] In an 1866 article in *The Sword and the Trowel,* Spurgeon listed piety as the first of the College's admission standards, writing, "The selection of candidates for admission is principally determined by evidences of

---

[1] C. H. Spurgeon, ed., *The Sword and the Trowel* (London: Passmore and Alabaster, June, 1889), 311.

eminent piety, of adaptation to public teaching, of great zeal for the salvation of souls, and of instances of actual usefulness."[2]

When it comes to pastoral ministry, it could be said, character is king. To a generation that is too easily impressed with charisma, professional competence, and personal magnetism, Spurgeon's call for ministers to nurture spiritual vigor and a close walk with God ought to come with fresh force. Churches should desire more in their pastors than personal charm and slick presentation. Too many are willing to wink at men who are lax with respect to piety, as long as they are urbane, competent, and able to keep the machinery of the church in good working order. However, Spurgeon reminds us that true pastors must be those who walk with God and evidence the fruit of a secret history with Him in the way they live and minister.

Furthermore, in a context in which many men have disqualified themselves or become enshrouded in scandal and controversy, Spurgeon's emphasis on godly character in pastors should invite our heartiest approval. Only men of true godliness and eminent holiness are qualified to serve the church as her leaders. The qualifications given in 1 Timothy 3:1-7 and Titus 1:5-9 are not negotiable. They are given as filters through which every ministerial candidate must pass. Spurgeon reminds us that the church must insist on Christ-likeness in her ministers in order to preserve the witness of the church, provide an example to the flock, and lead God's people in their mission

---

[2] Spurgeon, *The Sword and the Trowel* (March, 1866), 135.

The Minister's Self-Watch

Every workman knows the necessity of keeping his tools in a good state of repair, for "if the iron be blunt, and he do not whet the edge, then must he put to more strength." If the workman lose the edge from his adze, he knows that there will be a greater draught upon his energies, or his work will be badly done. Michael Angelo,[1] the elect of the fine arts, understood so well the importance of his tools, that he always made his own brushes with his own hands, and in this he gives us an illustration of the God of grace, who with special care fashions for himself all true ministers. It is true that the Lord, like Quintin Mastys[2] in the story of the Antwerp well-cover, can work with the faultiest kind of instrumentality, as he does when he occasionally makes very foolish preaching to be useful in conversion; and he can even work without agents, as he does when he saves men without a preacher at all, applying the word directly by his Holy Spirit; but we cannot regard God's absolutely sovereign acts as a rule for our action. He may, in his own absoluteness, do as pleases him best, but we must act as his plainer dispensations instruct us; and one of the facts which is clear enough is this, that the Lord usually adapts means to ends, from which the plain lesson is, that we shall be likely to accomplish most when we are in the best spiritual condition; or in other words, we shall usually do our Lord's work best when our gifts and graces are in good order, and we shall do worst when they are most out of trim. This is a practical truth for our guidance, when the Lord makes exceptions, they do but prove the rule.

---

[1] Michelangelo (1475-1564) was a renowned Italian painter, sculptor, and architect.

[2] Quinten Matsys (1466-1530) was a well-known Flemish painter.

We are, in a certain sense, our own tools, and therefore must keep ourselves in order. If I want to preach the gospel, I can only use my own voice; therefore I must train my vocal powers. I can only think with my own brains, and feel with my own heart, and therefore I must educate my intellectual and emotional faculties. I can only weep and agonise for souls in my own renewed nature, therefore must I watchfully maintain the tenderness which was in Christ Jesus. It will be in vain for me to stock my library, or organise societies, or project schemes, if I neglect the culture of myself; for books, and agencies, and systems, are only remotely the instruments of my holy calling; my own spirit, soul, and body, are my nearest machinery for sacred service; my spiritual faculties, and my inner life, are my battle axe and weapons of war. M'Cheyne,[3] writing to a ministerial friend, who was travelling with a view to perfecting himself in the German tongue, used language identical with our own,

> I know you will apply hard to German, but do not forget the culture of the inner man—I mean of the heart. How diligently the cavalry officer keeps his sabre clean and sharp; every stain he rubs off with the greatest care. Remember you are God's sword, his instrument—I trust, a chosen vessel unto him to bear his name. In great measure, according to the purity and perfection of the instrument, will be the success. It is not great talents God blesses so much as likeness to Jesus. A holy minister is an awful weapon in the hand of God.[4]

---

[3] Robert Murray M'Cheyne (1813–1843) was a prominent minister in the Church of Scotland. He was educated at the University of Edinburgh and pastored St. Peter's Church of Dundee, Scotland from 1836 until his death in 1843; Spurgeon's knowledge of M'Cheyne would have been based largely on Andrew A. Bonar, *Memoir and Remains of the Rev. R. M. M'Cheyne: Minister of St. Peter's Church, Dundee* (London: Hamilton, Adams, & Co., and J. Nisbet & Co., 1845).

[4] Bonar, *Memoir and Remains of the Rev. R. M. M'Cheyne*, 243.

The Minister's Self-Watch

For the herald of the gospel to be spiritually out of order in his own proper person is, both to himself and to his work, a most serious calamity, and yet, my brethren, how easily is such an evil produced, and with what watchfulness must it be guarded against! Travelling one day by express from Perth to Edinburgh, on a sudden we came to a dead stop, because a very small screw in one of the engines—every railway locomotive consisting virtually of two engines—had been broken, and when we started again we were obliged to crawl along with one piston-rod at work instead of two. Only a small screw was gone, if that had been right the train would have rushed along its iron road, but the absence of that insignificant piece of iron disarranged the whole. A train is said to have been stopped on one of the United States' railways by flies in the grease-boxes of the carriage wheels. The analogy is perfect; a man in all other respects fitted to be useful, may by some small defect be exceedingly hindered, or even rendered utterly useless. Such a result is all the more grievous, because it is associated with the gospel, which in the highest sense is adapted to effect the grandest results. It is a terrible thing when the healing balm loses its efficacy through the blunderer who administers it. You all know the injurious effects frequently produced upon water through flowing along leaden pipes.

Even so the gospel itself, in flowing through men who are spiritually unhealthy, may be debased until it grows injurious to their hearers. It is to be feared that Calvinistic doctrine becomes most evil teaching when it is set forth by men of ungodly lives, and exhibited as if it were a cloak for licentiousness; and Arminianism, on the other hand, with its wide sweep of the offer of mercy, may do most serious damage to the souls of men, if the careless tone of the preacher leads his hearers to believe that they can repent whenever they please, and that, therefore, no urgency surrounds the gospel message. Moreover, when a preacher is poor in grace, any lasting good which may be the result of his ministry, will usually be feeble and utterly out of proportion with what might have been expected. Much sowing will be followed by little reaping; the interest upon the talents will be inappreciably small. In two or three of the battles which were lost in the late American war, the result is said to have been due to the bad gunpowder which was served out by certain "shoddy" contractors to the army, so that the due effect of a cannonade was not produced. So it may be with us. We may miss our mark, lose our end and aim, and waste our time, through not possessing true vital force within ourselves, or not possessing it in such a degree that God could consistently bless us. Beware of being "shoddy" preachers.

Ministers must be converted themselves
It should be one of our first cares that we ourselves be saved men.

That a teacher of the gospel should first be a partaker of it is a simple truth, but at the same time a rule of the most weighty importance. We are not among those who accept the apostolical succession of young men simply because they assume it. If their college experience has been rather vivacious than spiritual, if their honours have been connected rather with athletic exercises than with labours for Christ, we demand evidence of another kind than they are able to present to us. No amount of fees paid to learned doctors, and no amount of classics received in return, appear to us to be evidences of a call from above. True and genuine piety is necessary as the first indispensable requisite. Whatever "call" a man may pretend to have, if he has not been called to holiness, he certainly has not been called to the ministry.

"First be trimmed thyself, and then adorn thy brother," say the rabbins. "The hand," saith Gregory, "that means to make another clean, must not itself be dirty."[5] If your salt be unsavoury

---

[5] It is not clear to whom Spurgeon refers to here, nor is the origin of the quote known.

The Minister's Self-Watch

how can you season others? Conversion is a sine qua non in a minister. Ye aspirants to our pulpits, "ye must be born again" (John 3:7). Nor is the possession of this first qualification a thing to be taken for granted by any man, for there is very great possibility of our being mistaken as to whether we are converted or not. Believe me, it is no child's play to "make your calling and election sure" (2 Pet. 1:10). The world is full of counterfeits, and swarms with panderers to carnal self-conceit, who gather around a minister as vultures around a carcass. Our own hearts are deceitful, so that truth lies not on the surface, but must be drawn up from the deepest well. We must search ourselves very anxiously and very thoroughly, lest by any means after having preached to others we ourselves should be castaways.

The perils of an unconverted ministry
How horrible to be a preacher of the gospel and yet to be unconverted! Let each man here whisper to his own inmost soul, "What a dreadful thing it will be for me if I should be ignorant of the power of the truth which I am preparing to proclaim!" Unconverted ministry involves the most unnatural relationships. A graceless pastor is a blind man elected to a professorship of optics, philosophising upon light and vision, discoursing upon and distinguishing to others the nice shades and delicate blendings of the prismatic colours, while he himself is absolutely in the dark. He is a dumb man elevated to the chair of music; a deaf man fluent upon symphonies and harmonies. He is a mole professing to educate eaglets; a limpet elected to preside over angels. To such a relationship one might apply the most absurd and grotesque metaphors, except that the subject is too solemn. It is a dreadful position for a man to stand in, for he has undertaken a work for which he is totally, wholly, and altogether unqualified, but from the responsibilities of which this unfitness will not screen him, because he wilfully incurred them. Whatever his natural gifts, whatever his

mental powers may be, he is utterly out of court for spiritual work if he has no spiritual life; and it is his duty to cease the ministerial office till he has received this first and simplest of qualifications for it.

Unconverted ministry must be equally dreadful in another respect. If the man has no commission, what a very unhappy position for him to occupy! What can he see in the experience of his people to give him comfort? How must he feel when he hears the cries of penitents; or listens to their anxious doubts and solemn fears? He must be astonished to think that his words should be owned to that end. The word of an unconverted man may be blessed to the conversion of souls, since the Lord, while he disowns the man, will still honour his own truth. How perplexed such a man must be when he is consulted concerning the difficulties of mature Christians. In the pathway of experience, in which his own regenerate hearers are led, he must feel himself quite at a loss. How can he listen to their deathbed joys, or join in their rapturous fellowships around the table of their Lord?

In many instances of young men put to a trade which they cannot endure, they have run away to sea sooner than follow an irksome business; but where shall that man flee who is apprenticed for life to this holy calling, and yet is a total stranger to the power of godliness? How can he daily bid men come to Christ, while he himself is a stranger to his dying love? O sirs, surely this must be perpetual slavery. Such a man must hate the sight of a pulpit as much as a galley-slave hates the oar.

And how unserviceable such a man must be. He has to guide travellers along a road which he has never trodden, to navigate a vessel along a coast of which he knows none of the landmarks. He is called to instruct others, being himself a fool. What can he be but a cloud without rain, a tree with leaves only. As when the caravan in the wilderness, all athirst and ready to die beneath the broiling sun, comes to the long desired well, and, horror of horrors, finds it without a drop of water; so when souls thirsting after God come to a graceless ministry, they are ready to perish because the water of life is not to be found. Better abolish pulpits than fill them with men who have no experimental knowledge of what they teach.

Alas, the unregenerate pastor becomes terribly mischievous too, for of all the causes which create infidelity, ungodly ministers must be ranked among the first. I read the other day, that no phase of evil presented so marvellous a power for destruction, as the unconverted minister of a parish, with a £1200 organ, a choir of ungodly singers, and an aristocratic congregation. It was the opinion of the writer, that there could be no greater instrument for damnation out of hell than that. People go to their place of worship and sit down comfortably, and think they must be Christians, when all the time all that their religion consists in, is listening to an orator, having their ears tickled with music, and perhaps their eyes amused with graceful action and fashionable manners; the whole being no better than what they hear and see at the opera—not so good, perhaps, in point of aesthetic beauty, and not an atom more spiritual. Thousands are congratulating themselves, and even blessing God that they are devout worshippers, when at the same time they are living in an unregenerate Christless state, having the form of godliness, but denying the power thereof. He who presides over a system which aims at nothing higher than formalism, is far more a servant of the devil than a minister of God.

A formal preacher is mischievous while he preserves his outward equilibrium, but as he is without the preserving balance of godliness, sooner or later he is almost sure to make a trip in his moral character, and what a position is he in then. How is God blasphemed, and the gospel abused!

A solemn warning to unconverted ministers

Terrible is it to consider what a death must await such a man, and what must be his after-condition. The prophet pictures the king of Babylon going down to hell, and all the kings and princes whom he had destroyed, and whose capitals he had laid waste, rising up from their places in Pandemonium, and saluting the fallen tyrant with the cutting sarcasm, "Art thou become like unto us?" (Isa. 14:10). And cannot you suppose a man who has been a minister, but who has lived without Christ in his heart, going down to hell, and all the imprisoned spirits who used to hear him, and all the ungodly of his parish rising up and saying to him in bitter tones, "Art thou also become as we are? Physician, didst thou not heal thyself? Art thou who claimed to be a shining light cast down into the darkness for ever?" Oh, if one must be lost, let it not be in this fashion! To be lost under the shadow of a pulpit is dreadful, but how much more so to perish from the pulpit itself!

There is an awful passage in John Bunyan's[6] treatise, entitled "Sighs from Hell," which full often rings in my ears,

> How many souls have blind priests been the means of destroying by their ignorance? Preaching that was no better for their souls than ratsbane to the body. Many of them, it is to be feared, have whole towns to answer for. Ah! friend, I tell thee, thou that hast taken in hand to preach to the people, it may be thou hast taken in hand thou canst not tell what. Will

---

[6] John Bunyan (1628–1688) was a seventeenth century Puritan pastor who ministered in Bedfordshire. He is best known for his allegorical book, *The Pilgrim's Progress*, which Spurgeon claimed to have read over 100 times. Spurgeon famously said of Bunyan, "Read anything of his, and you will see that it is almost like reading the Bible itself.... He cannot give us his Pilgrim's Progress—that sweetest of all prose poems—without continually making us feel and say, 'Why, this man is a living Bible!' Prick him anywhere; and you will find that his blood is Bibline, the very essence of the Bible flows from him. He cannot speak without quoting a text, for his soul is full of the Word of God." See C. H. Spurgeon, *C. H. Spurgeon's Autobiography, Compiled from his Diary, Letters, and Records by His Wife and His Private Secretary*, vol. 4 (London: Passmore and Alabaster, 1897), 268.

The Minister's Self-Watch

it not grieve thee to see thy whole parish come bellowing after thee into hell? crying out, "This we have to thank thee for, thou wast afraid to tell us of our sins, lest we should not put meat fast enough into thy mouth. O cursed wretch, who wast not content, blind guide as thou wast, to fall into the ditch thyself, but hast also led us thither with thee."[7]

Richard Baxter,[8] in his *Reformed Pastor*, amid much other solemn matter, writes as follows:

Take heed to yourselves lest you should be void of that saving grace of God which you offer to others, and be strangers to the effectual working of that gospel which you preach; and lest, while you proclaim the necessity of a Saviour to the world, your hearts should neglect him, and you should miss of an interest in him and his saving benefits. Take heed to yourselves, lest you perish while you call upon others to take heed of perishing, and lest you famish yourselves while you prepare their food. Though there be a promise of shining as stars to those that turn many to righteousness (Dan. 12:3), this is but on supposition that they be first turned to it themselves: such promises are made *caeteris paribus, et suppositis supponendis*. Their own sincerity in the faith is the condition of their glory simply considered, though their great ministerial labours may be a condition of the promise of their greater glory. Many men have warned others that they come not to that place of torment, which yet they hasted to themselves; many a preacher is now in hell, that hath an hundred times called upon his hearers to use the utmost care and diligence to escape it. Can any reasonable man imagine that

---

[7] John Bunyan, "Sighs from Hell," in *The Entire Works of John Bunyan, Author of "The Pilgrim's Progress"*, edited with original introduction, notes, and memoir of the author, by Henry Stebbing, D. D., F. R. S., etc. vol. 1 (London: John Hirst, 1861), 155.

[8] Richard Baxter (1615–1691) was a prominent seventeenth century Puritan pastor whose most well-known books are *The Reformed Pastor*, *The Saint's Everlasting Rest*, and *A Call to the Unconverted*. Spurgeon was especially impacted by *A Call to the Unconverted* as a boy before he came to faith. See Spurgeon, *Autobiography*, vol. 1 (London: Passmore and Alabaster, 1897), 80.

God should save men for offering salvation to others, while they refused it themselves, and for telling others those truths which they themselves neglected and abused? Many a tailor goes in rags that maketh costly clothes for others; and many a cook scarce licks his fingers, when he hath dressed for others the most costly dishes. Believe it, brethren, God never saved any man for being a preacher, nor because he was an able preacher; but because he was a justified, sanctified man, and consequently faithful in his Master's work. Take heed, therefore, to yourselves first, that you be that which you persuade others to be, and believe that which you persuade them daily to believe, and have heartily entertained that Christ and Spirit which you offer unto others. He that bade you love your neighbours as yourselves, did imply that you should love yourselves and not hate and destroy both yourselves and them.[9]

My brethren, let these weighty sentences have due effect upon you. Surely there can be no need to add more, but let me pray you to examine yourselves, and so make good use of what has been addressed to you.

Ministers must be men of true piety

This first matter of true religion being settled, it is of the next importance to the minister that his piety be vigorous.

He is not to be content with being equal to the rank and file of Christians, he must be a mature and advanced believer, for the ministry of Christ has been truly called "the choicest of his choice, the elect of his election, a church picked out of the church." If he were called to an ordinary position, and to common work, common grace might perhaps satisfy him, though even then it would be an indolent satisfaction; but being elect to extraordinary

---

[9] Richard Baxter, *The Reformed Pastor*, ed. William Brown, 5th ed. (London: The Religious Tract Society, 1862), 20.

labours, and called to a place of unusual peril, he should be anxious to possess that superior strength which alone is adequate to his station. His pulse of vital godliness must beat strongly and regularly; his eye of faith must be bright; his foot of resolution must be firm; his hand of activity must be quick; his whole inner man must be in the highest degree of sanity.

It is said of the Egyptians that they chose their priests from the most learned of their philosophers, and then they esteemed their priests so highly, that they chose their kings from them. We require to have for God's ministers the pick of all the Christian host; such men indeed, that if the nation wanted kings they could not do better than elevate them to the throne. Our weakest-minded, most timid, most carnal, and most ill-balanced men are not suitable candidates for the pulpit. There are some works which we should never allot to the invalid or deformed. A man may not be qualified for climbing lofty buildings, his brain may be too weak, and elevated work might place him in great danger; by all means let him keep on the ground and find useful occupation where a steady brain is less important. There are brethren who have analogous spiritual deficiencies, they cannot be called to service which is conspicuous and elevated, because their heads are too weak. If they were permitted a little success they would be intoxicated with vanity—a vice all too common among ministers, and of all things the least becoming in them, and the most certain to secure them a fall. Should we as a nation be called to defend our hearths and homes, we should not send out our boys and girls with swords and guns to meet the foe, neither may the church send out every fluent novice or inexperienced zealot to plead for the faith. The fear of the Lord must teach the young man wisdom, or he is barred from the pastorate; the grace of God must mature his spirit, or he had better tarry till power be given him from on high.

Held to a higher standard

The highest moral character must be sedulously maintained. Many are disqualified for office in the church who are well enough as simple members. I hold very stern opinions with regard to Christian men who have fallen into gross sin. I rejoice that they may be truly converted, and may be with mingled hope and caution received into the church, but I question, gravely question whether a man who has grossly sinned should be very readily restored to the pulpit. As John Angell James[10] remarks, "When a preacher of righteousness has stood in the way of sinners, he should never again open his lips in the great congregation until his repentance is as notorious as his sin."[11] Let those who have been shorn by the sons of Ammon tarry at Jericho till their beards be grown; this has often been used as a taunt to beardless boys to whom it is evidently inapplicable, it is an accurate enough metaphor for dishonoured and characterless men, let their age be what it may. Alas, the beard of reputation once shorn is hard to grow again. Open immorality, in most cases, however deep the repentance, is a fatal sign that ministerial graces were never in the man's character. Caesar's wife must be beyond suspicion, and there must be no ugly rumours as to ministerial inconsistency in the past, or the hope of usefulness will be slender. Into the church such fallen ones are to be received as penitents, and into the ministry they may be received if God puts them there; my doubt is not about that, but as to whether God ever did place them there; and my belief is that we should be very slow to help back to the pulpit

---

[10] John Angell James (1785-1859) was a popular Congregationalist preacher. His most well-known book is *The Anxious Inquirer After Salvation Directed and Encouraged*, which had a significant impact on Spurgeon before he came to faith in Christ. See Spurgeon, *Autobiography*, vol. 1 (London: Passmore and Alabaster, 1897), 104, 208-209.

[11] John Angell James, *Christian Fellowship, or The Church Member's Guide: To Which is Added, A Pastoral Charge, Delivered to the Rev. Thomas James, at the Time of His Ordination in City Chapel, London* (Birmingham: B. Hudson, 1822), 55.

men, who having been once tried, have proved themselves to have too little grace to stand the crucial test of ministerial life.

For some work we choose none but the strong; and when God calls us to ministerial labour we should endeavour to get grace that we may be strengthened into fitness for our position, and not be mere novices carried away by the temptations of Satan, to the injury of the church and our own ruin. We are to stand equipped with the whole armour of God, ready for feats of valour not expected of others. To us self-denial, self-forgetfulness, patience, perseverance, longsuffering, must be every-day virtues, and who is sufficient for these things? We had need live very near to God, if we would approve ourselves in our vocation.

Recollect, as ministers, that your whole life, your whole pastoral life especially, will be affected by the vigour of your piety. If your zeal grows dull, you will not pray well in the pulpit; you will pray worse in the family, and worst in the study alone. When your soul becomes lean, your hearers, without knowing how or why, will find that your prayers in public have little savour for them; they will feel your barrenness, perhaps, before you perceive it yourself. Your discourses will next betray your declension. You may utter as well-chosen words, and as fitly-ordered sentences, as aforetime; but there will be a perceptible loss of spiritual force. You will shake yourselves as at other times, even as Samson did, but you will find that your great strength has departed. In your daily communion with your people, they will not be slow to mark the all-pervading decline of your graces. Sharp eyes will see the grey hairs here and there long before you do. Let a man be afflicted with a disease of the heart, and all evils are wrapped up in that one—stomach, lungs, viscera, muscles, and nerves will all suffer; and so, let a man have his heart weakened in spiritual things, and very soon his entire life will feel the withering influence. Moreover, as the result of your own decline, everyone of your hearers will suffer more or less; the vigorous amongst them will overcome the depressing tendency, but the weaker sort will be seriously damaged. It is with us and our hearers as it is with watches and the public clock; if our watch be wrong, very few will be misled by it but ourselves; but if the Horse Guards or Greenwich Observatory should go amiss, half London would lose its reckoning. So is it with the minister; he is the parish-clock, many take their time from him, and if he be incorrect, then they all go wrongly, more or less, and he is in a great measure accountable for all the sin which he occasions. This we cannot endure to think of, my brethren. It will not bear a moment's comfortable consideration, and yet it must be looked at that we may guard against it.

The unique dangers facing ministers
You must remember, too, that we have need of very vigorous piety, because our danger is so much greater than that of others. Upon the whole, no place is so assailed with temptation as the ministry. Despite the popular idea that ours is a snug retreat from temptation, it is no less true that our dangers are more numerous and more insidious than those of ordinary Christians. Ours may be a vantage-ground for height, but that height is perilous, and to many the ministry has proved a Tarpeian rock. If you ask what these temptations are, time might fail us to particularise them, but among them are both the coarser and the more refined. The coarser are such temptations as self-indulgence at the table, enticements to which are superabundant among a hospitable people; the temptations of the flesh, which are incessant with young unmarried men set on high among an admiring throng of young women; but enough of this, your own observation will soon reveal to you a thousand snares, unless indeed your eyes are blinded. There are more secret snares than these, from which we can less easily escape, and of these the worst is the temptation to ministerialism—the tendency to read our Bibles as ministers, to pray as ministers, to get into doing the whole of our religion as not

ourselves personally, but only relatively, concerned in it. To lose the personality of repentance and faith is a loss indeed. "No man," says John Owen,[12] "preaches his sermon well to others if he doth not first preach it to his own heart."[13] Brethren, it is eminently hard to keep to this. Our office, instead of helping our piety, as some assert, is through the evil of our natures turned into one of its most serious hindrances; at least, I find it so. How one kicks and struggles against officialism, and yet how easily doth it beset us, like a long garment which twists around the racer's feet and impedes his running. Beware, dear brethren, of this and all the other seductions of your calling; and if you have done so until now, continue still to watch till life's latest hour.

We have noted but one of the perils, but indeed they are legion. The great enemy of souls takes care to leave no stone unturned for the preacher's ruin. "Take heed to yourselves," says Baxter,

> because the tempter will make his first and sharpest onset upon you. If you will be the leaders against him, he will spare you no further than God restraineth him. He beareth you the greatest malice that are engaged to do him the greatest mischief. As he hateth Christ more than any of us, because he is the General of the field, and the "Captain of our salvation," and doth more than all the world besides against the kingdom of darkness; so doth he note the leaders under him more than the common soldiers, on the like account, in their proportion. He knows what a rout he may make among the rest, if the leaders fall before their eyes. He hath long tried that way of fighting, "neither with small nor great," comparatively, but these; and of "smiting the shepherds, that

---

[12] John Owen (1616-1683) was one of the most prominent Puritan theologians of the seventeenth century. He was a parish pastor, chaplain to Oliver Cromwell, Vice-Chancellor of Oxford University, and eventually a Nonconformist pastor after the "Great Ejection" of 1662. Owen's most famous books include *On the Mortification of Sin*, *On Communion with God*, and *On the Glories of Christ*.

[13] John Owen, *The Works of John Owen, D. D.*, ed. William H. Goold (London and Edinburgh: Johnstone and Hunter, 1851), 455.

he may scatter the flock." And so great has been his success this way, that he will follow it on as far as he is able. Take heed, therefore, brethren, for the enemy hath a special eye upon you. You shall have his most subtle insinuations, and incessant solicitations, and violent assaults. As wise and learned as you are, take heed to yourselves lest he overwit you. The devil is a greater scholar than you, and a nimbler disputant; he can "transform himself into an angel of light" to deceive. He will get within you and trip up your heels before you are aware; he will play the juggler with you undiscerned, and cheat you of your faith or innocency, and you shall not know that you have lost it; nay, he will make you believe it is multiplied or increased when it is lost. You shall see neither hook nor line, much less the subtle angler himself, while he is offering you his bait. And his baits shall be so fitted to your temper and disposition, that he will be sure to find advantages within you, and make your own principles and inclinations to betray you; and whenever he ruineth you, he will make you the instrument of your own ruin. Oh, what a conquest will he think he hath got, if he can make a minister lazy and unfaithful; if he can tempt a minister into covetousness or scandal! He will glory against the church, and say, "These are your holy preachers: you see what their preciseness is, and whither it will bring them." He will glory against Jesus Christ himself, and say, "These are thy champions! I can make thy chiefest servants to abuse thee; I can make the stewards of thy house unfaithful." If he did so insult against God upon a false surmise, and tell him he could make Job to curse him to his face (Job 1:2), what would he do if he should indeed prevail against us? And at last he will insult as much over you that ever he could draw you to be false to your great trust, and to blemish your holy profession, and to do him so much service that was your enemy. O do not so far gratify Satan; do not make him so much sport: suffer him not to use you as the Philistines did Samson—first to deprive you of your strength, and then to put out your eyes, and so to make you the matter of his triumph and derision.[14]

Once more. We must cultivate the highest degree of godliness because our work imperatively requires it. The labour of the Christian ministry is well performed in exact proportion to the vigour of our renewed nature. Our work is only well done when it is well with ourselves. As is the workman, such will the work be. To face the enemies of truth, to defend the bulwarks of the faith, to rule well in the house of God, to comfort all that mourn, to edify the saints, to guide the perplexed, to bear with the froward, to win and nurse souls—all these and a thousand other works beside are not for a Feeble-mind or a Ready-to-halt, but are reserved for Great-heart whom the Lord has made strong for himself.[15] Seek then strength from the Strong One, wisdom from the Wise One, in fact, all from the God of all.

Ministers must possess godly character
Thirdly, let the minister take care that his personal character agrees in all respects with his ministry.

We have all heard the story of the man who preached so well and lived so badly, that when he was in the pulpit everybody said he ought never to come out again, and when he was out of it they all declared he never ought to enter it again. From the imitation of such a Janus may the Lord deliver us. May we never be priests of God at the altar, and sons of Belial outside the tabernacle door; but on the contrary, may we, as Nazianzen says of Basil, "thunder in our doctrine, and lightning in our conversation."[16] We do not

---

[14] Baxter, *The Reformed Pastor*, 49–51.
[15] Here, Spurgeon references classic characters from John Bunyan, *The Pilgrim's Progress: From This World to That Which is to Come; Delivered Under the Similitude of a Dream* (Kettering: J. Toller, 1843), 311-333.
[16] Gregory of Nazianzus (329-390) was the Archbishop of Constantinople. Basil the Great (330-379) was the Bishop of Caesarea Both men along with Gregory of

trust those persons who have two faces, nor will men believe in those whose verbal and practical testimonies are contradictory. As actions, according to the proverb, speak louder than words, so an ill life will effectually drown the voice of the most eloquent ministry. After all, our truest building must be performed with our hands; our characters must be more persuasive than our speech. Here I would not alone warn you of sins of commission, but of sins of omission. Too many preachers forget to serve God when they are out of the pulpit, their lives are negatively inconsistent. Abhor, dear brethren, the thought of being clockwork ministers who are not alive by abiding grace within, but are wound up by temporary influences; men who are only ministers for the time being, under the stress of the hour of ministering, but cease to be ministers when they descend the pulpit stairs. True ministers are always ministers. Too many preachers are like those sand-toys we buy for our children; you turn the box upside down, and the little acrobat revolves and revolves till the sand is all run down, and then he hangs motionless; so there are some who persevere in the ministrations of truth as long as there is an official necessity for their work, but after that, no pay, no paternoster; no salary, no sermon.

It is a horrible thing to be an inconsistent minister. Our Lord is said to have been like Moses, for this reason, that he was "a prophet mighty in word and in deed." The man of God should imitate his Master in this; he should be mighty both in the word of his doctrine and in the deed of his example, and mightiest, if possible, in the second. It is remarkable that the only church history we have is, "The Acts of the apostles." The Holy Spirit has not preserved their sermons. They were very good ones, better

---

Nyssa are known as the Cappadocian Fathers, staunch defenders of Nicene orthodoxy. I have not been able to discover the original source of the quote Spurgeon mentions here, but it is contained in John Spencer, *Things New & Old: or, A Storehouse of Similes, Sentences, Allegories, Apophthegms, Adages, Apologues, Divine, Moral, Political, etc.*, vol. 2 (London: William Tegg, 1868), 130.

than we shall ever preach, but still the Holy Spirit has only taken care of their "acts." We have no books of the resolutions of the apostles; when we hold our church-meetings we record our minutes and resolutions, but the Holy Spirit only puts down the "acts." Our acts should be such as to bear recording, for recorded they will be. We must live as under the more immediate eye of God, and as in the blaze of the great all-revealing day.

The magnetic power of a holy life
Holiness in a minister is at once his chief necessity and his goodliest ornament. Mere moral excellence is not enough, there must be the higher virtue; a consistent character there must be, but this must be anointed with the sacred consecrating oil, or that which makes us most fragrant to God and man will be wanting. Old John Stoughton,[17] in his treatise entitled *The Preacher's Dignity and Duty*, insists upon the minister's holiness in sentences full of weight.

> If Uzzah must die but for touching the ark of God, and that to stay it when it was like to fall; if the men of Beth-shemesh for looking into it; if the very beasts that do but come near the holy mount be threatened; then what manner of persons ought they to be who shall be admitted to talk with God familiarly, to "stand before him," as the angels do, and "behold his face continually;" "to bear the ark upon their shoulders," "to bear his name before the Gentiles;" in a word, to be his ambassadors? 'Holiness becometh thy house, O Lord;' and were it not a ridiculous thing to imagine, that the vessels must be holy, the vestures must be holy, all must be holy, but only he upon whose very garments must be written "holiness to the Lord," might be unholy; that the bells of the horses should have an inscription of holiness upon them, in Zechariah, and the saints' bells, the

---

[17] John Stoughton (1593-1639) was an English Puritan pastor.

bells of Aaron, should be unhallowed? No, they must be "burning and shining lights," or else their influence will dart some malignant quality; they must "chew the cud and divide the hoof," or else they are unclean; they must "divide the word aright," and walk uprightly in their life, and so join life to learning. If holiness be wanting, the ambassadors dishonour the country from whence they come, and the prince from whom they come; and this dead Amasa, this dead doctrine not quickened with a good life, lying in the way, stops the people of the Lord, that they cannot go on cheerfully in their spiritual warfare.[18]

The life of the preacher should be a magnet to draw men to Christ, and it is sad indeed when it keeps them from him. Sanctity in ministers is a loud call to sinners to repent, and when allied with holy cheerfulness it becomes wondrously attractive. Jeremy Taylor[19] in his own rich language tell us,

> Herod's doves could never have invited so many strangers to their dove-cotes, if they had not been besmeared with opobalsamum: but, ἐὰν μύρῳ χρίσῃς τὰς περιστερὰς, καὶ ἔξωθεν ἄλλας ἄξουσιν, said Didymus; "make your pigeons smell sweet, and they will allure whole flocks;" and if your life be excellent, if your virtues be like a precious ointment, you will soon invite your charges to run "*in odorem unguentorum*," "after your precious odours:" but you must be excellent, not "*tanquam unus de populo*," but "*tanquam homo Dei*;" you must be a man of God, not after the common manner of men, but 'after God's own heart;' and men will strive to be like you, if you be like to God: but when you

---

[18] The original source of this citation is found in John Stoughton, "The Preachers Dignity and Duty" in *XV. Choice Sermons Preached Upon Selected Occasions, in Cambridge, viz. I. The Preacher's Dignity, and Duty, etc.* (London: R. B. for John Bellamie, Henry Overton, John Rothwell, and Ralph Smith, 1640), 89–91.

[19] Jeremy Taylor (1613–1667) was a prominent minister in the Church of England and served as the Bishop of Down and Connor in Ireland as well as the Vice-Chancellor of the University of Dublin.

only stand at the door of virtue, for nothing but to keep sin out, you will draw into the folds of Christ none but such as fear drives in. "*Ad majorem Dei gloriam,*" "To do what will most glorify God," that is the line you must walk by: for to do no more than all men needs must is servility, not so much as the affection of sons; much less can you be fathers to the people, when you go not so far as the sons of God: for a dark lantern, though there be a weak brightness on one side, will scarce enlighten one, much less will it conduct a multitude, or allure many followers by the brightness of its flame.[20]

Another equally admirable episcopal divine[21] has well and pithily said,

The star which led the wise men unto Christ, the pillar of fire which led the children unto Canaan, did not only shine, but go before them (Matt. 2:9; Exod. 13:21). The voice of Jacob will do little good if the hands be the hands of Esau. In the law, no person who had any blemish was to offer the oblations of the Lord (Lev. 21:17-20); the Lord thereby teaching us what graces ought to be in his ministers. The priest was to have in his robes bells and pomegranates; the one a figure of sound doctrine, and the other of a fruitful life (Exod. 28:33, 34). The Lord will be sanctified in all those that draw near unto him (Isa. 52:11); for the sins of the priests make the people abhor the offering of the Lord (1 Sam. 2:17); their wicked lives do shame their doctrine; *Passionem Christi annunciant profitendo, male agendo exhonorant,* as St. Austin speaks: with their doctrine they build, and with their lives they destroy. I conclude this point with that wholesome passage of *Hierom ad Nepotianum.* Let not, saith he, thy works shame thy doctrine, lest they who hear thee in the church tacitly answer, Why doest thou not thyself

---

[20] Jeremy Taylor, *The Works of Jeremy Taylor, D. D. with Some Account of His Life, Summary of Each Discourse, Notes, etc.*, ed. T. S. Hughes (London: A. J. Valpy, M.A., 1831), 155.

[21] Edward Reynolds (1599-1676) was the Bishop of Norwich from 1660 to 1676.

what thou teachest to others? He is too delicate a teacher who persuadeth others to fast with a full belly. A robber may accuse covetousness. *Sacerdotis Christi os, mens, manusque concordent;* a minister of Christ should have his tongue, and his heart, and his hand agree.[22]

Very quaint also is the language of Thomas Playfere[23] in his *Say Well, Do Well.*

There was a ridiculous actor in the city of Smyrna, who, pronouncing *O caelum*! O heaven! pointed with his finger towards the ground; which when Polemo, the chiefest man in the place, saw, he could abide to stay no longer, but went from the company in a great chafe, saying 'This fool hath made a solecism with his hand, he has spoken false Latin with his finger.' And such are they who teach well and do ill; that however they have heaven at their tongue's end, yet the earth is at their finger's end; such as do not only speak false Latin with their tongue, but false divinity with their hands; such as live not according to their preaching. But he that sits in the heaven will laugh them to scorn, and hiss them off the stage, if they do not mend their action.[24]

Attention to detail

Even in little things the minister should take care that his life is consistent with his ministry. He should be especially careful never to fall short of his word. This should be pushed even to scrupulosity; we cannot be too careful; truth must not only be in us, but shine from us. A celebrated doctor of divinity in London, who is now in heaven I have no doubt—a very excellent and godly man—

---

[22] Edward Reynolds, *The Whole Works of the Right Rev. Edwards Reynolds, D. D., Lord Bishop of Norwich, etc.*, vol. 5 (London: B. Holdsworth, 1826), 404-405.

[23] Thomas Playfere (1561-1609) was an Anglican theologian, professor at Cambridge University, and chaplain to King James I.

[24] John Spencer, *Things New & Old: or, A Storehouse of Similes, Sentences, Allegories, Apophthegms, Adages, Apologues, Divine, Moral, Political, etc.*, vol. 1 (London: William Tegg, 1867), 337.

The Minister's Self-Watch

gave notice one Sunday that he intended to visit all his people, and said, that in order to be able to get round and visit them and their families once in the year, he should take all the seatholders in order. A person well known to me, who was then a poor man, was delighted with the idea that the minister was coming to his house to see him, and about a week or two before he conceived it would be his turn, his wife was very careful to sweep the hearth and keep the house tidy, and the man ran home early from work, hoping each night to find the doctor there. This went on for a considerable time. He either forgot his promise, or grew weary in performing it, or for some other reason never went to this poor man's house, and the result was this, the man lost confidence in all preachers, and said, "They care for the rich, but they do not care for us who are poor." That man never settled down to any one place of worship for many years, till at last he dropped into Exeter Hall and remained my hearer for years till providence removed him. It was no small task to make him believe that any minister could be an honest man, and could impartially love both rich and poor. Let us avoid doing such mischief, by being very particular as to our word.

We must remember that we are very much looked at. Men hardly have the impudence to break the law in the open sight of their fellows, yet in such publicity we live and move. We are watched by a thousand eagle eyes. Let us so act that we shall never need to care if all heaven, and earth, and hell, swelled the list of spectators. Our public position is a great gain if we are enabled to exhibit the fruits of the Spirit in our lives. Take heed, brethren, that you throw not away the advantage.

When we say to you, my dear brethren, take care of your life, we mean be careful of even the minutiae of your character. Avoid little debts, unpunctuality, gossiping, nicknaming, petty quarrels, and all other of those little vices which fill the ointment with flies. The self-indulgences which have lowered the repute of many must not be tolerated by us. The familiarities which have laid others under suspicion, we must chastely avoid. The roughnesses which have rendered some obnoxious, and the fopperies which have made others contemptible, we must put away. We cannot afford to run great risks through little things. Our care must be to act on the rule, "giving no offence in anything, that the ministry be not blamed" (2 Cor. 6:3).

By this is not intended that we are to hold ourselves bound by every whim or fashion of the society in which we move. As a general rule, I hate the fashions of society, and detest conventionalities, and if I conceived it best to put my foot through a law of etiquette, I should feel gratified in having it to do. No, we are men, not slaves, and are not to relinquish our manly freedom, to be the lacqueys of those who affect gentility or boast refinement. Yet, brethren, anything that verges upon the coarseness which is akin to sin, we must shun as we would a viper. The rules of Chesterfield are ridiculous to us, but not the example of Christ, and he was never coarse, low, discourteous, or indelicate.

Even in your recreations, remember that you are ministers. When you are off the parade you are still officers in the army of Christ, and as such demean yourselves. But if the lesser things must be looked after, how careful should you be in the great matters of morality, honesty, and integrity! Here the minister must not fail. His private life must ever keep good tune with his ministry, or his day will soon set with him, and the sooner he retires the better, for his continuance in his office will only dishonour the cause of God and ruin himself.

2
The Call to the Ministry

Introduction

Some of Spurgeon's most distinctive contributions to the discipline of pastoral theology appear in his treatment of the subject of the call to the ministry. In this lecture on the topic, which is among his most well-known, Spurgeon identifies four main elements of a call to pastoral ministry. The first is what he calls "an intense, all-absorbing desire for the work" and "an irresistible, overwhelming craving and raging thirst" to preach the gospel. In this first element, it is almost impossible to imagine that Spurgeon's own personality and temperament did not affect his thinking. Spurgeon simply could not conceive of a man stepping into the ministry with anything less than an all-consuming, insatiable appetite for the work of preaching and pastoral care. What he termed "soul-winning" was like necessary food to Spurgeon, and preaching Christ like needed drink.

Spurgeon identifies aptness to teach as the second element contributing to a call to the ministry. As a matter of policy, the Pastors' College under Spurgeon's leadership only received into admission students who demonstrated at least two years of preaching experience before applying.[1] As he says in the lecture, "We never tried to make a minister, and should fail if we did; we receive none into the College but those who profess to be ministers already." Spurgeon himself had about a year of preaching experience under his belt before he took up his first pastorate in the

---

[1] C. H. Spurgeon, *C. H. Spurgeon's Autobiography, compiled from His Diary, Letters, and Records by His Wife and his Private Secretary*, vol. 2 (London: Passmore and Alabaster, 1898), 148–149.

small village of Waterbeach as a seventeen-year-old. By the time he arrived in London at the age of nineteen to pastor the New Park Street Chapel he had already preached over 600 sermons.[2]

The third indicator that a man is called to the ministry, according to Spurgeon, is that souls are actually saved under his preaching. He believed the ultimate aim of the ministry was soul-winning, and thus, it was simply to be expected that if a man was indeed called to the ministry, God would supply the fruit of conversion as an endorsement of that call. Thus, Spurgeon held the conversions of souls to be one of surest indications of a man's call to ministry.

Spurgeon asserts that the final seal of a call to ministry is found in what might be called the "external call." This call is conferred by the collective judgement of a local church congregation. Spurgeon believed that the congregation's approval was an altogether necessary part of a man's call to ministry. It was not enough for the man himself to feel an all-absorbing, internal desire for the work. His own sense of his call must meet also with the approval of the congregation, which ultimately has the final say in the man's call to the ministry.

Spurgeon was unswerving in his conviction that all four of these conditions must be met if indeed a man was to be properly called to pastoral ministry.

---

[2] Eric W. Hayden, "Did you know," *Christian History*, 29, no. 1 (1991): 2.

The Call to the Ministry

Any Christian has a right to disseminate the gospel who has the ability to do so; and more, he not only has the right, but it is his duty so to do as long as he lives (Rev. 22:17). The propagation of the gospel is left, not to a few, but to all the disciples of the Lord Jesus Christ. According to the measure of grace entrusted to him by the Holy Spirit, each man is bound to minister in his day and generation, both to the church and among unbelievers. Indeed, this question goes beyond men, and even includes the whole of the other sex; whether believers are male or female, they are all bound, when enabled by divine grace, to exert themselves to the utmost to extend the knowledge of the Lord Jesus Christ. Our service, however, need not take the particular form of preaching—certainly, in some cases it must not, as for instance in the case of females, whose public teaching is expressly prohibited (1 Cor. 14:34; 1 Tim. 2:12). But yet if we have the ability to preach, we are bound to exercise it. I do not, however, in this lecture allude to occasional preaching, or any other form of ministry common to all the saints, but to the work and office of the bishopric, in which is included both teaching and bearing rule in the church, which requires the dedication of a man's entire life to spiritual work, and separation from every secular calling, (2 Tim. 2:4); and entitles the man to cast himself for temporal supplies upon the church of God since he gives up all his time, energies, and endeavours, for the good of those over whom he presides (1 Cor. 9:11; 1 Tim. 5:18). Such a man is addressed by Peter in the words, "Feed the flock of God which is among you, taking the oversight thereof" (1 Pet. 5:2). Now, all in a church cannot oversee, or rule—there must be some to be overseen and ruled, and we believe that the Holy Ghost appoints in the church of God some to act as overseers, while others are made willing to be watched over for their good. All are not called to labour in word and doctrine, or to be elders, or to exercise the office of a bishop; nor should all aspire to such works, since the gifts necessary are nowhere promised to all, but those should addict themselves to such important engagements who feel, like the apostle, that they have "received this ministry" (2 Cor. 4:1). No man may intrude into the sheep-fold as an under-shepherd; he must have an eye to the chief Shepherd, and wait his beck and command. Or ever a man stands forth as God's ambassador, he must wait for the call from above, and if he does not so, but rushes into the sacred office, the Lord will say of him and others like him, "I sent them not, neither commanded them; therefore they shall not profit this people at all, saith the Lord" (Jer. 23:32).

Old Testament ministers

By reference to the Old Testament, you will find the messengers of God in the old dispensation claiming to hold commissions from Jehovah. Isaiah tells us that one of the seraphim touched his lips with a live coal from off the altar, and the voice of the Lord said, "Whom shall I send, and who will go for us?" (Isa. 6:8). Then said the prophet, "Here am I, send me." He ran not before he had been thus especially visited of the Lord and qualified for his mission. "How shall they preach, except they be sent?" were words as yet unuttered, but their solemn meaning was well understood. Jeremiah details his call in his first chapter:

> Then the word of the Lord came unto me, saying, Before I formed thee in the belly I knew thee; and before thou camest forth out of the womb, I sanctified thee, and I ordained thee a prophet unto the nations. Then said I, Ah, Lord God! behold, I cannot speak: for I am a child. But the Lord said unto me, Say not, I am a child: for thou shalt go to all that I shall send thee, and whatsoever I command thee thou shalt

The Call to the Ministry

speak. Be not afraid of their faces: for I am with thee to deliver thee, saith the Lord. Then the Lord put forth his hand, and touched my mouth; and the Lord said unto me, Behold, I have put my words in thy mouth. See, I have this day set thee over the nations and over the kingdoms, to root out, and to pull down, and to destroy, and to throw down, and to build, and to plant (Jer. 1:4-10).

Varying in its outward form, but to the same purport, was the commission of Ezekiel; it runs thus in his own words: "And he said unto me, Son of man, stand upon thy feet, and I will speak unto thee. And the Spirit entered into me when he spake unto me, and set me upon my feet, that I heard him that spake unto me. And he said unto me, Son of man, I send thee to the children of Israel, to a rebellious nation that hath rebelled against me: they and their fathers have transgressed against me, even unto this very day" (Ezek. 2:1-3). "Moreover he said unto me, Son of man, eat that thou findest; eat this roll, and go speak unto the house of Israel. So I opened my mouth, and he caused me to eat that roll. And he said unto me, Son of man, cause thy belly to eat, and fill thy bowels with this roll that I give thee. Then did I eat it; and it was in my mouth as honey for sweetness. And he said unto me, Son of man, go, get thee unto the house of Israel, and speak with my words unto them" (Ezek. 3:1-4). Daniel's call to prophesy, although not recorded, is abundantly attested by the visions granted to him, and the exceeding favour which he had with the Lord, both in his solitary meditations and public acts. It is not needful to pass all the other prophets in review, for they all claimed to speak with "thus saith the Lord." In the present dispensation, the priesthood is common to all the saints; but to prophesy, or what is analogous thereto, namely, to be moved by the Holy Ghost to give oneself up wholly to the proclamation of the gospel, is, as a matter of fact, the gift and calling of only a comparatively small number; and surely these need to be as sure of the rightfulness of their position as were the prophets; and yet how can they justify their office, except by a similar call?

New Testament ministers

Nor need any imagine that such calls are a mere delusion, and that none are in this age separated for the peculiar work of teaching and overseeing the church, for the very names given to ministers in the New Testament imply a previous call to their work. The apostle says, "Now then we are ambassadors for God" (2 Cor. 5:20), but does not the very soul of the ambassadorial office lie in the appointment which is made by the monarch represented? An ambassador unsent would be a laughing-stock. Men who dare to avow themselves ambassadors for Christ, must feel most solemnly that the Lord has "committed" to them the word of reconciliation (2 Cor. 5:18, 19). If it be said that this is restricted to the apostles, I answer that the epistle is written not in the name of Paul only, but of Timothy also, and hence includes other ministry besides apostleship. In the first epistle to the Corinthians we read, "Let a man so account of us (the us here meaning Paul and Sosthenes, 1 Cor. 1:1), as of the ministers of Christ, and stewards of the mysteries of God" (1 Cor. 4:1). Surely a steward must hold his office from the Master. He cannot be a steward merely because he chooses to be so, or is so regarded by others. If any of us should elect ourselves stewards to the Marquis of Westminster, and proceed to deal with his property, we should have our mistake very speedily pointed out to us in the most convincing manner. There must evidently be authority ere a man can legally become a bishop, "the steward of God" (Titus 1:7).

The Apocalyptic title of Angel (Rev. 2:1) means a messenger, and how shall men be Christ's heralds, unless by his election and ordination? If the reference of the word Angel to the minister be questioned, we should be glad to have it shown that it can relate to any one else. To whom would the Spirit write in the church as

The Call to the Ministry

its representative, but to some one in a position analogous to that of the presiding elder?

Titus was bidden to make full proof of his ministry—there was surely something to prove. Some are "vessels unto honour, sanctified and meet for the Master's use, and prepared unto every good work" (2 Tim. 2:21). The Master is not to be denied the choice of the vessels which he uses, he will still say of certain men as he did of Saul of Tarsus, "He is a chosen vessel unto me, to bear my name before the Gentiles" (Acts 9:15). When our Lord ascended on high he gave gifts unto men, and it is noteworthy that these gifts were men set apart for various works, "He gave some, apostles; and some, prophets; and some, evangelists; and some, pastors and teachers" (Eph. 4:11); from which it is evident that certain individuals are, as the result of our Lord's ascension, bestowed upon the churches as pastors. They are given of God, and consequently not self-elevated to their position. Brethren, I trust you may be able one day to speak of the flock over whom "the Holy Ghost has made you overseers" (Acts 20:28), and I pray that every one of you may be able to say with the apostle of the Gentiles, that your ministry is not of man, neither by man, but that you have received it of the Lord (Gal. 1:1). In you may that ancient promise be fulfilled, "I will give them pastors according to mine heart" (Jer. 3:15). "I will set up shepherds over them, which shall feed them" (Jer. 23:4). May the Lord himself fulfil in your several persons his own declaration, "I have set watchmen upon thy walls, O Jerusalem, which shall never hold their peace day nor night" (Isa. 62:6). May you take forth the precious from the vile, and so be as God's mouth (Jer. 15:19). May the Lord make manifest by you the savour of the knowledge of Jesus in every place, and make you "unto God a sweet savour of Christ, in them that are saved, and in them that perish" (2 Cor. 2:15). Having a priceless treasure in earthen vessels, may the excellency of the divine power rest upon you, and so may you both glorify God and clear yourselves from the blood of all men. As the Lord Jesus went up to the Mount and called to him whom he would, and then sent them forth to preach (Mark 3:13), even so may he select you, call you upward to commune with himself, and send you forth as his elect servants to bless both the church and the world.

Discerning a call to ministry

How may a young man know whether he is called or not? That is a weighty enquiry, and I desire to treat it most solemnly. O for divine guidance in so doing! That hundreds have missed their way, and stumbled against a pulpit is sorrowfully evident from the fruitless ministries and decaying churches which surround us. It is a fearful calamity to a man to miss his calling, and to the church upon whom he imposes himself, his mistake involves an affliction of the most grievous kind. It would be a curious and painful subject for reflection—the frequency with which men in the possession of reason mistake the end of their existence, and aim at objects which they were never intended to pursue. The writer who penned the following lines must surely have had his eye upon many ill-occupied pulpits,

> Declare, ye sages, if ye find
> 'Mongst animals of every kind,
> Of each condition, sort, and size,
> From whales and elephants to flies,
> A creature that mistakes his plan,
> And errs so constantly as man!
>
> Each kind pursues its proper good,
> And seeks enjoyment, rest and food,
> As nature points, and never errs
> In what it chooses or prefers;
> Man only blunders, though possessed
> Of reason far above the rest.
> Descend to instances and try:

The Call to the Ministry

An ox will not attempt to fly,
Or leave his pasture in the wood
With fishes to explore the flood.
Man only acts of every creature
In opposition to his nature.[1]

When I think upon the all but infinite mischief which may result from a mistake as to our vocation for the Christian pastorate, I feel overwhelmed with fear lest any of us should be slack in examining our credentials, and I had rather that we stood too much in doubt, and examined too frequently, than that we should become cumberers of the ground. There are not lacking many exact methods by which a man may test his call to the ministry if he earnestly desires to do so. It is imperative upon him not to enter the ministry until he has made solemn quest and trial of himself as to this point. His own personal salvation being secure, he must investigate as to the further matter of his call to office; the first is vital to himself as a Christian, the second equally vital to him as a pastor. As well be a professor without conversion, as a pastor without calling. In both cases there is a name and nothing more.

An all-absorbing desire

The first sign of the heavenly call is an intense, all-absorbing desire for the work. In order to a true call to the ministry there must be an irresistible, overwhelming craving and raging thirst for telling to others what God has done to our own souls. What if I call it a kind of στοργη, such as birds have for rearing their young when the season is come; when the mother-bird would sooner die than leave her nest. It was said of Alleine[2] by one who knew him

---

[1] William Wilkie, "The Boy and the Rainbow," in *The British Poets Including Translations In One Hundred Volumes, LXXI. Jenyns. Wilkie. Graeme* (Chiswick: C. Whittingham, 1822), 185.

[2] Joseph Alleine (1634–1668) was an English Puritan pastor best known for his book *An Alarm to the Unconverted*. Spurgeon was deeply impacted by Alleine's book as

intimately, that "he was infinitely and insatiably greedy of the conversion of souls." When he might have had a fellowship at his university, he preferred a chaplaincy, because he was "inspired with an impatience to be occupied in direct ministerial work."[3]

"Do not enter the ministry if you can help it," was the deeply sage advice of a divine to one who sought his judgment. If any student in this room could be content to be a newspaper editor, or a grocer, or a farmer, or a doctor, or a lawyer, or a senator, or a king, in the name of heaven and earth let him go his way; he is not the man in whom dwells the Spirit of God in its fulness, for a man so filled with God would utterly weary of any pursuit but that for which his inmost soul pants. If on the other hand, you can say that for all the wealth of both the Indies you could not and dare not espouse any other calling so as to be put aside from preaching the gospel of Jesus Christ, then, depend upon it, if other things be equally satisfactory, you have the signs of this apostleship. We must feel that woe is unto us if we preach not the gospel. The word of God must be unto us as fire in our bones, otherwise, if we undertake the ministry, we shall be unhappy in it, shall be unable to bear the self-denials incident to it, and shall be of little service to those among whom we minister. I speak of self-denials, and well I may, for the true pastor's work is full of them, and without a love to his calling he will soon succumb, and either leave the drudgery, or move on in discontent, burdened with a monotony as tiresome as that of a blind horse in a mill.

> There is a comfort in the strength of love;
> 'Twill make a thing endurable which else

---

a boy. See C. H. Spurgeon, *C. H. Spurgeon's Autobiography, Compiled from his Diary, Letters, and Records by His Wife and His Private Secretary*, vol. 1 (London: Passmore and Alabaster, 1897), 80.

[3] These two quotes were possibly drawn from Charles Stanford, *Joseph Alleine: His Companions & Times; A Memorial of "Glack Bartholomew," 1662* (London: Jackon, Walford, and Hodder, 1861), 140 and 61 respectively.

The Call to the Ministry

Would break the heart.[4]

Girt with that love, you will be undaunted, divested of that more than magic-belt of irresistible vocation, you will pine away in wretchedness.

This desire must be a thoughtful one. It should not be a sudden impulse unattended by anxious consideration. It should be the outgrowth of our heart in its best moments, the object of our reverent aspirations, the subject of our most fervent prayers. It must continue with us when tempting offers of wealth and comfort come into conflict with it, and remain as a calm, clear-headed resolve after everything has been estimated at its right figure, and the cost thoroughly counted. When living as a child at my grandfather's in the country, I saw a company of huntsmen in their red coats riding through his fields after a fox. I was delighted! My little heart was excited. I was ready to follow the hounds over hedge and ditch. I have always felt a natural taste for that sort of business, and, as a child, when asked what I would be, I usually said I was going to be a huntsman. A fine profession, truly! Many young men have the same idea of being parsons as I had of being a huntsman—a mere childish notion that they would like the coat and the horn-blowing; the honour, the respect, the ease; and they are probably even fools enough to think, the riches of the ministry (ignorant beings they must be if they look for wealth in connection with the Baptist ministry). The fascination of the preacher's office is very great to weak minds, and hence I earnestly caution all young men not to mistake whim for inspiration, and a childish preference for a call of the Holy Spirit.

Mark well, that the desire I have spoken of must be thoroughly disinterested. If a man can detect, after the most earnest self-

---

[4] From the poem "Michael" by William Wordsworth (1770–1850). See William Wordsworth, *The Poetical Works of William Wordsworth*, ed. William Knight, LL. D. (Edinburgh: William Paterson, 1882), 142.

examination, any other motive than the glory of God and the good of souls in his seeking the bishopric, he had better turn aside from it at once, for the Lord will abhor the bringing of buyers and sellers into his temple. The introduction of anything mercenary, even in the smallest degree, will be like the fly in the pot of ointment, and will spoil it all.

This desire should be one which continues with us, a passion which bears the test of trial, a longing from which it is quite impossible for us to escape, though we may have tried to do so; a desire, in fact, which grows more intense by the lapse of years, until it becomes a yearning, a pining, a famishing to proclaim the Word. This intense desire is so noble and beautiful a thing, that whenever I perceive it glowing in any young man's bosom, I am always slow to discourage him, even though I may have my doubts as to his abilities. It may be needful, for reasons to be given you further on, to repress the flame, but it should always be reluctantly and wisely done. I have such a profound respect for this "fire in the bones," that if I did not feel it myself, I must leave the ministry at once. If you do not feel the consecrated glow, I beseech you return to your homes and serve God in your proper spheres; but if assuredly the coals of juniper blaze within, do not stifle them, unless, indeed, other considerations of great moment should prove to you that the desire is not a fire of heavenly origin.

Aptness to teach
In the second place, combined with the earnest desire to become a pastor, there must be aptness to teach and some measure of the other qualities needful for the office of a public instructor. A man to prove his call must make a successful trial of these. I do not claim that the first time a man rises to speak he must preach as well as Robert Hall did in his later days. If he preaches no worse than that great man did at the first, he must not be condemned. You are aware that Robert Hall broke down altogether three

The Call to the Ministry

times, and cried, "If this does not humble me, nothing will." Some of the noblest speakers were not in their early days the most fluent. Even Cicero at first suffered from a weak voice and a difficulty of utterance. Still, a man must not consider that he is called to preach until he has proved that he can speak. God certainly has not created behemoth to fly; and should leviathan have a strong desire to ascend with the lark, it would evidently be an unwise aspiration, since he is not furnished with wings. If a man be called to preach, he will be endowed with a degree of speaking ability, which he will cultivate and increase. If the gift of utterance be not there in a measure at the first, it is not likely that it will ever be developed.

I have heard of a gentleman who had a most intense desire to preach, and pressed his suit upon his minister, until after a multitude of rebuffs he obtained leave to preach a trial sermon. That opportunity was the end of his importunity, for upon announcing his text he found himself bereft of every idea but one, which he delivered feelingly, and then descended the rostrum. "My brethren," said he, "if any of you think it an easy thing to preach, I advise you to come up here and have all the conceit taken out of you." The trial of your powers will go far to reveal to you your deficiency, if you have not the needed ability. I know of nothing better. We must give ourselves a fair trial in this matter, or we cannot assuredly know whether God has called us or not; and during the probation we must often ask ourselves whether, upon the whole, we can hope to edify others with such discourses.

We must, however, do much more than put it to our own conscience and judgment, for we are poor judges. A certain class of brethren have a great facility for discovering that they have been very wonderfully and divinely helped in their declamations. I should envy them their glorious liberty and self-complacency if there were any ground for it; for alas! I very frequently have to bemoan and mourn over my non-success and shortcomings as a speaker. There is not much dependence to be placed upon our own opinion, but much may be learned from judicious, spiritual-minded persons. It is by no means a law which ought to bind all persons, but still it is a good old custom in many of our country churches for the young man who aspires to the ministry to preach before the church. It can hardly ever be a very pleasant ordeal for the youthful aspirant, and, in many cases, it will scarcely be a very edifying exercise for the people; but still it may prove a most salutary piece of discipline, and save the public exposure of rampant ignorance. The church book at Arnsby contains the following entry,

A short account of the Call of Robert Hall, Junior, to the work of the Ministry, by the Church at Arnsby, August 13th, 1780.

The said Robert Hall was born at Arnsby, May 2nd, 1764; and was, even from his childhood, not only serious, and given to secret prayer before he could speak plain, but was always wholly inclined to the work of the ministry. He began to compose hymns before he was quite seven years old, and therein discovered marks of piety, deep thought, and genius. Between eight and nine years he made several hymns, which were much admired by many, one of which was printed in the Gospel Magazine about that time. He wrote his thoughts on various religious subjects, and select portions of Scripture. He was likewise possessed of an intense inclination for learning, and made such progress that the country master under whom he was could not instruct him any further. He was then sent to Northampton boarding school, under the care of the Rev. John Ryland, where he continued about a year and a-half, and made great progress in Latin and Greek.

In October, 1778, he went to the Academy at Bristol, under the care of the Rev. Mr. Evans; and on August 13th, 1780, was sent out to the ministry by this church, being

The Call to the Ministry

sixteen years and three months old. The manner in which the church obtained satisfaction with his abilities for the great work, was his speaking in his turn at conference meetings from various portions of Scripture; in which, and in prayer, he had borne a part for upwards of four years before; and having when at home, at their request, frequently preached on Lord's-day mornings, to their great satisfaction. They therefore earnestly and unanimously requested his being in a solemn manner set apart to public employ.

Accordingly, on the day aforesaid, he was examined by his father before the church, respecting his inclination, motives, and end, in reference to the ministry, and was likewise desired to make a declaration of his religious sentiments. All which being done, to the entire satisfaction of the church, they therefore set him apart by lifting up their right hands, and by solemn prayer. His father then delivered a discourse to him from 2 Tim. 2:1, "Thou therefore, my son, be strong in the grace that is in Christ Jesus." Being thus sent forth, he preached in the afternoon from 2 Thessalonians 1:7, 8. "May the Lord bless him, and grant him great success!"[5]

Considerable weight is to be given to the judgment of men and women who live near to God, and in most instances their verdict will not be a mistaken one. Yet this appeal is not final nor infallible, and is only to be estimated in proportion to the intelligence and piety of those consulted. I remember well how earnestly I was dissuaded from preaching by as godly a Christian matron as ever breathed. The value of her opinion I endeavoured to estimate with candour and patience—but it was outweighed by the judgment of persons of wider experience. Young men in doubt will do well to take with them their wisest friends when next they go out to the country chapel or village meeting-room and essay to deliver the

---

[5] J. M. Morris, *Biographical Recollections of the Rev. Robert Hall, A. M.* (London: George Wightman, 1833), 44–45.

Word. I have noted—and our venerable friend, Mr. Rogers,[6] has observed the same—that you, gentlemen, students, as a body, in your judgment of one another, are seldom if ever wrong. There has hardly ever been an instance, take the whole house through, where the general opinion of the entire college concerning a brother has been erroneous. Men are not quite so unable to form an opinion of each other as they are sometimes supposed to be. Meeting as you do in class, in prayer-meeting, in conversation, and in various religious engagements, you gauge each other, and a wise man will be slow to set aside the verdict of the house.

I should not complete this point if I did not add, that mere ability to edify, and aptness to teach is not enough, there must be other talents to complete the pastoral character. Sound judgment and solid experience must instruct you. Gentle manners and loving affections must sway you, firmness and courage must be manifest, and tenderness and sympathy must not be lacking. Gifts administrative in ruling well will be as requisite as gifts instructive in teaching well. You must be fitted to lead, prepared to endure, and able to persevere. In grace, you should be head and shoulders above the rest of the people, able to be their father and counsellor. Read carefully the qualifications of a bishop, given in 1 Timothy 3:2-7, and in Titus 1:6-9. If such gifts and graces be not in you and abound, it may be possible for you to succeed as an evangelist, but as a pastor you will be of no account.

The fruit of conversion

In order further to prove a man's call, after a little exercise of his gifts, such as I have already spoken of, he must see a measure of conversion-work going on under his efforts, or he may conclude that he has made a mistake, and, therefore, may go back by the

---

[6] George Rogers was a Congregationalist minister and the first Principal of the Pastors' College. He served in the latter role from 1856 to 1881.

best way he can. It is not to be expected that upon the first or even twentieth effort in public we shall be apprized of success, and a man may even give himself a life trial of preaching if he feels called to do so, but it seems to me, that as a man to be set apart to the ministry, his commission is without seals until souls are won by his instrumentality to the knowledge of Jesus. As a worker, he is to work on whether he succeeds or no, but as a minister he cannot be sure of his vocation till results are apparent. How my heart leaped for joy when I heard tidings of my first convert! I could never be satisfied with a full congregation, and the kind expressions of friends. I longed to hear that hearts had been broken, that tears had been seen streaming from the eyes of penitents. How did I rejoice, as one that findeth great spoil, over one poor labourer's wife who confessed that she felt the guilt of sin, and had found the Saviour under my discourse on Sunday afternoon. I have the cottage in which she lived in my eye now; believe me, it always appears picturesque. I remember well her being received into the church, and her dying, and her going home to heaven. She was the first seal to my ministry, and, I can assure you, a very precious one indeed. No mother was ever more full of happiness at the sight of her first-born son. Then could I have sung the song of the Virgin Mary, for my soul did magnify the Lord for remembering my low estate, and giving me the great honour to do a work for which all generations should call me blessed, for so I counted the conversion of one soul. There must be some measure of conversion-work in your irregular labours before you can believe that preaching is to be your life-work. Remember the Lord's words by the prophet Jeremiah, they are very much to the point, and should alarm all fruitless preachers. "I have not sent these prophets, yet they ran; I have not spoken to them, yet they prophesied. But if they had stood in my counsel, and had caused my people to hear my words, then they should have turned them from their evil way, and from the evil of their doings" (Jer. 23:21–22). It is a marvel to me how men continue at ease in preaching year after year without conversions. Have they no bowels of compassion for others? No sense of responsibility upon themselves? Dare they, by a vain misrepresentation of divine sovereignty, cast the blame on their Master? Or is it their belief that Paul plants and Apollos waters, and that God gives no increase? Vain are their talents, their philosophy, their rhetoric, and even their orthodoxy, without the signs following. How are they sent of God who bring no men to God? Prophets whose words are powerless, sowers whose seed all withers, fishers who take no fish, soldiers who give no wounds—are these God's men? Surely it were better to be a mud-raker, or a chimney-sweep, than to stand in the ministry as an utterly barren tree. The meanest occupation confers some benefit upon mankind, but the wretched man who occupies a pulpit and never glorifies his God by conversions is a blank, a blot, an eyesore, a mischief. He is not worth the salt he eats, much less his bread; and if he writes to newspapers to complain of the smallness of his salary, his conscience, if he has any, might well reply, "And what you have is undeserved." Times of drought there may be; ay, and years of leanness may consume the former years of usefulness, but still there will be fruit in the main, and fruit to the glory of God, and meanwhile the transient barrenness will fill the soul with unutterable anguish. Brethren, if the Lord gives you no zeal for souls, keep to the lapstone or the trowel, but avoid the pulpit as you value your heart's peace and your future salvation.

The external call
A step beyond all this is however needful in our enquiry. The will of the Lord concerning pastors is made known through the prayerful judgment of his church. It is needful as a proof of your vocation that your preaching should be acceptable to the people of God. God usually opens doors of utterance for those whom he calls to speak in his name. Impatience would push open or break down the

The Call to the Ministry

door, but faith waits upon the Lord, and in due season her opportunity is awarded her. When the opportunity comes then comes our trial. Standing up to preach, our spirit will be judged of the assembly, and if it be condemned, or if, as a general rule, the church is not edified, the conclusion may not be disputed, that we are not sent of God. The signs and marks of a true bishop are laid down in the Word for the guidance of the church, and if in following such guidance the brethren see not in us the qualifications, and do not elect us to office, it is plain enough that however well we may evangelise, the office of the pastor is not for us. Churches are not all wise, neither do they all judge in the power of the Holy Ghost, but many of them judge after the flesh; yet I had sooner accept the opinion of a company of the Lord's people than my own upon so personal a subject as my own gifts and graces. At any rate, whether you value the verdict of the church or no, one thing is certain, that none of you can be pastors without the loving consent of the flock, and therefore this will be to you a practical indicator if not a correct one. If your call from the Lord be a real one you will not long be silent. As surely as the man wants his hour, so surely the hour wants its man. The church of God is always urgently in need of living ministers; to her a man is always more precious than the gold of Ophir. Formal officials do lack and suffer hunger, but the anointed of the Lord need never be without a charge, for there are quick ears which will know them by their speech, and ready hearts to welcome them to their appointed place. Be fit for your work, and you will never be out of it. Do not run about inviting yourselves to preach here and there. Be more concerned about your ability than your opportunity, and more earnest about your walk with God than about either. The sheep will know the God-sent shepherd; the porter of the fold will open to you, and the flock will know your voice.

The perspective of John Newton

At the time of my first delivery of this lecture, I had not read John Newton's[7] admirable letter to a friend on this subject; it so nearly tallies with my own thoughts, that at the risk of being thought to be a copyist, which I certainly am not in this instance, I will read you the letter:—

> Your case reminds me of my own; my first desires towards the ministry were attended with great uncertainties and difficulties, and the perplexity of my own mind was heightened by the various and opposite judgments of my friends. The advice I have to offer is the result of painful experience and exercise, and for this reason, perhaps, may not be unacceptable to you. I pray our gracious Lord to make it useful.
>
> I was long distressed, as you are, about what was or was not a proper call to the ministry. It now seems to me an easy point to solve; but, perhaps, it will not be so to you, till the Lord shall make it clear to yourself in your own case. I have not room to say so much as I could. In brief, I think it principally includes three things:—
>
> 1. A warm and earnest desire to be employed in this service. I apprehend the man who is once moved by the Spirit of God to this work, will prefer it, if attainable, to thousands of gold and silver; so that, though he is at times intimidated by a sense of its importance and difficulty, compared with his own great insufficiency (for it is to be presumed a call of this sort, if indeed from God, will be accompanied with humility and self-abasement), yet he cannot give it up. I hold it a good rule to enquire in this point, whether the desire to preach is most fervent in our most lively and spiritual

---

[7] John Newton (1725–1807) was a dissolute sailor and slave-trader who eventually became an evangelical Christian, Anglican minister, and hymn-writer. He ministered in Olney, Buckinghamshire from 1764 to 1779 and then became the rector of St. Mary Woolnoth in London where he ministered from 1779 until his death in 1807. He is best known as the author of the most famous hymn in the English-speaking world, "Amazing Grace." He is also known and appreciated today as in his own day for his many published letters.

frames, and when we are most laid in the dust before the Lord? If so, it is a good sign. But if, as is sometimes the case, a person is very earnest to be a preacher to others, when he finds but little hungerings and thirstings after grace in his own soul, it is then to be feared his zeal springs rather from a selfish principle than from the Spirit of God.

2. Besides this affectionate desire and readiness to preach, there must in due season appear some competent sufficiency as to gifts, knowledge, and utterance. Surely, if the Lord sends a man to teach others, he will furnish him with the means. I believe many have intended well in setting up for preachers, who yet went beyond or before their call in so doing. The main difference between a minister and a private Christian, seems to consist in those ministerial gifts, which are imparted to him, not for his own sake, but for the edification of others. But then I say these are to appear in due season; they are not to be expected instantaneously, but gradually, in the use of proper means. They are necessary for the discharge of the ministry, but not necessary as prerequisites to warrant our desires after it. In your case, you are young, and have time before you; therefore, I think you need not as yet perplex yourself with enquiring if you have these gifts already. It is sufficient if your desire is fixed, and you are willing, in the way of prayer and diligence, to wait upon the Lord for them; as yet you need them not.

3. That which finally evidences a proper call, is a correspondent opening in providence, by a gradual train of circumstances pointing out the means, the time, the place, of actually entering upon the work. And until this coincidence arrives, you must not expect to be always clear from hesitation in your own mind. The principal caution on this head is, not to be too hasty in catching at first appearances. If it be the Lord's will to bring you into his ministry, he has already appointed your place and service, and though you know it not at present, you shall at a proper time. If you had the talents of an angel, you could do no good with them till his hour is come, and till he leads you to the people whom he has determined to bless by your means. It is very difficult

to restrain ourselves within the bounds of prudence here, when our zeal is warm: a sense of the love of Christ upon our hearts, and a tender compassion for poor sinners, is ready to prompt us to break out too soon; but he that believeth shall not make haste. I was about five years under this constraint; sometimes I thought I must preach, though it was in the streets. I listened to everything that seemed plausible, and to many things which were not so. But the Lord graciously, and as it were insensibly, hedged up my way with thorns; otherwise, if I had been left to my own spirit, I should have put it quite out of my power to have been brought into such a sphere of usefulness, as he in his good time has been pleased to lead me to.

And I can now see clearly, that at the time I would first have gone out, though my intention was, I hope, good in the main, yet I overrated myself, and had not that spiritual judgment and experience which are requisite for so great a service.[8]

Evaluating men for ministry

Thus much may suffice, but the same subject will be before you if I detail a little of my experience in dealing with aspirants for the ministry. I have constantly to fulfill the duty which fell to the lot of Cromwell's Triers. I have to form an opinion as to the advisability of aiding certain men in their attempts to become pastors. This is a most responsible duty, and one which requires no ordinary care. Of course, I do not set myself up to judge whether a man shall enter the ministry or not, but my examination merely aims at answering the question whether this institution shall help him, or leave him to his own resources. Certain of our charitable neighbours accuse us of having "a parson manufactory" here, but the charge is not true at all. We never tried to make a minister, and should fail if we did; we receive none into the College but those

---

[8] John Newton, *Cardiphonia: Or, The Utterance of the Heart; in the Course of a Real Correspondence*, vol. 2 (Edinburgh: Andrew Balfour, 1814), 49-51.

The Call to the Ministry

who profess to be ministers already. It would be nearer the truth if they called me a parson killer, for a goodly number of beginners have received their quietus from me, and I have the fullest ease of conscience in reflecting upon what I have so done. It has always been a hard task for me to discourage a hopeful young brother who has applied for admission to the College. My heart has always leaned to the kindest side, but duty to the churches has compelled me to judge with severe discrimination. After hearing what the candidate has had to say, having read his testimonials and seen his replies to questions, when I have felt convinced that the Lord had not called him, I have been obliged to tell him so. Certain of the cases are types of all. Young brethren apply who earnestly desire to enter the ministry, but it is painfully apparent that their main motive is an ambitious desire to shine among men. These men are from a common point of view to be commended for aspiring, but then the pulpit is never to be the ladder by which ambition is to climb. Had such men entered the army they would never have been satisfied till they had reached the front rank, for they are determined to push their way up—all very laudable and very proper so far, but they have embraced the idea that if they entered the ministry they would be greatly distinguished. They have felt the buddings of genius, and have regarded themselves as greater than ordinary persons, and, therefore, they have looked upon the ministry as a platform upon which to display their supposed abilities. Whenever this has been visible I have felt bound to leave the man "to gang his ain gate," as the Scotch say, believing that such spirits always come to nought if they enter the Lord's service. We find that we have nothing whereof to glory, and if we had, the very worst place in which to hang it out would be a pulpit; for there we are brought daily to feel our own insignificance and nothingness.

Men who since conversion have betrayed great feebleness of mind and are readily led to embrace strange doctrines, or to fall into evil company and gross sin, I never can find it in my heart to encourage to enter the ministry, let their professions be what they may. Let them, if truly penitent, keep in the rear ranks. Unstable as water they will not excel.

So, too, those who cannot endure hardness, but are of the kid-gloved order, I refer elsewhere. We want soldiers, not fops, earnest labourers, not genteel loiterers. Men who have done nothing up to their time of application to the college, are told to earn their spurs before they are publicly dubbed as knights. Fervent lovers of souls do not wait till they are trained, they serve their Lord at once.

Certain good men appeal to me who are distinguished by enormous vehemence and zeal, and a conspicuous absence of brains; brethren who would talk for ever and ever upon nothing—who would stamp and thump the Bible, and get nothing out of it all; earnest, awfully earnest, mountains in labour of the most painful kind; but nothing comes of it all, not even the *ridiculus mus*. There are zealots abroad who are not capable of conceiving or uttering five consecutive thoughts, whose capacity is most narrow and their conceit most broad, and these can hammer, and bawl, and rave, and tear, and rage, but the noise all arises from the hollowness of the drum. I conceive that these brethren will do quite as well without education as with it, and therefore I have usually declined their applications.

Another exceedingly large class of men seek the pulpit they know not why. They cannot teach and will not learn, and yet must fain be ministers. Like the man who slept on Parnassus, and ever after imagined himself a poet, they have had impudence enough once to thrust a sermon upon an audience, and now nothing will do but preaching. They are so hasty to leave off sewing garments, that they will make a rent in the church of which they are members to accomplish their design. The counter is distasteful, and a pulpit cushion is coveted. The scales and weights they are weary of, and must needs try their hands at the balances of the sanctuary. Such

The Call to the Ministry

men, like raging waves of the sea usually foam forth their own shame, and we are happy when we bid them adieu.

Physical infirmities raise a question about the call of some excellent men. I would not, like Eusthenes,[9] judge men by their features, but their general physique is no small criterion. That narrow chest does not indicate a man formed for public speech. You may think it odd, but still I feel very well assured, that when a man has a contracted chest, with no distance between his shoulders, the all-wise Creator did not intend him habitually to preach. If he had meant him to speak he would have given him in some measure breadth of chest, sufficient to yield a reasonable amount of lung force. When the Lord means a creature to run, he gives it nimble legs, and if he means another creature to preach, he will give it suitable lungs. A brother who has to pause in the middle of a sentence and work his air-pump, should ask himself whether there is not some other occupation for which he is better adapted. A man who can scarcely get through a sentence without pain, can hardly be called to "Cry aloud and spare not" (Isa. 58:1). There may be exceptions, but is there not weight in the general rule? Brethren with defective mouths and imperfect articulation are not usually called to preach the gospel. The same applies to brethren with no palate, or an imperfect one.

Application was received some short time ago from a young man who had a sort of rotary action of his jaw of the most painful sort to the beholder. His pastor commended him as a very holy young man, who had been the means of bringing some to Christ, and he expressed the hope that I would receive him, but I could not see the propriety of it. I could not have looked at him while preaching without laughter if all the gold of Tarshish had been my reward, and in all probability nine out of ten of his hearers would

---

[9] Eusthenes was an ancient practitioner of physiognomy, which is the philosophy or practice of discerning one's character from one's outward appearance.

have been more sensitive than myself. A man with a big tongue which filled up his mouth and caused indistinctness, another without teeth, another who stammered, another who could not pronounce all the alphabet, I have had the pain of declining on the ground that God had not given them those physical appliances, which are as the prayer-book would put it, "generally necessary."

One brother I have encountered—one did I say? I have met ten, twenty, a hundred brethren, who have pleaded that they were sure, quite sure that they were called to the ministry—they were quite certain of it, because they had failed in everything else. This is a sort of model story: "Sir, I was put into a lawyer's office, but I never could bear the confinement, and I could not feel at home in studying law; Providence clearly stopped up my road, for I lost my situation." "And what did you do then?" "Why sir, I was induced to open a grocer's shop." "And did you prosper?" "Well, I do not think, sir, I was ever meant for trade, and the Lord seemed quite to shut my way up there, for I failed and was in great difficulties. Since then I have done a little in life-assurance agency, and tried to get up a school, besides selling tea, but my path is hedged up, and something within me makes me feel that I ought to be a minister." My answer generally is, "Yes, I see, you have failed in everything else, and therefore you think the Lord has especially endowed you for his service, but I fear you have forgotten that the ministry needs the very best of men, and not those who cannot do anything else." A man who would succeed as a preacher would probably do right well either as a grocer, or a lawyer, or anything else. A really valuable minister would have excelled at anything. There is scarcely anything impossible to a man who can keep a congregation together for years, and be the means of edifying them for hundreds of consecutive Sabbaths. He must be possessed of some abilities, and be by no means a fool or ne'er-do-well. Jesus Christ deserves the best men to preach his cross, and not the empty-headed and the shiftless.

The Call to the Ministry

One young gentleman with whose presence I was once honoured, has left on my mind the photograph of his exquisite self. That same face of his looked like the title-page to a whole volume of conceit and deceit. He sent word into my vestry one Sabbath morning that he must see me at once. His audacity admitted him, and when he was before me he said, "Sir, I want to enter your College, and should like to enter it at once." "Well, sir," said I, "I fear we have no room for you at present, but your case shall be considered." "But mine is a very remarkable case, sir; you have probably never received such an application as mine before." "Very good, we'll see about it; the secretary will give you one of the application papers, and you can see me on Monday." He came on the Monday bringing with him the questions, answered in a most extraordinary manner. As to books, he claimed to have read all ancient and modern literature, and after giving an immense list he added, "this is but a selection; I have read most extensively in all departments." As to his preaching, he could produce the highest testimonials, but hardly thought they would be needed, as a personal interview would convince me of his ability at once. His surprise was great when I said, "Sir, I am obliged to tell you that I cannot receive you." "Why not, sir?" "I will tell you plainly. You are so dreadfully clever that I could not insult you by receiving you into our College, where we have none but rather ordinary men; the president, tutors, and students, are all men of moderate attainments, and you would have to condescend too much in coming among us." He looked at me very severely, and said with dignity, "Do you mean to say, that because I have an unusual genius, and have produced in myself a gigantic mind such as is rarely seen, I am refused admittance into your College?" "Yes," I replied, as calmly as I could, considering the overpowering awe which his genius inspired, "for that very reason." "Then, sir, you ought to allow me a trial of my preaching abilities; select me any text you like, or suggest any subject you please, and here in this very room

I will speak upon it, or preach upon it without deliberation, and you will be surprised." "No, thank you, I would rather not have the trouble of listening to you." "Trouble, sir! I assure you it would be the greatest possible pleasure you could have." I said it might be, but I felt myself unworthy of the privilege, and so bade him a long farewell. The gentleman was unknown to me at the time, but he has since figured in the police court as too clever by half.

We have occasionally had applications at which, perhaps, you would be amazed, from men who are evidently fluent enough, and who answer all our questions very well, except those upon their doctrinal views, to which repeatedly we have had this answer: "Mr. So-and-so is prepared to receive the doctrines of the College whatever they may be!" In all such cases we never deliberate a moment, the instantaneous negative is given. I mention it, because it illustrates our conviction that men are not called to the ministry who have no knowledge and no definite belief. When young fellows say that they have not made up their minds upon theology, they ought to go back to the Sunday-school until they have. For a man to come shuffling into a College, pretending that he holds his mind open to any form of truth, and that he is eminently receptive, but has not settled in his mind such things as whether God has an election of grace, or whether he loves his people to the end, seems to me to be a perfect monstrosity. "Not a novice," says the apostle; yet a man who has not made up his mind on such points as these, is confessedly and egregiously "a novice," and ought to be relegated to the catechism-class till he has learned the first truths of the gospel.

Proving one's call
After all, gentlemen, we shall have to prove our call by the practical proof of our ministry in after life, and it will be a lamentable thing for us to start in our course without due examination; for if

The Call to the Ministry

so, we may have to leave it in disgrace. On the whole, experience is our surest test, and if God upholds us from year to year, and gives us his blessing, we need make no other trial of our vocation. Our moral and spiritual fitnesses will be tried by the labour of our ministry, and this is the most trustworthy of all tests. From some one or other I heard in conversation of a plan adopted by Matthew Wilks,[10] for examining a young man who wanted to be a missionary; the drift, if not the detail of the test, commends itself to my judgment though not to my taste. The young man desired to go to India as a missionary in connection with the London Missionary Society. Mr. Wilks was appointed to consider his fitness for such a post. He wrote to the young man, and told him to call upon him at six o'clock the next morning. The brother lived many miles off, but he was at the house at six o'clock punctually. Mr. Wilks did not, however, enter the room till hours after. The brother waited wonderingly, but patiently. At last, Mr. Wilks arrived, and addressed the candidate thus, in his usual nasal tones, "Well, young man, so you want to be a missionary?" "Yes, Sir." "Do you love the Lord Jesus Christ?" "Yes, Sir, I hope I do." "And have you had any education?" "Yes, Sir, a little." "Well, now, we'll try you; can you spell 'cat'?" The young man looked confused, and hardly knew how to answer so preposterous a question. His mind evidently halted between indignation and submission, but in a moment he replied steadily, "C, a, t, cat." "Very good," said Mr. Wilks; "now, can you spell 'dog'?" Our young martyr hesitated, but Mr. Wilks said in his coolest manner, "Oh, never mind; don't be bashful; you spelt the other word so well that I should think you will be able to spell this. High as the attainment is, it is not so elevated but what you might do it without blushing." The youthful

---

[10] Matthew Wilks (1746–1829) was a well-known London preacher and was involved in the founding of the London Missionary Society and the publication of the Evangelical Magazine. His son, John Wilks (1776–1854) was a Whig member of the House of Commons from 1830 to 1837.

Job replied, "D, o, g, dog." "Well, that is right; I see you will do in your spelling, and now for your arithmetic; how many are twice two?" It is a wonder that Mr. Wilks did not receive "twice two" after the fashion of muscular Christianity, but the patient youth gave the right reply and was dismissed. Matthew Wilks at the committee meeting said, "I cordially recommend that young man; his testimonials and character I have duly examined, and besides that, I have given him a rare personal trial such as few could bear. I tried his self-denial, he was up in the morning early; I tried his temper, and I tried his humility; he can spell 'cat' and 'dog,' and can tell that 'twice two make four,' and he will do for a missionary exceedingly well."

Now, what the old gentleman is thus said to have done with exceedingly bad taste, we may with much propriety do with ourselves. We must try whether we can endure brow-beating, weariness, slander, jeering, and hardship; and whether we can be made the off-scouring of all things, and be treated as nothing for Christ's sake. If we can endure all these, we have some of those points which indicate the possession of the rare qualities which should meet in a true servant of the Lord Jesus Christ. I gravely question whether some of us will find our vessels, when far out at sea, to be quite so seaworthy as we think them. O my brethren, make sure work of it while you are yet in this retreat; and diligently labour to fit yourselves for your high calling. You will have trials enough, and woe to you if you do not go forth armed from head to foot with armour of proof. You will have to run with horsemen, let not the footmen weary you while in your preliminary studies. The devil is abroad, and with him are many. Prove your own selves, and may the Lord prepare you for the crucible and the furnace which assuredly await you. Your tribulation may not in all respects be so severe as that of Paul and his companions, but you must be ready for a like ordeal. Let me read you his memorable words, and let

The Call to the Ministry

me entreat you to pray, while you hear them, that the Holy Ghost may strengthen you for all that lies before you.

> Giving no offence in anything, that the ministry be not blamed: but in all things approving ourselves as the ministers of God, in much patience, in affliction, in necessities, in distresses, in stripes, in imprisonments, in tumults, in labours, in watchings, in fastings; by pureness, by knowledge, by long-suffering, by kindness, by the Holy Ghost, by love unfeigned, by the word of truth, by the power of God, by the armour of righteousness on the right hand and on the left, by honour and dishonour, by evil report and good report: as deceivers, and yet true; as unknown, and yet well known; as dying, and, behold, we live; as chastened, and not killed; as sorrowful, yet always rejoicing; as poor, yet making many rich; as having nothing, and yet possessing all things.[11]

---

[11] 2 Corinthians 6:3–10.

3
The Preacher's Private Prayer

Introduction

In the original edition of *Lectures to My Students*, Spurgeon includes the lecture below on "The Preacher's Private Prayer" and another lecture entitled "Our Public Prayer." The latter address, though not included in this volume, is an excellent lecture and focuses on how to lead God's people in prayer particularly in public worship.[1] Spurgeon's best-known published work on prayer is his short volume entitled, *Only a Prayer Meeting*.[2] The book is a collection of addresses Spurgeon gave at various prayer meetings that were held at the Metropolitan Tabernacle over the years. Also in print, one can find various collections of Spurgeon's actual Sunday morning prayers as well as collections of his sermons on the subject of prayer.[3]

The lecture below on the preacher's private prayer focuses primarily on prayer in connection with the minister's personal communion with God as well as the role of prayer in relation to preaching. Throughout the lecture, Spurgeon warns against negligence in personal devotion and urges his students to cultivate the habit of regular and earnest private prayer. His main point is that prayer

---

[1] C. H. Spurgeon, *Lectures to My Students*, First Series (London: Passmore and Alabaster, 1881), 53–71.

[2] Christian Focus has recently published a new edition of this classic work with a foreword by Mark Dever, C. H. Spurgeon, *Only a Prayer Meeting: Studies on Prayer Meetings and Prayer Meeting Addresses* (Scotland, UK: Christian Focus Publications, 2022).

[3] For examples see, C. H. Spurgeon, *Spurgeon's Prayers: Including Advice on How to Improve Prayer Meetings* (Scotland, UK; Christian Focus Publications, 2017); C. H. Spurgeon, *Twelve Sermons on Prayer* (Grand Rapids, MI: Baker Publishing Group, 1989); Jason K. Allen, ed., *Spurgeon on the Priority of Prayer* (Chicago, IL: Moody Publishers, 2021).

readies men for usefulness in ministry like nothing else. He says, "To you, as the ambassadors of God, the mercy-seat has a virtue beyond all estimate. The more familiar you are with the court of heaven the better shall you discharge your heavenly trust."

Spurgeon gives special attention to prayer in connection with preaching. He argues that prayer is vital to a man's preparation to preach. Prayer awakens the preacher's mind to spiritual realities and invites fresh wisdom and insight from God. It also best prepares a man to receive unction and an anointing from the Holy Spirit. Though Spurgeon always maintained that this blessing from the Spirit can never be summoned in some kind of mechanical fashion, he believed nonetheless that prayer cultivates a proper readiness to receive such an anointing. Thus, prayer should be seen as essential to a man's preparation to preach. But Spurgeon also believed prayer must continue after the preaching event and that God must be entreated to bring lasting fruit from the Word preached. Pastors must pray for the success of their labors and for the ongoing health and growth of the flock.

Spurgeon reminds ministers today that prayer is foundational to the work of the ministry. No amount of busyness, even in the most worthwhile endeavors, should crowd out a minister's focused devotion and private prayer. In the face of thousands of distractions and temptations, pastors should imitate the resolve of the early Apostles who said, "we will devote ourselves to prayer and to the ministry of the Word" (Acts 6:4).

The Preacher's Private Prayer

Of course the preacher is above all others distinguished as a man of prayer. He prays as an ordinary Christian, else he were a hypocrite. He prays more than ordinary Christians, else he were disqualified for the office which he has undertaken. "It would be wholly monstrous," says Bernard,[1] "for a man to be highest in office and lowest in soul; first in station and last in life."[2] Over all his other relationships the pre-eminence of the pastor's responsibility casts a halo, and if true to his Master, he becomes distinguished for his prayerfulness in them all. As a citizen, his country has the advantage of his intercession; as a neighbour those under his shadow are remembered in supplication. He prays as a husband and as a father; he strives to make his family devotions a model for his flock; and if the fire on the altar of God should burn low anywhere else, it is well tended in the house of the Lord's chosen servant—for he takes care that the morning and evening sacrifice shall sanctify his dwelling. But there are some of his prayers which concern his office, and of those our plan in these lectures leads us to speak most. He offers peculiar supplications as a minister, and he draws near to God in this respect, over and above all his approaches in his other relationships.

Praying without ceasing

I take it that as a minister he is always praying. Whenever his mind turns to his work, whether he is in it or out of it, he ejaculates a petition, sending up his holy desires as well-directed arrows to the

---

[1] Bernard of Clairvaux (1090–1153) was a Cistercian monk and the Abbot of Clairvaux. He was canonized by the church not long after his death.
[2] I was unable to find the original source for this quote.

skies. He is not always in the act of prayer, but he lives in the spirit of it. If his heart be in his work, he cannot eat or drink, or take recreation, or go to his bed, or rise in the morning, without evermore feeling a fervency of desire, a weight of anxiety, and a simplicity of dependence upon God. Thus, in one form or other he continues in prayer. If there be any man under heaven, who is compelled to carry out the precept, "Pray without ceasing" (1 Thess. 5:17), surely it is the Christian minister. He has peculiar temptations, special trials, singular difficulties, and remarkable duties; he has to deal with God in awful relationships, and with men in mysterious interests; he therefore needs much more grace than common men, and as he knows this, he is led constantly to cry to the strong for strength, and say, "I will lift up mine eyes unto the hills, from whence cometh my help" (Ps. 121:1). Alleine once wrote to a dear friend,

> Though I am apt to be unsettled and quickly set off the hinges, yet, methinks, I am like a bird out of the nest, I am never quiet till I am in my old way of communion with God; like the needle in the compass, that is restless till it be turned towards the pole. I can say, through grace, with the church, "With my soul have I desired thee in the night, and with my spirit within me have I sought thee early." My heart is early and late with God; 'tis the business and delight of my life to seek him.[3]

Such must be the even tenor of your way, O men of God. If you as ministers are not very prayerful, you are much to be pitied. If, in the future, you shall be called to sustain pastorates, large or small, if you become lax in secret devotion, not only will you need to be pitied, but your people also; and, in addition to that, you shall be

---

[3] Joseph Alleine, *The Works of the Truly Pious and Learned Mr. Joseph Allan; Sometime Minister of the Gospel at Taunton in Somerset-shire, etc.* (Dalry: John Shaw, 1806), 630.

blamed, and the day cometh in which you shall be ashamed and confounded.

It may scarcely be needful to commend to you the sweet uses of private devotion, and yet I cannot forbear. To you, as the ambassadors of God, the mercy-seat has a virtue beyond all estimate. The more familiar you are with the court of heaven the better shall you discharge your heavenly trust. Among all the formative influences which go to make up a man honoured of God in the ministry, I know of none more mighty than his own familiarity with the mercy-seat. All that a college course can do for a student is coarse and external compared with the spiritual and delicate refinement obtained by communion with God. While the unformed minister is revolving upon the wheel of preparation, prayer is the tool of the great potter by which he moulds the vessel. All our libraries and studies are mere emptiness compared with our closets. We grow, we wax mighty, we prevail in private prayer.

Prayer as preparation
Your prayers will be your ablest assistants while your discourses are yet upon the anvil. While other men, like Esau, are hunting for their portion, you, by the aid of prayer, will find the savoury meat near at home, and may say in truth what Jacob said so falsely, "The Lord brought it to me" (Gen. 27:20). If you can dip your pens into your hearts, appealing in earnestness to the Lord, you will write well; and if you can gather your matter on your knees at the gate of heaven, you will not fail to speak well. Prayer, as a mental exercise, will bring many subjects before the mind, and so help in the selection of a topic, while as a high spiritual engagement it will cleanse your inner eye that you may see truth in the light of God. Texts will often refuse to reveal their treasures till you open them with the key of prayer. How wonderfully were the books opened to Daniel when he was in supplication! How much Peter learned upon the housetop! The closet is the best study. The

commentators are good instructors, but the Author himself is far better, and prayer makes a direct appeal to him and enlists him in our cause. It is a great thing to pray one's self into the spirit and marrow of a text; working into it by sacred feeding-thereon, even as the worm bores its way into the kernel of the nut. Prayer supplies a leverage for the uplifting of ponderous truths. One marvels how the stones of Stonehenge could have been set in their places; it is even more to be enquired after whence some men obtained such admirable knowledge of mysterious doctrines. Was not prayer the potent machinery which wrought the wonder? Waiting upon God often turns darkness into light. Persevering enquiry at the sacred oracle uplifts the veil and gives grace to look into the deep things of God. A certain Puritan divine at a debate was observed frequently to write upon the paper before him; upon others curiously seeking to read his notes, they found nothing upon the page but the words, "More light, Lord," "More light, Lord," repeated scores of times; a most suitable prayer for the student of the Word when preparing his discourse.

You will frequently find fresh streams of thought leaping up from the passage before you, as if the rock had been struck by Moses' rod; new veins of precious ore will be revealed to your astonished gaze as you quarry God's Word and use diligently the hammer of prayer. You will sometimes feel as if you were entirely shut up, and then suddenly a new road will open before you. He who hath the key of David openeth, and no man shutteth. If you have ever sailed down the Rhine, the water scenery of that majestic river will have struck you as being very like in effect to a series of lakes. Before and behind the vessel appears to be enclosed in massive walls of rock, or circles of vine-clad terraces, till on a sudden you turn a corner, and before you the rejoicing and abounding river flows onward in its strength. So the laborious student often finds it with a text; it appears to be fast closed against you, but prayer propels your vessel, and turns its prow into fresh waters,

The Preacher's Private Prayer

and you behold the broad and deep stream of sacred truth flowing in its fulness, and bearing you with it. Is not this a convincing reason for abiding in supplication? Use prayer as a boring rod, and wells of living water will leap up from the bowels of the Word. Who will be content to thirst when living waters are so readily to be obtained!

The best and holiest men have ever made prayer the most important part of pulpit preparation. It is said of M'Cheyne,

> Anxious to give his people on the Sabbath what had cost him somewhat, he never, without an urgent reason, went before them without much previous meditation and prayer. His principle on this subject was embodied in a remark he made to some of us who were conversing on the matter. Being asked his view of diligent preparation for the pulpit, he reminded us of Exodus 27:20. "Beaten oil—beaten oil for the lamps of the sanctuary." And yet his prayerfulness was greater still. Indeed, he could not neglect fellowship with God before entering the congregation. He needed to be bathed in the love of God. His ministry was so much a bringing out of views that had first sanctified his own soul, that the healthiness of his soul was absolutely needful to the vigour and power of his ministrations.[4]

"With him the commencement of all labour invariably consisted in the preparation of his own soul. The walls of his chamber were witnesses of his prayerfulness and of his tears, as well as of his cries."[5]

---

[4] Andrew A. Bonar, *Memoir and Remains of the Rev. R. M. M'Cheyne: Minister of St. Peter's Church, Dundee* (London: Hamilton, Adams, & Co., and J. Nisbet & Co., 1845), 51. In this original lecture as it appears in *Lectures to My Students*, Spurgeon includes the following in a footnote: "This is one of the best and most profitable volumes ever published. Every minister should read it often." See C. H. Spurgeon, *Lectures to My Students: A Selection from Addresses Delivered to the Students of the Pastors' College, Metropolitan Tabernacle*, First Series (London: Passmore and Alabaster, 1881), 43.

[5] Bonar, *Memoir and Remains of the Rev. Robert Murray M'Cheyne*, 33.

Prayer will singularly assist you in the delivery of your sermon; in fact, nothing can so gloriously fit you to preach as descending fresh from the mount of communion with God to speak with men. None are so able to plead with men as those who have been wrestling with God on their behalf. It is said of Alleine, "He poured out his very heart in prayer and preaching. His supplications and his exhortations were so affectionate, so full of holy zeal, life and vigour, that they quite overcame his hearers; he melted over them, so that he thawed and mollified, and sometimes dissolved the hardest hearts."[6] There could have been none of this sacred dissolving of heart if his mind had not been previously exposed to the tropical rays of the Sun of Righteousness by private fellowship with the risen Lord. A truly pathetic delivery, in which there is no affectation, but much affection, can only be the offspring of prayer. There is no rhetoric like that of the heart, and no school for learning it but the foot of the cross. It were better that you never learned a rule of human oratory, but were full of the power of heavenborn love, than that you should master Quintilian, Cicero, and Aristotle, and remain without the apostolic anointing.

Prayer may not make you eloquent after the human mode, but it will make you truly so, for you will speak out of the heart; and is not that the meaning of the word eloquence? It will bring fire from heaven upon your sacrifice, and thus prove it to be accepted of the Lord.

As fresh springs of thought will frequently break up during preparation in answer to prayer, so will it be in the delivery of the sermon. Most preachers who depend upon God's Spirit will tell you that their freshest and best thoughts are not those which were premeditated, but ideas which come to them, flying as on the wings of angels; unexpected treasures brought on a sudden by

---

[6] The Religious Tract Society, *Life of the Rev. Joseph Alleine of Taunton, Author of "The Alarm to the Unconverted."* (London: Religious Tract Society, 1832), 9.

celestial hands, seeds of the flowers of paradise, wafted from the mountains of myrrh. Often and often when I have felt hampered, both in thought and expression, my secret groaning of heart has brought me relief, and I have enjoyed more than usual liberty. But how dare we pray in the battle if we have never cried to the Lord while buckling on the harness! The remembrance of his wrestlings at home comforts the fettered preacher when in the pulpit. God will not desert us unless we have deserted him. You, brethren, will find that prayer will ensure you strength equal to your day.

As the tongues of fire came upon the apostles, when they sat watching and praying, even so will they come upon you. You will find yourselves, when you might perhaps have flagged, suddenly upborne, as by a seraph's power. Wheels of fire will be fastened to your chariot, which had begun to drag right heavily, and steeds angelic will be in a moment harnessed to your fiery car, till you climb the heavens like Elijah, in a rapture of flaming inspiration.

Pray after preaching
After the sermon, how would a conscientious preacher give vent to his feelings and find solace for his soul if access to the mercy-seat were denied him? Elevated to the highest pitch of excitement, how can we relieve our souls but in importunate pleadings. Or depressed by a fear of failure, how shall we be comforted but in moaning out our complaint before our God. How often have some of us tossed to and fro upon our couch half the night because of conscious shortcomings in our testimony! How frequently have we longed to rush back to the pulpit again to say over again more vehemently, what we have uttered in so cold a manner! Where could we find rest for our spirits but in confession of sin, and passionate entreaty that our infirmity or folly might in no way hinder the Spirit of God! It is not possible in a public assembly to pour out all our heart's love to our flock. Like Joseph, the affectionate minister will seek where to weep. His emotions, however freely he

may express himself, will be pent up in the pulpit, and only in private prayer can he draw up the sluices and bid them flow forth. If we cannot prevail with men for God, we will, at least, endeavour to prevail with God for men. We cannot save them, or even persuade them to be saved, but we can at least bewail their madness and entreat the interference of the Lord. Like Jeremiah, we can make it our resolve, "If ye will not hear it, my soul shall weep in secret places for your pride, and mine eye shall weep sore and run down with tears" (Jer. 13:17). To such pathetic appeals the Lord's heart can never be indifferent; in due time the weeping intercessor will become the rejoicing winner of souls.

There is a distinct connection between importunate agonising and true success, even as between the travail and the birth, the sowing in tears and the reaping in joy. "How is it that your seed comes up so soon?" said one gardener to another. "Because I steep it," was the reply. We must steep all our teachings in tears, "when none but God is nigh," and their growth will surprise and delight us. Could any one wonder at Brainerd's[7] success, when his diary contains such notes as this: "Lord's Day, April 25th—This morning spent about two hours in sacred duties, and was enabled, more than ordinarily, to agonize for immortal souls; though it was early in the morning, and the sun scarcely shone at all, yet my body was quite wet with sweat."[8] The secret of Luther's[9] power lay in the same direction. Theodorus said of him: "I overheard him in prayer, but, good God, with what life and spirit did he pray! It was with so much reverence, as if he were speaking to God, yet with

---

[7] David Brainerd (1718-1749) was a missionary among Native Americans in New Jersey. The account of his life is famously told in Jonathan Edwards' *An Account of the Life of the Late Reverend Mr. David Brainerd*.

[8] Jonathan Edwards, *An Account of the Life of the Late Reverend Mr. David Brainerd* (Edinburgh: John Gray and Gavin Alston, 1765), 26.

[9] Martin Luther (1483-1546) was a German monk and theologian who eventually became the leading protestant reformer and the founder of Lutheranism.

The Preacher's Private Prayer

so much confidence as if he were speaking to his friend."[10] My brethren, let me beseech you to be men of prayer. Great talents you may never have, but you will do well enough without them if you abound in intercession. If you do not pray over what you have sown, God's sovereignty may possibly determine to give a blessing, but you have no right to expect it, and if it comes it will bring no comfort to your own heart. I was reading yesterday a book by Father Faber,[11] late of the Oratory, at Brompton, a marvellous compound of truth and error. In it he relates a legend to this effect. A certain preacher, whose sermons converted men by scores, received a revelation from heaven that not one of the conversions was owing to his talents or eloquence, but all to the prayers of an illiterate lay-brother, who sat on the pulpit steps, pleading all the time for the success of the sermon. It may in the all-revealing day be so with us. We may discover, after having laboured long and wearily in preaching, that all the honour belongs to another builder, whose prayers were gold, silver, and precious stones, while our sermonisings being apart from prayer, were but hay and stubble.

Interceding for the flock

When we have done with preaching, we shall not, if we are true ministers of God, have done with praying, because the whole church, with many tongues, will be crying, in the language of the Macedonian, "Come over and help us" in prayer. If you are enabled to prevail in prayer you will have many requests to offer for others who will flock to you, and beg a share in your intercessions, and so you will find yourselves commissioned with errands to the

---

[10] I was unable to find the original source for this quote, but it's possible Spurgeon drew the quotation from Thomas Watson, *The Christian Soldier; or, Heaven Taken by Storm, Shewing the Holy Violence a Christian is to Put Forth in Pursuit After Glory, etc.* (New York; Robert Moore, 1810), 30.

[11] Frederick William Faber (1814-1863) was a Catholic theologian and hymn-writer and was the founder and first Provost of the London Oratory.

mercy-seat for friends and hearers. Such is always my lot, and I feel it a pleasure to have such requests to present before my Lord. Never can you be short of themes for prayer, even if no one should suggest them to you. Look at your congregation. There are always sick folk among them, and many more who are soul-sick. Some are unsaved, others are seeking and cannot find. Many are desponding, and not a few believers are backsliding or mourning. There are widows' tears and orphans' sighs to be put into our bottle, and poured out before the Lord. If you are a genuine minister of God you will stand as a priest before the Lord, spiritually wearing the ephod and the breast-plate whereon you bear the names of the children of Israel, pleading for them within the veil. I have known brethren who have kept a list of persons for whom they felt bound especially to pray, and I doubt not such a record often reminded them of what might otherwise have slipped their memory. Nor will your people wholly engross you; the nation and the world will claim their share. The man who is mighty in prayer may be a wall of fire around his country, her guardian angel and her shield. We have all heard how the enemies of the Protestant cause dreaded the prayers of Knox[12] more than they feared armies of ten thousand men. The famous Welch[13] was also a great intercessor for his country. He used to say, "he wondered how a Christian could lie in his bed all night and not rise to pray."[14] When his wife, fearing that he would take cold, followed him into the room to which he had withdrawn, she heard him pleading in broken sentences, "Lord, wilt thou not grant me Scotland?" O that we were thus

---

[12] John Knox (1514-1572) was a famous sixteenth century Scottish reformer and founder of the Presbyterian Church of Scotland.

[13] John Welch (or Welsh) (c. 1570-1622) was a minister in the Presbyterian Church of Scotland.

[14] Thomas Boys, *The Suppressed Evidence: Or, Proofs of the Miraculous Faith and Experience of the Church of Christ in All Ages, etc.* (London: Hamilton, Adams, and Co., 1832), 348.

wrestling at midnight, crying, "Lord, wilt thou not grant us our hearers' souls?"

The minister who does not earnestly pray over his work must surely be a vain and conceited man. He acts as if he thought himself sufficient of himself, and therefore needed not to appeal to God. Yet what a baseless pride to conceive that our preaching can ever be in itself so powerful that it can turn men from their sins, and bring them to God without the working of the Holy Ghost. If we are truly humble-minded we shall not venture down to the fight until the Lord of Hosts has clothed us with all power, and said to us, "Go in this thy might" (Judg. 6:14). The preacher who neglects to pray much must be very careless about his ministry. He cannot have comprehended his calling. He cannot have computed the value of a soul, or estimated the meaning of eternity. He must be a mere official, tempted into a pulpit because the piece of bread which belongs to the priest's office is very necessary to him, or a detestable hypocrite who loves the praise of men, and cares not for the praise of God. He will surely become a mere superficial talker, best approved where grace is least valued and a vain show most admired. He cannot be one of those who plough deep and reap abundant harvests. He is a mere loiterer, not a labourer. As a preacher he has a name to live and is dead. He limps in his life like the lame man in the Proverbs, whose legs were not equal, for his praying is shorter than his preaching.

Negligence in prayer

I am afraid that, more or less, most of us need self-examination as to this matter. If any man here should venture to say that he prays as much as he ought, as a student, I should gravely question his statement; and if there be a minister, deacon, or elder present who can say that he believes he is occupied with God in prayer to the full extent to which he might be, I should be pleased to know him. I can only say, that if he can claim this excellence, he leaves me far behind, for I can make no such claim. I wish I could, and I make the confession with no small degree of shame-facedness and confusion, but I am obliged to make it. If we are not more negligent than others, this is no consolation to us. The shortcomings of others are no excuses for us. How few of us could compare ourselves with Mr. Joseph Alleine, whose character I have mentioned before? "At the time of his health," writes his wife,

> he did rise constantly at or before four of the clock, and would be much troubled if he heard smiths or other craftsmen at their trades before he was at communion with God; saying to me often, "How this noise shames me. Does not my Master deserve more than theirs?," From four till eight he spent in prayer, holy contemplation, and singing of psalms, in which he much delighted and did daily practise alone, as well as in the family. Sometimes he would suspend the routine of parochial engagements, and devote whole days to these secret exercises, in order to which, he would contrive to be alone in some void house, or else in some sequestered spot in the open valley. Here there would be much prayer and meditation on God and heaven.[15]

Could we read Jonathan Edwards'[16] description of David Brainerd and not blush? "His life," says Edwards,

> shows the right way to success in the works of the ministry. He sought it as a resolute soldier seeks victory in a siege or battle; or as a man that runs a race for a great prize. Animated with love to Christ and souls, how did he labour always fervently, not only in word and doctrine, in public and

---

[15] Charles Stanford, *Joseph Alleine: His Companions and Times; A Memorial of "Black Bartholomew," 1662* (London: Jackson, Walford, and Hodder, 1861), 155-156. Spurgeon adds the comment in his own footnote, "An admirable biography." See Spurgeon, *Lectures to My Students*, First Series, 48.

[16] Jonathan Edwards (1703-1758) was an American pastor and theologian associated with the first Great Awakening.

private, but in prayers day and night, "wrestling with God" in secret, and "travailing in birth," with unutterable groans and agonies! "until Christ were formed" in the hearts of the people to whom he was sent! How did he thirst for a blessing upon his ministry, "and watch for souls as one that must give account!" How did he "go forth in the strength of the Lord God, seeking and depending on the special influence of the Spirit to assist and succeed him!" And what was the happy fruit at last, after long waiting and many dark and discouraging appearances: like a true son of Jacob, he persevered in wrestling through all the darkness of the night, until the breaking of the day.[17]

Might not Henry Martyn's[18] journal shame us, where we find such entries as these,

Sept. 24th—The determination with which I went to bed last night, of devoting this day to prayer and fasting, I was enabled to put into execution. In my first prayer for deliverance from worldly thoughts, depending on the power and promises of God, for fixing my soul while I prayed, I was helped to enjoy much abstinence from the world for nearly an hour. Then read the history of Abraham, to see how familiarly God had revealed himself to mortal men of old. Afterwards, in prayer for my own sanctification, my soul breathed freely and ardently after the holiness of God, and this was the best season of the day.[19]

We might perhaps more truly join with him in his lament after the first year of his ministry that "he judged he had dedicated too

---

[17] Edwards, *An Account of the Life of the Late Reverend Mr. David Brainerd*, 309.

[18] Henry Martyn (1781–1812) was an Anglican missionary to India and Persia. He was one of the first missionaries sent out by the Church Missionary Society.

[19] John Sargent, *A Memoir of the Rev. Henry Martyn, B. D. Fellow of St. John's College, Cambridge; and Chaplain to the Hon. East India Company* (London: Seeleys, 1852), 118.

much time to public ministrations, and too little to private communion with God."[20]

How much of blessing we may have missed through remissness in supplication we can scarcely guess, and none of us can know how poor we are in comparison with what we might have been if we had lived habitually nearer to God in prayer. Vain regrets and surmises are useless, but an earnest determination to amend will be far more useful. We not only ought to pray more, but we must. The fact is, the secret of all ministerial success lies in prevalence at the mercy-seat.

Prayer and the Spirit's anointing
One bright benison which private prayer brings down upon the ministry is an indescribable and inimitable something, better understood than named; it is a dew from the Lord, a divine presence which you will recognise at once when I say it is "an unction from the holy One." What is it? I wonder how long we might beat our brains before we could plainly put into words what is meant by preaching with unction; yet he who preaches knows its presence, and he who hears soon detects its absence; Samaria, in famine, typifies a discourse without it; Jerusalem, with her feasts of fat things full of marrow, may represent a sermon enriched with it. Everyone knows what the freshness of the morning is when orient pearls abound on every blade of grass, but who can describe it, much less produce it of itself? Such is the mystery of spiritual anointing; we know, but we cannot tell to others what it is. It is as easy as it is foolish to counterfeit it, as some do who use expressions which are meant to betoken fervent love, but oftener indicate sickly sentimentalism or mere cant. "Dear Lord!" "Sweet Jesus!" "Precious Christ!" are by them poured out wholesale, till one is nauseated. These familiarities may have been not only

---

[20] Sargent, *A Memoir of the Rev. Henry Martyn*, 49.

tolerable, but even beautiful when they first fell from a saint of God, speaking, as it were, out of the excellent glory, but when repeated flippantly they are not only intolerable, but indecent, if not profane. Some have tried to imitate unction by unnatural tones and whines; by turning up the whites of their eyes, and lifting their hands in a most ridiculous manner. M'Cheyne's tone and rhythm one hears from Scotchmen continually. We much prefer his spirit to his mannerism; and all mere mannerism without power is as foul carrion of all life bereft, obnoxious, mischievous. Certain brethren aim at inspiration through exertion and loud shouting; but it does not come. Some we have known to stop the discourse, and exclaim, "God bless you," and others gesticulate wildly, and drive their finger nails into the palms of their hands as if they were in convulsions of celestial ardour. Bah! The whole thing smells of the green-room and the stage. The getting up of fervour in hearers by the simulation of it in the preacher is a loathsome deceit to be scorned by honest men. "To affect feeling," says Richard Cecil,[21] "is nauseous and soon detected, but to feel is the readiest way to the hearts of others."[22] Unction is a thing which you cannot manufacture, and its counterfeits are worse than worthless; yet it is in itself priceless, and beyond measure needful if you would edify believers and bring sinners to Jesus. To the secret pleader with God this secret is committed. Upon him rests the dew of the Lord. About him is the perfume which makes glad the heart. If the anointing which we bear come not from the Lord of hosts we are deceivers, and since only in prayer can we obtain it, let us continue instant, constant, fervent in supplication. Let your fleece lie on the threshing-floor of supplication till it is wet with the dew of heaven.

---

[21] Richard Cecil (1748-1810) was a prominent evangelical Anglican minister in London.

[22] Richard Cecil, *Remains of the Rev. Richard Cecil, M. A., Late Rector of Bisley; Vicar of Chobham, Surrey; And Minister of St. John's Chapel, Bedford-Row, London etc.* (London: A. Simpson, 1840), 48.

Servants of Christ, Lovers of Men

Go not to minister in the temple till you have washed in the laver. Think not to be a messenger of grace to others till you have seen the God of grace for yourselves, and had the word from his mouth.

Time spent in quiet prostration of soul before the Lord is most invigorating. David "sat before the Lord;" it is a great thing to hold these sacred sittings; the mind being receptive, like an open flower drinking in the sunbeams, or the sensitive photographic plate accepting the image before it. Quietude, which some men cannot abide, because it reveals their inward poverty, is as a palace of cedar to the wise, for along its hallowed courts the King in his beauty deigns to walk.

> Sacred silence! thou that art
> Floodgate of the deeper heart,
> Offspring of a heavenly kind;
> Frost o' the mouth, and thaw o' the mind.[23]

Priceless as the gift of utterance may be, the practice of silence in some aspects far excels it. Do you think me a Quaker? Well, be it so. Herein I follow George Fox[24] most lovingly, for I am persuaded that we most of us think too much of speech, which after all is but the shell of thought. Quiet contemplation, still worship, unuttered rapture, these are mine when my best jewels are before me. Brethren, rob not your heart of the deep sea joys. Miss not the far-down life, by for ever babbling among the broken shells and foaming surges of the shore.

I would seriously recommend to you, when settled in the ministry, the celebration of extraordinary seasons of devotion. If your ordinary prayers do not keep up the freshness and vigour of your souls, and you feel that you are flagging, get alone for a week, or

---

[23] Charles Lamb, "A Quaker's Meeting," in *Poems and Essays of Charles Lamb* (London: Frederick Warne and Co., 1879), 190.

[24] George Fox (1624–1691) was the founder of the Religious Society of Friends, often referred to simply as Quakers or Friends.

The Preacher's Private Prayer

even a month if possible. We have occasional holidays, why not frequent holy days? We hear of our richer brethren finding time for a journey to Jerusalem; could we not spare time for the less difficult and far more profitable journey to the heavenly city? Isaac Ambrose,[25] once pastor at Preston, who wrote that famous book, "Looking unto Jesus," always set apart one month in the year for seclusion in a hut in a wood at Garstang. No wonder that he was so mighty a divine, when he could regularly spend so long a time in the mount with God. I notice that the Romanists are accustomed to secure what they call "Retreats," where a number of priests will retire for a time into perfect quietude, to spend the whole of the time in fasting and prayer, so as to inflame their souls with ardour. We may learn from our adversaries. It would be a great thing every now and then for a band of truly spiritual brethren to spend a day or two with each other in real burning agony of prayer. Pastors alone could use much more freedom than in a mixed company. Times of humiliation and supplication for the whole church will also benefit us if we enter into them heartily. Our seasons of fasting and prayer at the Tabernacle have been high days indeed; never has heaven-gate stood wider; never have our hearts been nearer the central glory. I look forward to our month of special devotion, as mariners reckon upon reaching land. Even if our public work were laid aside to give us space for special prayer, it might be a great gain to our churches. A voyage to the golden rivers of fellowship and meditation would be well repaid by a freight of sanctified feeling and elevated thought. Our silence might be better than our voices if our solitude were spent with God. That was a grand action of old Jerome,[26] when he laid all his pressing engagements aside to achieve a purpose to which he felt

---

[25] Isaac Ambrose (1604–1664) was a prominent English Puritan.

[26] Jerome (c. 342–420) was one of the most influential theologians of the early church. He is best known for his Latin translation of the Bible, often referred to as the Latin Vulgate.

a call from heaven. He had a large congregation, as large a one as any of us need want; but he said to his people, "Now it is of necessity that the New Testament should be translated, you must find another preacher: the translation must be made; I am bound for the wilderness, and shall not return till my task is finished."[27] Away he went with his manuscripts, and prayed and laboured, and produced a work—the Latin Vulgate—which will last as long as the world stands; on the whole a most wonderful translation of Holy Scripture. As learning and prayerful retirement together could thus produce an immortal work, if we were sometimes to say to our people when we felt moved to do so, "Dear friends, we really must be gone for a little while to refresh our souls in solitude," our profiting would soon be apparent, and if we did not write Latin Vulgates, yet we should do immortal work, such as would abide the fire.

---

[27] I was unable to find the original source for this quote.

4
Sermons—Their Matter

Introduction

The centrality of preaching in Spurgeon's view of his own life and ministry was unmistakable. Mark Hopkins notes, "Preaching never strayed from its central place in Spurgeon's life and work: it must be the starting point for an examination of the various means by which his influence made itself felt."[1] R. J. Helmstadter writes, "His was a preaching ministry; his sermons, above all else were the central feature of the religious life of the Tabernacle."[2] More than anything else, Spurgeon was a preacher, and he gave himself to this work with unparalleled ardor, often preaching seven times per week, and occasionally preaching more than ten times per week.[3] Spurgeon devoted himself to preaching because he believed preaching was at the very heart of the call to the ministry.

Spurgeon's sermon preparation process has become the stuff of legend. He often did not work at all on his Sunday sermon until Saturday evening. Most of that time was spent selecting a text for the sermon. Once he had the text in hand, Spurgeon put together a simple outline that he sketched on a small card which is all he

---

[1] Mark Hopkins, *Nonconformity's Romantic Generation: Evangelical and Liberal Theologies in Victorian England* (Eugene, OR: Wipf and Stock Publishers, 2006), 152.

[2] R. J. Helmstadter, "Spurgeon in Outcast London," in P. T. Phillips ed., *The View From the Pulpit: Victorian Ministers and Society* (Toronto, ON: Macmillan of Canada, 1978), 165.

[3] Eric W. Hayden, *Highlights in the Life of C. H. Spurgeon* (Pasadena, TX: Pilgrim Publications, 1990), 12; George Needham, *The Life and Labors of Charles H. Spurgeon: The Faithful Preacher, the Devoted Pastor, the Noble Philanthropist, the Beloved college President, and the Voluminous Writer, Author, Etc., Etc.* (Boston, MA: D. L. Guernsey, 1887), 41.

brought with him into the pulpit. Anyone who has ever read a full manuscript of one of Spurgeon's sermons can appreciate what a marvel it is that he preached only with a few lines before him.

Spurgeon began publishing his weekly sermons in 1855 with the help of his publishers Joseph Passmore and James Alabaster. This effort would continue throughout the rest of his life and after his death until 1917 when a national paper shortage brought the project to a halt. By 1870, his sermons were selling an average of 25,000 copies per week.[4]

The preparation of Spurgeon's sermons for publishing involved the work of a number of others in addition to the preacher. Peter Morden describes the typical process by which the sermons went from Spurgeon's few scribbled notes on a small piece of paper to the final publication,

> Each week someone sat in the Tabernacle congregation and took down Spurgeon's message, word for word, in longhand. The many people who have enjoyed reading Spurgeon's sermons down the years owe them a significant debt. The preacher would be given these longhand notes on the Monday. These he would proceed to edit, usually quite lightly. The edited notes would then be typeset by his publishers.... The next phase involved returning the draft printed pages to Spurgeon. Spurgeon would work from these galley proofs, doing any further editing he thought was required. It was the corrected galley proof that was the basis of the final published message.... The process by which the preached sermon became the printed text was so well honed that Sunday's sermon could be available to buy and read before the week was out.[5]

---

[4] Christian T. George, "Timeline 1800–1910," in C. H. Spurgeon *The Lost Sermons of C. H. Spurgeon: His Earliest Outlines and Sermons Between 1851 and 1854*, Edited with Introduction and Notes by Christian George, vol. 1, (Nashville, TN: B&H Academic, 2016), xliv.

[5] Peter J. Morden, *C. H. Spurgeon: The People's Preacher* (Farnham, UK: CWR, 2009), 112.

Sermons—Their Matter

Clearly the printing of his sermons week by week involved no small amount of work on Spurgeon's part, and required the assistance of many helpers.

In the lecture below, Spurgeon teaches his students concerning the content of sermons. He encourages his students to preach sermons that are scripturally rich and theologically robust. He urges them to pack their sermons full of truth upon which the sheep can feed to the nourishment of their souls. He also gives practical advice on how to organize material in the sermon and to keep the preaching fresh week by week. Spurgeon's aim was to train ministers who could preach sermons that were powerful with Scriptural argument and doctrinal force, and could do so in their churches weekly in a manner that was spiritually gripping and compelling.

Sermons — Their Matter

Sermons should have real teaching in them, and their doctrine should be solid, substantial, and abundant. We do not enter the pulpit to talk for talk's sake; we have instructions to convey important to the last degree, and we cannot afford to utter pretty nothings. Our range of subjects is all but boundless, and we cannot, therefore, be excused if our discourses are threadbare and devoid of substance. If we speak as ambassadors for God, we need never complain of want of matter, for our message is full to overflowing. The entire gospel must be presented from the pulpit; the whole faith once delivered to the saints must be proclaimed by us. The truth as it is in Jesus must be instructively declared, so that the people may not merely hear, but know, the joyful sound. We serve not at the altar of "the unknown God," but we speak to the worshippers of him of whom it is written, "they that know thy name will put their trust in thee." To divide a sermon well may be a very useful art, but how if there is nothing to divide? A mere division maker is like an excellent carver with an empty dish before him. To be able to deliver an exordium which shall be appropriate and attractive, to be at ease in speaking with propriety during the time allotted for the discourse, and to wind up with a respectable peroration, may appear to mere religious performers to be all that is requisite; but the true minister of Christ knows that the true value of a sermon must lie, not in its fashion and manner, but in the truth which it contains. Nothing can compensate for the absence of teaching; all the rhetoric in the world is but as chaff to the wheat in contrast to the gospel of our salvation. However beautiful the sower's basket it is a miserable mockery if it be without seed. The grandest discourse ever delivered is an ostentatious failure if the doctrine of the grace of God be absent from it; it sweeps over men's heads like a cloud, but it distributes no rain upon the thirsty earth; and therefore the remembrance of it to souls taught wisdom by an experience of pressing need is one of disappointment, or worse. A man's style may be as fascinating as that of the authoress of whom one said, "that she should write with a crystal pen dipped in dew upon silver paper, and use for pounce the dust of a butterfly's wing"; but to an audience whose souls are in instant jeopardy, what will mere elegance be but "altogether lighter than vanity?"

Weigh your sermons

Horses are not to be judged by their bells or their trappings, but by limb and bone and blood; and sermons, when criticised by judicious hearers, are largely measured by the amount of gospel truth and force of gospel spirit which they contain. Brethren, weigh your sermons. Do not retail them by the yard, but deal them out by the pound. Set no store by the quantity of words which you utter, but strive to be esteemed for the quality of your matter. It is foolish to be lavish in words and niggardly in truth. He must be very destitute of wit who would be pleased to hear himself described after the manner of the world's great poet,[1] who says, "Gratiano speaks an infinite deal of nothing, more than any man in all Venice: his reasons are as two grains of wheat hidden in two bushels of chaff; you shall seek all day ere you find them; and when you have them they are not worth the search."[2]

---

[1] This reference is to William Shakespeare (1564–1616), the famous English playwright and poet. Spurgeon greatly admired Shakespeare and read all of his plays, some several times. See William Williams, *Personal Reminiscences of Charles Haddon Spurgeon* (London: The Religious Tract Society, 1895), 81.

[2] William Shakespeare, *The Merchant of Venice, with Introduction, and Notes Explanatory and Critical. For Use in Schools and Classes. By the Rev. Hendry N. Hudson, LL. D.* (Boston: Ginn & Company, 1887), 85.

Sermons—Their Matter

Rousing appeals to the affections are excellent, but if they are not backed up by instruction they are a mere flash in the pan, powder consumed and no shot sent home. Rest assured that the most fervid revivalism will wear itself out in mere smoke, if it be not maintained by the fuel of teaching. The divine method is to put the law in the mind, and then write it on the heart; the judgment is enlightened, and then the passions subdued. Read Hebrews 8:10, and follow the model of the covenant of grace. Gouge's[3] note on that place may with fitness be quoted here: "Ministers are herein to imitate God, and, to their best endeavour, to instruct people in the mysteries of godliness, and to teach them what to believe and practise, and then to stir them up in act and deed, to do what they are instructed to do. Their labour otherwise is like to be in vain. Neglect of this course is a main cause that men fall into many errors as they do in these days."[4] I may add that this last remark has gained more force in our times; it is among uninstructed flocks that the wolves of popery make havoc; sound teaching is the best protection from the heresies which ravage right and left among us.

Sound information upon scriptural subjects your hearers crave for, and must have. Accurate explanations of Holy Scripture they are entitled to, and if you are "an interpreter, one of a thousand," a real messenger of heaven, you will yield them plenteously. Whatever else may be present, the absence of edifying, instructive truth, like the absence of flour from bread, will be fatal. Estimated by their solid contents rather than their superficial area, many sermons are very poor specimens of godly discourse. I believe the remark is too well grounded that if you attend to a

---

[3] William Gouge (1575-1653) was an English Puritan who was minister at St. Ann Blackfriars in London and was also a member of the Westminster Assembly.

[4] William Gouge, *A Commentary on the Whole Epistle to the Hebrews, Being the Substance of Thirty Years' Wednesday's Lectures at Blackfriars, London, etc.* (London: James Nisbet and Co., 1866), 195-196.

lecturer on astronomy or geology, during a short course you will obtain a tolerably clear view of his system; but if you listen, not only for twelve months, but for twelve years, to the common run of preachers, you will not arrive at anything like an idea of their system of theology. If it be so, it is a grievous fault, which cannot be too much deplored. Alas, the indistinct utterances of many concerning the grandest of eternal realities, and the dimness of thought in others with regard to fundamental truths, have given too much occasion for the criticism! Brethren, if you are not theologians you are in your pastorates just nothing at all. You may be fine rhetoricians, and be rich in polished sentences; but without knowledge of the gospel, and aptness to teach it, you are but a sounding brass and a tinkling cymbal. Verbiage is too often the fig-leaf which does duty as a covering for theological ignorance. Sounding periods are offered instead of sound doctrine, and rhetorical flourishes in the place of robust thought. Such things ought not to be. The abounding of empty declamation, and the absence of food for the soul, will turn a pulpit into a box of bombast, and inspire contempt instead of reverence. Unless we are instructive preachers, and really feed the people, we may be great quoters of elegant poetry, and mighty retailers of second-hand windbags, but we shall be like Nero of old, fiddling while Rome was burning, and sending vessels to Alexandria to fetch sand for the arena while the populace starved for want of corn.

We insist upon it, that there must be abundance of matter in sermons, and next, that this matter must be congruous to the text. The discourse should spring out of the text as a rule, and the more evidently it does so the better; but at all times, to say the least, it should have a very close relationship thereto. In the matter of spiritualising and accommodation very large latitude is to be allowed; but liberty must not degenerate into license, and there must always be a connection, and something more than a remote connection—a real relationship between the sermon and its text. I heard

Sermons—Their Matter

the other day of a remarkable text, which was appropriate or inappropriate, as you may think. A squire of a parish had given away a number of flaming scarlet cloaks to the oldest matrons of the parish. These resplendent beings were required to attend the parish church on the following Sunday, and to sit in front of the pulpit, from which one of the avowed successors of the apostles edified the saints from the words, "Solomon in all his glory was not arrayed like one of these" (Matt. 6:29). It is reported that on a subsequent occasion, when the same benefactor of the parish had given a bushel of potatoes to every man who had a family, the topic on the following Sunday was, "And they said, it is manna" (Exod. 16:15). I cannot tell whether the matter in that case was congruous to the selection of the text; I suppose it may have been, for the probabilities are that the whole performance was foolish throughout. Some brethren have done with their text as soon as they have read it. Having paid all due honour to that particular passage by announcing it, they feel no necessity further to refer to it. They touch their hats, as it were, to that part of Scripture, and pass on to fresh fields and pastures new. Why do such men take a text at all? Why limit their own glorious liberty? Why make Scripture a horsing-block by which to mount upon their unbridled Pegasus? Surely the words of inspiration were never meant to be boot hooks to help a Talkative[5] to draw on his seven-leagued boots in which to leap from pole to pole.

Preaching the text

The surest way to maintain variety is to keep to the mind of the Holy Spirit in the particular passage under consideration. No two texts are exactly similar; something in the connection or drift of the passage gives to each apparently identical text a shade of

---

[5] Here, Spurgeon references the character Talkative from John Bunyan, *The Pilgrim's Progress: From This World to That Which is to Come; Delivered Under the Similitude of a Dream* (Kettering: J. Toller, 1843), 87–99.

difference. Keep to the Spirit's track and you will never repeat yourself or be short of matter; his paths drop fatness. A sermon, moreover, comes with far greater power to the consciences of the hearers when it is plainly the very word of God—not a lecture about the Scripture, but Scripture itself opened up and enforced. It is due to the majesty of inspiration that when you profess to be preaching from a verse you do not thrust it out of sight to make room for your own thinkings.

Brethren, if you are in the habit of keeping to the precise sense of the Scripture before you, I will further recommend you to hold to the *ipsissima verba,* the very words of the Holy Ghost; for, although in many cases topical sermons are not only allowable, but very proper, those sermons which expound the exact words of the Holy Spirit are the most useful and the most agreeable to the major part of our congregations. They love to have the words themselves explained and expounded. The many are not always sufficiently capable of grasping the sense apart from the language—of gazing, so to speak, upon the truth disembodied; but when they hear the precise words reiterated again and again, and each expression dwelt upon after the manner of such preachers as Mr. Jay, of Bath,[6] they are more edified, and the truth fixes itself more firmly upon their memories. Let your matter, then, be copious, and let it grow out of the inspired word, as violets and primroses spring up naturally from the sod, or as the virgin honey drops from the comb.

Take care that your deliverances are always weighty, and full of really important teaching. Build not with wood, hay, and stubble, but with gold, silver, and precious stones. It is scarcely needful to warn you against the grosser degradations of pulpit

---

[6] William Jay (1769-1853) was a English Congregationalist who ministered for sixty years at Argyle Chapel in Bath.

Sermons—Their Matter

eloquence, or the example of the notorious orator Henley[7] might be instanced. That loquacious adventurer, whom Pope has immortalized in his "Dunciad,"[8] was wont to make the passing events of the week the themes of his buffoonery on week days, and theological topics suffered the same fate on Sundays. His forte lay in his low wit and in tuning his voice and balancing his hands. The satirist says of him, "How fluent nonsense trickles from his tongue." Gentlemen, it were better never to have been born, than to have the like truthfully said of us; we are on peril of our souls bound to deal with the solemnities of eternity and with no earth-born topics. There are, however, other and more inviting methods of wood and hay-building, and it behoves you not to be duped by them. This remark is necessary, especially to those gentlemen who mistake highflying sentences for eloquence, and latinized utterances for great depth of thought. Certain homiletical instructors, by their example, if not by their precepts, encourage rhodomontade and great swelling words, and, therefore, are most perilous to young preachers. Think of a discourse commencing with such an amazing and stupendous assertion as the following, which by its native grandeur will strike you at once with a sense of the sublime and beautiful: "Man is moral." This genius might have added, "A cat has four feet." There would have been as much novelty in the one information as the other.

I remember a sermon by a would-be profound writer which quite stunned the reader with grenadier words of six-feet length, but which, when properly boiled down, came to as much essence of meat as this—Man has a soul, his soul will live in another world, and therefore he should take care that it occupies a happy place. No one can object to the teaching, but it is not so novel as to need

---

[7] John Henley (1692–1756), known as "Orator Henley," was an especially eccentric English preacher.

[8] Alexander Pope, *The Dunciad, Complete in Four Books, According to Mr. Pope's Last Improvements, etc.* (London: Mr. Warburton, 1749).

a blast of trumpets and a procession of bedizened phrases to introduce it to public attention. The art of saying commonplace things elegantly, pompously, grandiloquently, bombastically, is not lost among us, although its utter extinction were "a consummation devoutly to be wished."[9] Sermons of this sort have been held up as models, and yet they are mere bits of bladder which would lie on your finger-nail, blown out until they remind you of those coloured balloons which itinerant dealers carry about the streets to sell at a halfpenny a-piece for the delectation of the extremely juvenile; the parallel, I am sorry to say, holding good a little further, for in some cases these discourses contain just a tinge of poison by way of colouring, which some of the weaker sort have found out to their cost. It is infamous to ascend your pulpit and pour over your people rivers of language, cataracts of words, in which mere platitudes are held in solution like infinitesimal grains of homeopathic medicine in an Atlantic of utterance. Better far give the people masses of unprepared truth in the rough, like pieces of meat from a butcher's block, chopped off anyhow, bone and all, and even dropped down in the sawdust, than ostentatiously and delicately hand them out upon a china dish a delicious slice of nothing at all, decorated with the parsley of poetry, and flavoured with the sauce of affectation.

Doctrinal preaching

It will be a happy circumstance if you are so guided by the Holy Spirit as to give a clear testimony to all the doctrines which constitute or lie around the gospel. No truth is to be kept back. The doctrine of reserve, so detestable in the mouths of Jesuits, is not one whit the less villainous when accepted by Protestants. It is not true that some doctrines are only for the initiated; there is nothing

---

[9] William Shakespeare, *Hamlet: Prince of Denmark, with Introduction and Notes by K. Deighton* (London: Macmillan and Co., 1891), 53.

Sermons—Their Matter

in the Bible which is ashamed of the light. The sublimest views of divine sovereignty have a practical bearing, and are not, as some think, mere metaphysical subtleties; the distinctive utterances of Calvinism have their bearing upon every-day life and ordinary experience, and if you hold such views, or the opposite, you have no dispensation permitting you to conceal your beliefs. Cautious reticence is, in nine cases out of ten, cowardly betrayal. The best policy is never to be politic, but to proclaim every atom of the truth so far as God has taught it to you. Harmony requires that the voice of one doctrine shall not drown the rest, and it also demands that the gentler notes shall not be omitted because of the greater volume of other sounds. Every note appointed by the great minstrel must be sounded; each note having its own proportionate power and emphasis, the passage marked with forte must not be softened, and those with piano must not be rolled out like thunder, but each must have its due hearing. All revealed truth in harmonious proportion must be your theme.

Brethren, if you resolve in your pulpit utterances to deal with important verities, you must not forever hover around the mere angles of truth. Those doctrines which are not vital to the soul's salvation, nor even essential to practical Christianity, are not to be considered upon every occasion of worship. Bring in all the features of truth in due proportion, for every part of Scripture is profitable, and you are not only to preach the truth, but the whole truth. Do not insist perpetually upon one truth alone. A nose is an important feature in the human countenance, but to paint a man's nose alone is not a satisfactory method of taking his likeness: a doctrine may be very important, but an exaggerated estimate of it may be fatal to an harmonious and complete ministry. Do not make minor doctrines main points. Do not paint the details of the background of the gospel picture with the same heavy brush as the great objects in the foreground of it. For instance, the great problems of sublapsarianism and supralapsarianism, the trenchant debates concerning eternal filiation, the earnest dispute concerning the double procession, and the pre or post millenarian schemes, however important some may deem them, are practically of very little concern to that godly widow woman, with seven children to support by her needle, who wants far more to hear of the loving-kindness of the God of providence than of these mysteries profound. If you preach to her on the faithfulness of God to his people, she will be cheered and helped in the battle of life; but difficult questions will perplex her or send her to sleep. She is, however, the type of hundreds of those who most require your care. Our great master theme is the good news from heaven; the tidings of mercy through the atoning death of Jesus, mercy to the chief of sinners upon their believing in Jesus.

We must throw all our strength of judgment, memory, imagination, and eloquence into the delivery of the gospel and not give to the preaching of the cross our random thoughts while wayside topics engross our deeper meditations. Depend upon it, if we brought the intellect of a Locke[10] or a Newton,[11] and the eloquence of a Cicero,[12] to bear upon the simple doctrine of "believe and live," we should find no surplus strength. Brethren, first and above all things, keep to plain evangelical doctrines; whatever else you do or do not preach, be sure incessantly to bring forth the soul-saving truth of Christ and him crucified. I know a minister whose shoe-latchet I am unworthy to unloose, whose preaching is often little better than sacred miniature painting—I might almost say holy trifling. He is great upon the ten toes of the beast, the four faces of the cherubim, the mystical meaning of badgers' skins, and the typical bearings of the staves of the ark, and the windows of

---

[10] John Locke (1632-1704) was an English philosopher and one of the foremost Enlightenment thinkers. He is often referred to as the "Father of Liberalism."

[11] Isaac Newton (1642-1727) was an English mathematician, physicist, and philosopher and a leading Enlightenment thinker.

[12] Cicero (106-43 BC) was a Roman statesman and rhetorician. He is widely regarded today as one of the most important philosophers in history.

Sermons—Their Matter

Solomon's temple, but the sins of business men, the temptations of the times, and the needs of the age, he scarcely ever touches upon. Such preaching reminds me of a lion engaged in mouse-hunting, or a man-of-war cruising after a lost water-butt. Topics scarcely in importance equal to what Peter calls "old wives' fables,"[13] are made great matters of by those microscopic divines to whom the nicety of a point is more attractive than the saving of souls. You will have read in Todd's "Student's Manual"[14] that Harcatius, king of Persia, was a notable mole-catcher; and Briantes, king of Lydia, was equally *au fait* at filing needles; but these trivialities by no means prove them to have been great kings. It is much the same in the ministry, there is such a thing as meanness of mental occupation unbecoming the rank of an ambassador of heaven.

Among a certain order of minds at this time the Athenian desire of telling or hearing some new thing appears to be predominant. They boast of new light, and claim a species of inspiration which warrants them in condemning all who are out of their brotherhood, and yet their grand revelation relates to a mere circumstantial of worship, or to an obscure interpretation of prophecy; so that, at sight of their great fuss and loud cry concerning so little, we are reminded of,

> Ocean into tempest toss'd
> To waft a feather or to drown a fly.[15]

---

[13] Spurgeon appears to incorrectly attribute this quote to the Apostle Peter, when the original reference is likely from the Apostle Paul in 1 Timothy 4:7. It is possible Spurgeon had 2 Peter 1:16 in mind when he made this reference.

[14] John Todd, *The Student's Manual; Designed, by Specific Direction, to Aid in Forming and Strengthening the Intellectual and Moral Character and Habits of the Student* (London: Simpkin, Marshall, & Co., 1840).

[15] Edward Young, *Night-Thoughts, With Life and Critical Dissertation by the Rev. George Gilfillan*, ed. Charles Cowden Clarke (London: James Nisbet and Co., 1865), 10.

Worse still are those who waste time in insinuating doubts concerning the authenticity of texts, or the correctness of Biblical statements concerning natural phenomena. Painfully do I call to mind hearing one Sabbath evening a deliverance called a sermon, of which the theme was a clever enquiry as to whether an angel did actually descend, and stir the pool at Bethesda, or whether it was an intermitting spring, concerning which Jewish superstition had invented a legend. Dying men and women were assembled to hear the way of salvation and they were put off with such vanity as this! They came for bread, and received a stone; the sheep looked up to the shepherd, and were not fed. Seldom do I hear a sermon, and when I do I am grievously unfortunate, for one of the last I was entertained with was intended to be a justification of Joshua for destroying the Canaanites, and another went to prove that it was not good for man to be alone. How many souls were converted in answer to the prayers before these sermons I have never been able to ascertain, but I shrewdly suspect that no unusual rejoicing disturbed the serenity of the golden streets.

Arranging the content of the sermon

Believing my next remark to be almost universally unneeded, I bring it forward with diffidence—do not overload a sermon with too much matter. All truth is not to be comprised in one discourse. Sermons are not to be bodies of divinity. There is such a thing as having too much to say, and saying it till hearers are sent home loathing rather than longing. An old minister walking with a young preacher, pointed to a cornfield, and observed, "Your last sermon had too much in it, and it was not clear enough, or sufficiently well-arranged; it was like that field of wheat, it contained much crude food, but none fit for use. You should make your sermons like a loaf of bread, fit for eating, and in convenient form." It is to be feared that human heads (speaking phrenologically) are not so capacious for theology as they once were, for our forefathers

Sermons—Their Matter

rejoiced in sixteen ounces of divinity, undiluted and unadorned, and could continue receiving it for three or four hours at a stretch, but our more degenerate, or perhaps more busy, generation requires about an ounce of doctrine at a time, and that must be the concentrated extract or essential oil, rather than the entire substance of divinity. We must in these times say a great deal in a few words, but not too much, nor with too much amplification. One thought fixed on the mind will be better than fifty thoughts made to flit across the ear. One tenpenny nail driven home and clenched will be more useful than a score of tin-tacks loosely fixed, to be pulled out again in an hour.

Our matter should be well arranged according to the true rules of mental architecture. Not practical inferences at the basis and doctrines as the topstones; not metaphors in the foundations, and propositions at the summit; not the more important truths first and the minor teachings last, after the manner of an anticlimax; but the thought must climb and ascend; one stair of teaching leading to another; one door of reasoning conducting to another, and the whole elevating the hearer to a chamber from whose windows truth is seen gleaming in the light of God. In preaching, have a place for everything, and everything in its place. Never suffer truths to fall from you pell-mell. Do not let your thoughts rush as a mob, but make them march as a troop of soldiery. Order, which is heaven's first law, must not be neglected by heaven's ambassadors.

Your doctrinal teaching should be clear and unmistakable. To be so it must first of all be clear to yourself. Some men think in smoke and preach in a cloud. Your people do not want a luminous haze, but the solid *terra firma* of truth. Philosophical speculations put certain minds into a semi-intoxicated condition, in which they either see everything double, or see nothing at all. The head of a certain college in Oxford was years ago asked by a stranger what was the motto of the arms of that university. He told him that it was "*Dominus illuminatio mea.*" But he also candidly informed the stranger that, in his private opinion, a motto more appropriate might be, "*Aristoteles mea tenebrae.*" Sensational writers have half crazed many honest men who have conscientiously read their lucubrations out of a notion that they ought to be abreast of the age, as if such a necessity might not also require us to attend the theatres in order to be able to judge the new plays, or frequent the turf that we might not be too bigoted in our opinions upon racing and gambling. For my part, I believe that the chief readers of heterodox books are ministers, and that if they would not notice them they would fall still-born from the press. Let a minister keep clear of mystifying himself, and then he is on the road to becoming intelligible to his people. No man can hope to be felt who cannot make himself understood. If we give our people refined truth, pure Scriptural doctrine, and all so worded as to have no needless obscurity about it, we shall be true shepherds of the sheep, and the profiting of our people will soon be apparent.

Variety, richness, and force in preaching
Endeavour to keep the matter of your sermonising as fresh as you can. Do not rehearse five or six doctrines with unvarying monotony of repetition. Buy a theological barrel-organ, brethren, with five tunes accurately adjusted, and you will he qualified to practise as an ultra-Calvinistic preacher at Zoar and Jireh, if you also purchase at some vinegar factory a good supply of bitter, acrid abuse of Arminians, and duty-faith men. Brains and grace are optional, but the organ and the wormwood are indispensable. It is ours to perceive and rejoice in a wider range of truth. All that these good men hold of grace and sovereignty we maintain as firmly and boldly as they; but we dare not shut our eyes to other teachings of the word, and we feel bound to make full proof of our ministry, by declaring the whole counsel of God. With abundant themes diligently illustrated by fresh metaphors and experiences, we shall not

Sermons—Their Matter

weary, but, under God's hand, shall win our hearers' ears and hearts.

Let your teachings grow and advance; let them deepen with your experience, and rise with your soul-progress. I do not mean preach new truths; for, on the contrary, I hold that man happy who is so well taught from the first that, after fifty years of ministry, he has never had to recant a doctrine or to mourn an important omission; but I mean, let our depth and insight continually increase, and where there is spiritual advance it will be so. Timothy could not preach like Paul. Our earlier productions must be surpassed by those of our riper years; we must never make these our models; they will be best burned, or only preserved to be mourned over because of their superficial character. It were ill, indeed, if we knew no more after being many years in Christ's school; our progress may be slow, but progress there must be, or there will be cause to suspect that the inner life is lacking or sadly unhealthy. Set it before you as most certain that you have not yet attained, and may grace be given you to press forward towards that which is yet beyond. May you all become able ministers of the New Testament, and not a whit behind the very chief of preachers, though in yourselves you will still be nothing.

The word "sermon" is said to signify a thrust, and, therefore, in sermonising it must be our aim to use the subject in hand with energy and effect, and the subject must be capable of such employment. To choose mere moral themes will be to use a wooden dagger; but the great truths of revelation are as sharp swords. Keep to doctrines which stir the conscience and the heart. Remain unwaveringly the champions of a soul-winning gospel. God's truth is adapted to man, and God's grace adapts man to it. There is a key which, under God, can wind up the musical box of man's nature; get it, and use it daily. Hence I urge you to keep to the old-fashioned gospel, and to that only, for assuredly it is the power of God unto salvation.

Servants of Christ, Lovers of Men

Of all I would wish to say this is the sum: my brethren, preach Christ, always and evermore. He is the whole gospel. His person, offices, and work must be our one great, all-comprehending theme. The world needs still to be told of its Saviour, and of the way to reach him. Justification by faith should be far more than it is the daily testimony of Protestant pulpits; and if with this master-truth there should be more generally associated the other great doctrines of grace, the better for our churches and our age. If with the zeal of Methodists we can preach the doctrine of Puritans a great future is before us. The fire of Wesley,[16] and the fuel of Whitfield,[17] will cause a burning which shall set the forests of error on fire, and warm the very soul of this cold earth. We are not called to proclaim philosophy and metaphysics, but the simple gospel. Man's fall, his need of a new birth, forgiveness through an atonement, and salvation as the result of faith, these are our battle-axe and weapons of war. We have enough to do to learn and teach these great truths, and accursed be that learning which shall divert us from our mission, or that wilful ignorance which shall cripple us in its pursuit. More and more am I jealous lest any views upon prophecy, church government, politics, or even systematic theology, should withdraw one of us from glorying in the cross of Christ. Salvation is a theme for which I would fain enlist every holy tongue. I am greedy after witnesses for the glorious gospel of the blessed God. O that Christ crucified were the universal burden of men of God. Your guess at the number of the beast, your Napoleonic speculations, your conjectures concerning a personal Antichrist—forgive me, I count them but mere bones for dogs; while men are dying, and hell is filling, it seems to me the veriest drivel to be muttering about an Armageddon at Sebastopol or

---

[16] John Wesley (1703–1791) was a famous English preacher of revival during the first Great Awakening and was also the founder of Methodism.

[17] George Whitefield (1714–1770) was a famous English itinerant preacher also associated with the first Great Awakening, who preached both in Britain and America.

Sermons—Their Matter

Sadowa or Sedan, and peeping between the folded leaves of destiny to discover the fate of Germany. Blessed are they who read and hear the words of the prophecy of the Revelation, but the like blessing has evidently not fallen on those who pretend to expound it, for generation after generation of them have been proved to be in error by the mere lapse of time, and the present race will follow to the same inglorious sepulchre. I would sooner pluck one single brand from the burning than explain all mysteries. To win a soul from going down into the pit is a more glorious achievement than to be crowned in the arena of theological controversy as Doctor Sufficientissimus; to have faithfully unveiled the glory of God in the face of Jesus Christ will be in the final judgment accounted worthier service than to have solved the problems of the religious Sphinx, or to have cut the Gordian knot of apocalyptic difficulty. Blessed is that ministry of which Christ is all.

5
The Minister's Fainting Fits

Introduction

Anyone who has studied Spurgeon's life and ministry in depth knows that he struggled mightily with melancholy and depression. At times his despondency was so severe that he doubted whether or not he was truly a child of God. He could very quickly and unpredictably swing between moods and often experienced unbeckoned emotions that were difficult to control. It was not uncommon for Spurgeon to weep uncontrollably without being able to identify the reason why. Many times, his depression sidelined him from ministry and forced him to withdraw to a secluded retreat in order to regain emotional and spiritual equilibrium.

To some, the fact that the mighty "Prince of Preachers" struggled with depression may come as a great surprise. The only thing perhaps more surprising is the fact that he shared these struggles publicly and candidly from the pulpit, which would have been largely unheard of in Victorian society. Spurgeon's struggles, and his openness about them, are a major contributing factor to his ongoing appeal to Christians today. Many have derived comfort and help from the fact that a man of such tremendous faithfulness was also familiar with severe bouts of melancholy and despondency. Of course, what is most encouraging is that Spurgeon ultimately wrestled successfully through his doubts and struggles and was enabled to hold fast to Christ by faith.[1]

---

[1] For those who wish to explore Spurgeon's struggles with depression in greater depth, Zack Eswine has produced an excellent little book on the subject. See Zack Eswine, *Spurgeon's Sorrows: Realistic Hope for those who Suffer from Depression* (Scotland, UK: Christian Focus, 2014).

Servants of Christ, Lovers of Men

In this lecture on "The Minister's Fainting Fits," one can immediately sense Spurgeon's sympathy with those who struggle with depression; a sympathy born of genuine personal experience. He does not stand aloof and removed from those who are afflicted, but speaks as one who has often been visited by dark nights of the soul and has accumulated treasures of the darkness over many long years. He begins by focusing on man's natural frailty, and candidly acknowledges the reality of human vulnerability to spiritual and emotional vicissitudes. This is part of man's natural condition. However, he suggests that ministers in particular are exposed to a number of unique pressures and temptations that can compound their experiences of melancholy. Because pastoral work involves a heightened degree of spiritual and emotional intensity, ministers can be unusually vulnerable to depression, anxiety, and despondency.

After highlighting some particular triggers to depression in ministry, Spurgeon speaks to God's purposes in the minister's fainting fits. Spurgeon suggests that God chooses to bring his servants through such trials as a means of humbling them and mortifying their pride. He also permits such struggles to promote their sanctification and their further usefulness in his kingdom. But most importantly, the Lord permits these trials of the soul to cultivate greater dependence on God and deeper fellowship with him. Spurgeon ultimately offers pastors a redemptive and hopeful perspective on depression and points them to the grace that God is working even in the midst of their greatest sorrows.

The Minister's Fainting Fits

As it is recorded that David, in the heat of battle, waxed faint, so may it be written of all the servants of the Lord. Fits of depression come over the most of us. Usually cheerful as we may be, we must at intervals be cast down. The strong are not always vigorous, the wise not always ready, the brave not always courageous, and the joyous not always happy. There may be here and there men of iron, to whom wear and tear work no perceptible detriment, but surely the rust frets even these; and as for ordinary men, the Lord knows, and makes them to know, that they are but dust. Knowing by most painful experience what deep depression of spirit means, being visited therewith at seasons by no means few or far between, I thought it might be consolatory to some of my brethren if I gave my thoughts thereon, that younger men might not fancy that some strange thing had happened to them when they became for a season possessed by melancholy; and that sadder men might know that one upon whom the sun has shone right joyously did not always walk in the light.

It is not necessary by quotations from the biographies of eminent ministers to prove that seasons of fearful prostration have fallen to the lot of most, if not all of them. The life of Luther might suffice to give a thousand instances, and he was by no means of the weaker sort. His great spirit was often in the seventh heaven of exultation, and as frequently on the borders of despair. His very death-bed was not free from tempests, and he sobbed himself into his last sleep like a great wearied child. Instead of multiplying cases, let us dwell upon the reasons why these things are permitted; why it is that the children of light sometimes walk in the thick darkness; why the heralds of the daybreak find themselves at times in tenfold night.

The reality of human frailty

Is it not first that they are men? Being men, they are compassed with infirmity, and heirs of sorrow. Well said the wise man in the Apocrypha,

> Great travail is created for all men, and a heavy yoke on the sons of Adam, from the day that they go out of their mother's womb unto that day that they return to the mother of all things—namely, their thoughts and fear of their hearts, and their imagination of things that they wail for, and the day of death. From him that sitteth in the glorious throne, to him that sitteth beneath in the earth and ashes; from him that is clothed in blue silk, and weareth a crown, to him that is clothed in simple linen—wrath, envy, trouble, and unquietness, and fear of death and rigour, and such things come to both man and beast, but sevenfold to the ungodly.[1]

Grace guards us from much of this, but because we have not more of grace we still suffer even from ills preventible. Even under the economy of redemption it is most clear that we are to endure infirmities, otherwise there were no need of the promised Spirit to help us in them. It is of need be that we are sometimes in heaviness. Good men are promised tribulation in this world, and ministers may expect a larger share than others, that they may learn sympathy with the Lord's suffering people, and so may be fitting shepherds of an ailing flock. Disembodied spirits might have been sent to proclaim the word, but they could not have entered into the feelings of those who, being in this body, do groan, being burdened. Angels might have been ordained evangelists, but their

---

[1] Ecclesiasticus 40:1–8.

The Minister's Fainting Fits

celestial attributes would have disqualified them from having compassion on the ignorant. Men of marble might have been fashioned, but their impassive natures would have been a sarcasm upon our feebleness, and a mockery of our wants. Men, and men subject to human passions, the all-wise God has chosen to be his vessels of grace; hence these tears, hence these perplexities and castings down.

Moreover, most of us are in some way or other unsound physically. Here and there we meet with an old man who could not remember that ever he was laid aside for a day; but the great mass of us labour under some form or other of infirmity, either in body or mind. Certain bodily maladies, especially those connected with the digestive organs, the liver, and the spleen, are the fruitful fountains of despondency; and, let a man strive as he may against their influence, there will be hours and circumstances in which they will for awhile overcome him. As to mental maladies, is any man altogether sane? Are we not all a little off the balance? Some minds appear to have a gloomy tinge essential to their very individuality; of them it may be said, "Melancholy marked them for her own;" fine minds withal, and ruled by noblest principles, but yet most prone to forget the silver lining, and to remember only the cloud. Such men may sing with the old poet,[2]

> Our hearts are broke, our harps unstringèd be,
> Our only music's sighs and groans,
> Our songs are to the tune of lachrymae,
> We're fretted all to skin and bones.[3]

These infirmities may be no detriment to a man's career of special usefulness; they may even have been imposed upon him by divine

---

[2] Thomas Washbourne (1606–1687) was an English poet and Anglican minister.

[3] Thomas Washbourne, "The Vine Wasted," in *The Poems of Thomas Washbourne, D. D. edited with Memorial-Introduction and Notes; by the Rev. Alexander B. Grosart* (Blackburn, Lancashire: C. Tiplady, 1868), 93.

wisdom as necessary qualifications for his peculiar course of service. Some plants owe their medicinal qualities to the marsh in which they grow; others to the shades in which alone they flourish. There are precious fruits put forth by the moon as well as by the sun. Boats need ballast as well as sail; a drag on the carriage-wheel is no hindrance when the road runs downhill. Pain has, probably, in some cases developed genius; hunting out the soul which otherwise might have slept like a lion in its den. Had it not been for the broken wing, some might have lost themselves in the clouds, some even of those choice doves who now bear the olive-branch in their mouths and show the way to the ark. But where in body and mind there are predisposing causes to lowness of spirit, it is no marvel if in dark moments the heart succumbs to them; the wonder in many cases is—and if inner lives could be written, men would see it so—how some ministers keep at their work at all, and still wear a smile upon their countenances. Grace has its triumphs still, and patience has its martyrs; martyrs none the less to be honoured because the flames kindle about their spirits rather than their bodies, and their burning is unseen of human eyes. The ministries of Jeremiahs are as acceptable as those of Isaiahs, and even the sullen Jonah is a true prophet of the Lord, as Nineveh felt full well. Despise not the lame, for it is written that they take the prey; but honour those who, being faint, are yet pursuing. The tender-eyed Leah was more fruitful than the beautiful Rachel, and the griefs of Hannah were more divine than the boastings of Peninnah. "Blessed are they that mourn" (Matt. 5:4), said the Man of Sorrows, and let none account them otherwise when their tears are salted with grace. We have the treasure of the gospel in earthen vessels, and if there be a flaw in the vessel here and there, let none wonder.

The Minister's Fainting Fits

The unique perils of ministry

Our work, when earnestly undertaken, lays us open to attacks in the direction of depression. Who can bear the weight of souls without sometimes sinking to the dust? Passionate longings after men's conversion, if not fully satisfied (and when are they?), consume the soul with anxiety and disappointment. To see the hopeful turn aside, the godly grow cold, professors abusing their privileges, and sinners waxing more bold in sin—are not these sights enough to crush us to the earth? The kingdom comes not as we would, the reverend name is not hallowed as we desire, and for this we must weep. How can we be otherwise than sorrowful, while men believe not our report, and the divine arm is not revealed? All mental work tends to weary and to depress, for much study is a weariness of the flesh; but ours is more than mental work—it is heart work, the labour of our inmost soul. How often, on Lord's-day evenings, do we feel as if life were completely washed out of us! After pouring out our souls over our congregations, we feel like empty earthen pitchers which a child might break. Probably, if we were more like Paul, and watched for souls at a nobler rate, we should know more of what it is to be eaten up by the zeal of the Lord's house. It is our duty and our privilege to exhaust our lives for Jesus. We are not to be living specimens of men in fine preservation, but living sacrifices, whose lot is to be consumed; we are to spend and to be spent, not to lay ourselves up in lavender, and nurse our flesh. Such soul-travail as that of a faithful minister will bring on occasional seasons of exhaustion, when heart and flesh will fail. Moses' hands grew heavy in intercession, and Paul cried out, "Who is sufficient for these things?" (2 Cor. 2:16). Even John the Baptist is thought to have had his fainting fits, and the apostles were once amazed, and were sore afraid.

Our position in the church will also conduce to this. A minister fully equipped for his work, will usually be a spirit by himself, above, beyond, and apart from others. The most loving of his people cannot enter into his peculiar thoughts, cares, and temptations. In the ranks, men walk shoulder to shoulder with many comrades, but as the officer rises in rank, men of his standing are fewer in number. There are many soldiers, few captains, fewer colonels, but only one commander-in-chief. So, in our churches, the man whom the Lord raises as a leader becomes, in the same degree in which he is a superior man, a solitary man. The mountain-tops stand solemnly apart, and talk only with God as he visits their terrible solitudes. Men of God who rise above their fellows into nearer communion with heavenly things, in their weaker moments feel the lack of human sympathy. Like their Lord in Gethsemane, they look in vain for comfort to the disciples sleeping around them; they are shocked at the apathy of their little band of brethren, and return to their secret agony with all the heavier burden pressing upon them, because they have found their dearest companions slumbering. No one knows, but he who has endured it, the solitude of a soul which has outstripped its fellows in zeal for the Lord of hosts, it dares not reveal itself, lest men count it mad. It cannot conceal itself, for a fire burns within its bones; only before the Lord does it find rest. Our Lord's sending out his disciples by two and two manifested that he knew what was in men; but for such a man as Paul, it seems to me that no helpmeet was found; Barnabas, or Silas, or Luke, were hills too low to hold high converse with such a Himalayan summit as the apostle of the Gentiles. This loneliness, which if I mistake not is felt by many of my brethren, is a fertile source of depression; and our ministers' fraternal meetings, and the cultivation of holy intercourse with kindred minds will, with God's blessing, help us greatly to escape the snare.

The Minister's Fainting Fits

There can be little doubt that sedentary habits have a tendency to create despondency in some constitutions. Burton,[4] in his *Anatomy of Melancholy*, has a chapter upon this cause of sadness; and, quoting from one of the myriad authors whom he lays under contribution, he says,

> Students are negligent of their bodies. Other men look to their tools; a painter will wash his pencils; a smith will look to his hammer, anvil, forge; a husbandman will mend his plough-irons, and grind his hatchet if it be dull; a falconer or huntsman will have an especial care of his hawks, hounds, horses, dogs, etc.; a musician will string and unstring his lute; only scholars neglect that instrument (their brain and spirits I mean) which they daily use. Well saith Lucan, "See thou twist not the rope so hard that it break."[5]

To sit long in one posture, poring over a book, or driving a quill, is in itself a taxing of nature; but add to this a badly-ventilated chamber, a body which has long been without muscular exercise, and a heart burdened with many cares, and we have all the elements for preparing a seething cauldron of despair, especially in the dim months of fog,

> When a blanket wraps the day,
> When the rotten woodland drips,
> And the leaf is stamped in clay.[6]

Let a man be naturally as blithe as a bird, he will hardly be able to bear up year after year against such a suicidal process; he will make his study a prison and his books the warders of a gaol, while

---

[4] Robert Burton (1577–1640) was a scholar and writer associated with Oxford University. He is best known for his book *The Anatomy of Melancholy*.

[5] Robert Burton, *The Anatomy of Melancholy, What it is, with All the Kinds, Causes, Symptoms, Prognostics, and Several cures of it, etc.* (London: William Tegg, 1863), 199.

[6] Alfred Tennyson, "The Vision of Sin," in *A Selection from the Works of Alfred Tennyson, D. C. L., Poet Laureate* (London: Edward Moxon & Co., 1865), 154.

nature lies outside his window calling him to health and beckoning him to joy. He who forgets the humming of the bees among the heather, the cooing of the wood-pigeons in the forest, the song of birds in the woods, the rippling of rills among the rushes, and the sighing of the wind among the pines, needs not wonder if his heart forgets to sing and his soul grows heavy. A day's breathing of fresh air upon the hills, or a few hours' ramble in the beech woods' umbrageous calm, would sweep the cobwebs out of the brain of scores of our toiling ministers who are now but half alive. A mouthful of sea air, or a stiff walk in the wind's face, would not give grace to the soul, but it would yield oxygen to the body, which is next best.

> Heaviest the heart is in a heavy air,
> Ev'ry wind that rises blows away despair.[7]

The ferns and the rabbits, the streams and the trouts, the fir trees and the squirrels, the primroses and the violets, the farm-yard, the new-mown hay, and the fragrant hops—these are the best medicine for hypochondriacs, the surest tonics for the declining, the best refreshments for the weary. For lack of opportunity, or inclination, these great remedies are neglected, and the student becomes a self-immolated victim.

Depression in relation to ministerial success

The times most favourable to fits of depression, so far as I have experienced, may be summed up in a brief catalogue. First among them I must mention the hour of great success. When at last a long-cherished desire is fulfilled, when God has been glorified greatly by our means, and a great triumph achieved, then we are apt to faint. It might be imagined that amid special favours our soul would soar to heights of ecstacy, and rejoice with joy

---

[7] Thomas T. Lynch, *The Rivulet: A Contribution to Sacred Song*, 5th ed. (London: James Clarke and Co., 1883), 38

unspeakable, but it is generally the reverse. The Lord seldom exposes his warriors to the perils of exultation over victory; he knows that few of them can endure such a test, and therefore dashes their cup with bitterness. See Elias after the fire has fallen from heaven, after Baal's priests have been slaughtered and the rain has deluged the barren land. For him no notes of self-complacent music, no strutting like a conqueror in robes of triumph; he flees from Jezebel, and feeling the revulsion of his intense excitement, he prays that he may die. He who must never see death, yearns after the rest of the grave, even as Caesar, the world's monarch, in his moments of pain cried like a sick girl. Poor human nature cannot bear such strains as heavenly triumphs bring to it; there must come a reaction. Excess of joy or excitement must be paid for by subsequent depressions. While the trial lasts, the strength is equal to the emergency; but when it is over, natural weakness claims the right to show itself. Secretly sustained, Jacob can wrestle all night, but he must limp in the morning when the contest is over, lest he boast himself beyond measure. Paul may be caught up to the third heaven and hear unspeakable things, but a thorn in the flesh, a messenger of Satan to buffet him, must be the inevitable sequel. Men cannot bear unalloyed happiness; even good men are not yet fit to have "their brows with laurel and with myrtle bound," without enduring secret humiliation to keep them in their proper place. Whirled from off our feet by a revival, carried aloft by popularity, exalted by success in soul-winning, we should be as the chaff which the wind driveth away, were it not that the gracious discipline of mercy breaks the ships of our vainglory with a strong east wind, and casts us shipwrecked, naked and forlorn, upon the Rock of Ages.

Before any great achievement, some measure of the same depression is very usual. Surveying the difficulties before us, our hearts sink within us. The sons of Anak stalk before us, and we are as grasshoppers in our own sight in their presence (Num. 13:33).

Servants of Christ, Lovers of Men

The cities of Canaan are walled up to heaven, and who are we that we should hope to capture them? We are ready to cast down our weapons and take to our heels. Nineveh is a great city, and we would flee unto Tarshish sooner than encounter its noisy crowds. Already we look for a ship which may bear us quietly away from the terrible scene, and only a dread of tempest restrains our recreant footsteps. Such was my experience when I first became a pastor in London. My success appalled me; and the thought of the career which it seemed to open up, so far from elating me, cast me into the lowest depth, out of which I uttered my miserere and found no room for a gloria in excelsis. Who was I that I should continue to lead so great a multitude? I would betake me to my village obscurity, or emigrate to America, and find a solitary nest in the backwoods, where I might be sufficient for the things which would be demanded of me. It was just then that the curtain was rising upon my life-work, and I dreaded what it might reveal. I hope I was not faithless, but I was timorous and filled with a sense of my own unfitness. I dreaded the work which a gracious providence had prepared for me. I felt myself a mere child, and trembled as I heard the voice which said, "Arise, and thresh the mountains, and make them as chaff" (Isa. 41:15). This depression comes over me whenever the Lord is preparing a larger blessing for my ministry; the cloud is black before it breaks, and overshadows before it yields its deluge of mercy. Depression has now become to me as a prophet in rough clothing, a John the Baptist, heralding the nearer coming of my Lord's richer benison. So have far better men found it. The scouring of the vessel has fitted it for the Master's use. Immersion in suffering has preceded the baptism of the Holy Ghost. Fasting gives an appetite for the banquet. The Lord is revealed in the backside of the desert, while his servant keepeth the sheep and waits in solitary awe. The wilderness is the way to Canaan. The low valley leads to the towering mountain. Defeat prepares for victory. The raven is sent forth before the dove. The darkest hour of the night precedes the day-dawn. The mariners go down to the depths, but the next wave makes them mount to the heaven; their soul is melted because of trouble before he bringeth them to their desired haven.

Depression in the context of overexertion
In the midst of a long stretch of unbroken labour, the same affliction may be looked for. The bow cannot be always bent without fear of breaking. Repose is as needful to the mind as sleep to the body. Our Sabbaths are our days of toil, and if we do not rest upon some other day we shall break down. Even the earth must lie fallow and have her Sabbaths, and so must we. Hence the wisdom and compassion of our Lord, when he said to his disciples, "Let us go into the desert and rest awhile" (Mark 6:31). What, when the people are fainting? When the multitudes are like sheep upon the mountains without a shepherd? Does Jesus talk of rest? When Scribes and Pharisees, like grievous wolves, are rending the flock, does he take his followers on an excursion into a quiet resting place? Does some red-hot zealot denounce such atrocious forgetfulness of present and pressing demands? Let him rave in his folly. The Master knows better than to exhaust his servants and quench the light of Israel. Rest time is not waste time. It is economy to gather fresh strength. Look at the mower in the summer's day, with so much to cut down ere the sun sets. He pauses in his labour—is he a sluggard? He looks for his stone, and begins to draw it up and down his scythe, with "rink-a-tink—rink-a-tink—rink-a-tink." Is that idle music—is he wasting precious moments? How much he might have mown while he has been ringing out those notes on his scythe. But he is sharpening his tool, and he will do far more when once again he gives his strength to those long sweeps which lay the grass prostrate in rows before him. Even thus a little pause prepares the mind for greater service in the good cause. Fishermen must mend their nets, and we must every now

and then repair our mental waste and set our machinery in order for future service. To tug the oar from day to day, like a galley-slave who knows no holidays, suits not mortal men. Mill-streams go on and on for ever, but we must have our pauses and our intervals. Who can help being out of breath when the race is continued without intermission? Even beasts of burden must be turned out to grass occasionally; the very sea pauses at ebb and flood; earth keeps the Sabbath of the wintry months; and man, even when exalted to be God's ambassador, must rest or faint; must trim his lamp or let it burn low; must recruit his vigour or grow prematurely old. It is wisdom to take occasional furlough. In the long run, we shall do more by sometimes doing less. On, on, on for ever, without recreation, may suit spirits emancipated from this "heavy clay," but while we are in this tabernacle, we must every now and then cry halt, and serve the Lord by holy inaction and consecrated leisure. Let no tender conscience doubt the lawfulness of going out of harness for awhile, but learn from the experience of others the necessity and duty of taking timely rest.

Other sources of depression
One crushing stroke has sometimes laid the minister very low. The brother most relied upon becomes a traitor. Judas lifts up his heel against the man who trusted him, and the preacher's heart for the moment fails him. We are all too apt to look to an arm of flesh, and from that propensity many of our sorrows arise. Equally overwhelming is the blow when an honoured and beloved member yields to temptation, and disgraces the holy name with which he was named. Anything is better than this. This makes the preacher long for a lodge in some vast wilderness, where he may hide his head for ever, and hear no more the blasphemous jeers of the ungodly. Ten years of toil do not take so much life out of us as we lose in a few hours by Ahithophel the traitor, or Demas the apostate. Strife, also, and division, and slander, and foolish censures,

The Minister's Fainting Fits

have often laid holy men prostrate, and made them go "as with a sword in their bones." Hard words wound some delicate minds very keenly. Many of the best of ministers, from the very spirituality of their character, are exceedingly sensitive—too sensitive for such a world as this. "A kick that scarce would move a horse would kill a sound divine." By experience the soul is hardened to the rough blows which are inevitable in our warfare; but at first these things utterly stagger us, and send us to our homes wrapped in a horror of great darkness. The trials of a true minister are not few, and such as are caused by ungrateful professors are harder to bear than the coarsest attacks of avowed enemies. Let no man who looks for ease of mind and seeks the quietude of life enter the ministry; if he does so he will flee from it in disgust.

To the lot of few does it fall to pass through such a horror of great darkness as that which fell upon me after the deplorable accident at the Surrey Music Hall.[8] I was pressed beyond measure and out of bounds with an enormous weight of misery. The tumult, the panic, the deaths, were day and night before me, and made life a burden. Then I sang in my sorrow,

> The tumult of my thoughts
> Doth but increase my woe,
> My spirit languisheth, my heart
> Is desolate and low.[9]

---

[8] Spurgeon refers here to the disaster at the Surrey Gardens Music Hall, which took place on October 19, 1856. Spurgeon rented the hall to accommodate the massive crowds that were coming out to hear him preach. The night of the first service in the Surrey Gardens Music Hall, someone in the crowd raised a false alarm by shouting, "Fire!" A mad shuffle ensued as people tried to flee the building. In the midst of all the commotion, a stairwell collapsed and seven people were trampled to death and twenty-eight more people were injured. See C. H. Spurgeon, *C. H. Spurgeon's Autobiography, Compiled from his Diary, Letters, and Records by His Wife and His Private Secretary*, vol. 2 (London: Passmore and Alabaster, 1897), 195-220.

[9] Isaac Watts, "Psalm 25," in *"Our Own Hymn-book": A Collection of Psalms and Hymns for Public, Social, and Private Worship*, ed. C. H. Spurgeon (London: Passmore and Alabaster, 1866), #25.

From that dream of horror I was awakened in a moment by the gracious application to my soul of the text, "Him hath God the Father exalted" (Acts 5:31). The fact that Jesus is still great, let his servants suffer as they may, piloted me back to calm reason and peace. Should so terrible a calamity overtake any of my brethren, let them both patiently hope and quietly wait for the salvation of God.

When troubles multiply, and discouragements follow each other in long succession, like Job's messengers, then, too, amid the perturbation of soul occasioned by evil tidings, despondency despoils the heart of all its peace. Constant dropping wears away stones, and the bravest minds feel the fret of repeated afflictions. If a scanty cupboard is rendered a severer trial by the sickness of a wife or the loss of a child, and if ungenerous remarks of hearers are followed by the opposition of deacons and the coolness of members, then, like Jacob, we are apt to cry, "All these things are against me" (Gen. 42:36). When David returned to Ziklag and found the city burned, goods stolen, wives carried off, and his troops ready to stone him, we read, "he encouraged himself in his God" (1 Sam. 30:6), and well was it for him that he could do so, for he would then have fainted if he had not believed to see the goodness of the Lord in the land of the living. Accumulated distresses increase each other's weight; they play into each other's hands, and, like bands of robbers, ruthlessly destroy our comfort. Wave upon wave is severe work for the strongest swimmer. The place where two seas meet strains the most seaworthy keel. If there were a regulated pause between the buffetings of adversity, the spirit would stand prepared; but when they come suddenly and heavily, like the battering of great hailstones, the pilgrim may well be amazed. The last ounce breaks the camel's back, and when that last ounce is laid upon us, what wonder if we for awhile are ready to give up the ghost!

The Minister's Fainting Fits

This evil will also come upon us, we know not why, and then it is all the more difficult to drive it away. Causeless depression is not to be reasoned with, nor can David's harp charm it away by sweet discoursings. As well fight with the mist as with this shapeless, undefinable, yet all-beclouding hopelessness. One affords himself no pity when in this case, because it seems so unreasonable, and even sinful to be troubled without manifest cause; and yet troubled the man is, even in the very depths of his spirit. If those who laugh at such melancholy did but feel the grief of it for one hour, their laughter would be sobered into compassion. Resolution might, perhaps, shake it off, but where are we to find the resolution when the whole man is unstrung? The physician and the divine may unite their skill in such cases, and both find their hands full, and more than full. The iron bolt which so mysteriously fastens the door of hope and holds our spirits in gloomy prison, needs a heavenly hand to push it back; and when that hand is seen we cry with the apostle, "Blessed be God, even the Father of our Lord Jesus Christ, the Father of mercies, and the God of all comfort; who comforteth us in all our tribulation, that we may be able to comfort them which are in any trouble, by the comfort wherewith we ourselves are comforted of God" (2 Cor. 1:3-4). It is the God of all consolation who can,

> With sweet oblivious antidote
> Cleanse our poor bosoms of that perilous stuff
> Which weighs upon the heart.[10]

Simon sinks till Jesus takes him by the hand. The devil within rends and tears the poor child till the word of authority commands him to come out of him. When we are ridden with horrible fears, and weighed down with an intolerable incubus, we need but the

---

[10] William Shakespeare, "Macbeth," in *The Works of William Shakespeare*, vol. 7, ed. Rev. Alexander Dyce (London, Bickers & Son, 1881), 284.

Servants of Christ, Lovers of Men

Sun of Righteousness to rise, and the evils generated of our darkness are driven away; but nothing short of this will chase away the nightmare of the soul. Timothy Rogers,[11] the author of a treatise on Melancholy, and Simon Browne,[12] the writer of some remarkably sweet hymns, proved in their own cases how unavailing is the help of man if the Lord withdraw the light from the soul.

God's purposes in the minister's fainting fits

If it be enquired why the valley of the shadow of death must so often be traversed by the servants of King Jesus, the answer is not far to find. All this is promotive of the Lord's mode of working, which is summed up in these words, "Not by might nor by power, but by my Spirit, saith the Lord" (Zech 4:6). Instruments shall be used, but their intrinsic weakness shall be clearly manifested; there shall be no division of the glory, no diminishing the honour due to the Great Worker. The man shall be emptied of self, and then filled with the Holy Ghost. In his own apprehension he shall be like a sere leaf driven of the tempest, and then shall be strengthened into a brazen wall against the enemies of truth. To hide pride from the worker is the great difficulty. Uninterrupted success and unfading joy in it would be more than our weak heads could bear. Our wine must needs be mixed with water, lest it turn our brains. My witness is, that those who are honoured of their Lord in public, have usually to endure a secret chastening, or to carry a peculiar cross, lest by any means they exalt themselves, and fall into the snare of the devil. How constantly the Lord calls Ezekiel, "Son of man," amid his soarings into the superlative splendours, just when with eye undimmed he is strengthened to gaze into the

---

[11] Timothy Rogers (1658–1728) was an English Nonconformist minister. The treatise Spurgeon refers to here is Timothy Rogers, *A Discourse on Trouble of Mind, and the Disease of Melancholy, With a Preface, Containing Several Advices to the Relations and Friends of Melancholy People* (London: Maxwell and Willson, 1808).

[12] Simon Brown (1680–1732) was an English Nonconformist minister and hymnwriter.

excellent glory, the word "Son of man" falls on his ears, sobering the heart which else might have been intoxicated with the honour conferred upon it. Such humbling but salutary messages our depressions whisper in our ears; they tell us in a manner not to be mistaken that we are but men, frail, feeble, apt to faint.

By all the castings down of his servants God is glorified, for they are led to magnify him when again he sets them on their feet, and even while prostrate in the dust their faith yields him praise. They speak all the more sweetly of his faithfulness, and are the more firmly established in his love. Such mature men as some elderly preachers are, could scarcely have been produced if they had not been emptied from vessel to vessel, and made to see their own emptiness and the vanity of all things round about them. Glory be to God for the furnace, the hammer, and the file. Heaven shall be all the fuller of bliss because we have been filled with anguish here below, and earth shall be better tilled because of our training in the school of adversity.

The lesson of wisdom is, be not dismayed by soul-trouble. Count it no strange thing, but a part of ordinary ministerial experience. Should the power of depression be more than ordinary, think not that all is over with your usefulness. Cast not away your confidence, for it hath great recompense of reward. Even if the enemy's foot be on your neck, expect to rise and overthrow him. Cast the burden of the present, along with the sin of the past and the fear of the future, upon the Lord, who forsaketh not his saints. Live by the day—ay, by the hour. Put no trust in frames and feelings. Care more for a grain of faith than a ton of excitement. Trust in God alone, and lean not on the reeds of human help. Be not surprised when friends fail you; it is a failing world. Never count upon immutability in man; inconstancy you may reckon upon without fear of disappointment. The disciples of Jesus forsook him; be not amazed if your adherents wander away to other teachers; as they were not your all when with you, all is not gone from you with their departure. Serve God with all your might while the candle is burning, and then when it goes out for a season, you will have the less to regret. Be content to be nothing, for that is what you are. When your own emptiness is painfully forced upon your consciousness, chide yourself that you ever dreamed of being full, except in the Lord. Set small store by present rewards; be grateful for earnests by the way, but look for the recompensing joy hereafter. Continue with double earnestness to serve your Lord when no visible result is before you. Any simpleton can follow the narrow path in the light; faith's rare wisdom enables us to march on in the dark with infallible accuracy, since she places her hand in that of her Great Guide. Between this and heaven there may be rougher weather yet, but it is all provided for by our covenant Head. In nothing let us be turned aside from the path which the divine call has urged us to pursue. Come fair or come foul, the pulpit is our watch-tower, and the ministry our warfare; be it ours, when we cannot see the face of our God, to trust under the shadow of his wings.

6
The Minister's Ordinary Conversation

Introduction

By all accounts, the Spurgeon home was a haven for warm hospitality and Christian fellowship. It was deliberately set up as a comfortable retreat and refuge for friends and visitors from far and wide. For many years, students of the Pastors' College enjoyed a standing invitation to visit Spurgeon in his garden on Saturday mornings for tea and conversation.[1] Spurgeon was completely at ease in these types of settings. He loved interacting with his students and always sought to turn the conversation for their spiritual profit. The Spurgeons also hosted many famous men of the day such as John Ruskin, Lord Shaftesbury, and the Prime Minister, William Gladstone. One of Spurgeon's biographers, J. C. Carlile, wrote,

> Mr. Spurgeon kept an ever-open door. No doubt his hospitality was not infrequently abused, and friends from other lands told wonderful stories of what they had heard and seen. Missionaries, preachers and public men from all over the world found their way to Westwood. Spurgeon was a great host, with dignity and courtesy and abounding generosity. He delighted to entertain his visitors.[2]

With warm Christian fellowship, hearty spiritual conversation, and an ever-buoyant sense of humor, Spurgeon charmed and refreshed his visitors. His personal interactions in private and

---

[1] J. C. Carlile, *C. H. Spurgeon: An Interpretive Biography* (London: Kingsgate Press, 1933), 193.
[2] Carlile, *C. H. Spurgeon: An Interpretive Biography*, 194.

unguarded moments only deepened his pastoral effectiveness and caused his ministry to shine all the brighter.

In this lecture, Spurgeon discusses the importance of the minister's conduct and speech outside the pulpit. He particularly has in mind occasions when pastors find themselves in more ordinary and casual socials contexts. Even in such settings, they must remember that they are still ministers and they must recognize that they are, in a sense, always on duty. Pastors must at all times maintain a reputation that is above reproach and continually model a holy and godly life before their people and before outsiders.

Spurgeon encourages pastors to endeavor to maintain the warmest disposition toward others. He believed strongly that ministers should be men of the people and should be natural and congenial in all contexts. They must be warm and accessible and should be men of popular sympathies if they are going to reach ordinary people with the gospel. It is in this lecture that we find Spurgeon's oft-quoted statement, "I love a minister whose face invites me to make him my friend—a man upon whose doorstep you read, 'Salve,' 'Welcome;' and feel that there is no need of that Pompeian warning, 'Cave Canem,' 'Beware of the dog.'" Spurgeon goes on to write,

> A man must have a great heart if he would have a great congregation. His heart should be as capacious as those noble harbours along our coast, which contain sea-room for a fleet. When a man has a large, loving heart, men go to him as ships to a haven, and feel at peace when they have anchored under the lee of his friendship.

Spurgeon concludes the lecture by encouraging ministers to be intentional and earnest in their conversations with others. They should always seek to turn the conversation toward spiritual subjects and should see every conversation as an opportunity to minister good to someone. Pastoral work is not limited to the

The Minister's Ordinary Conversation

pulpit, but extends to every interaction with the sheep. Opportunities to edify and encourage can be found in even the most ordinary contexts and conversations.

The Minister's Ordinary Conversation

Our subject is to be the minister's common conversation when he mingles with men in general, and is supposed to be quite at his ease. How shall he order his speech among his fellow-men? First and foremost, let me say, let him give himself no ministerial airs, but avoid everything which is stilted, official, fussy, and pretentious. "The Son of Man" is a noble title; it was given to Ezekiel, and to a greater than he; let not the ambassador of heaven be other than a son of man. In fact, let him remember that the more simple and unaffected he is, the more closely will he resemble that child-man, the holy child Jesus. There is such a thing as trying to be too much a minister, and becoming too little a man; though the more of a true man you are, the more truly will you be what a servant of the Lord should be. Schoolmasters and ministers have generally an appearance peculiarly their own; in the wrong sense, they "are not as other men are." They are too often speckled birds, looking as if they were not at home among the other inhabitants of the country; but awkward and peculiar. When I have seen a flamingo gravely stalking along, an owl blinking in the shade, or a stork demurely lost in thought, I have been irresistibly led to remember some of my dignified brethren of the teaching and preaching fraternity, who are so marvellously proper at all times that they are just a shade amusing. Their very respectable, stilted, dignified, important, self-restrained manner is easily acquired, but is it worth acquiring?

Servants of Christ, Lovers of Men

"Ministerial starch"

Theodore Hook[1] once stepped up to a gentleman who was parading the street with great pomposity, and said to him, "Sir, are you not a person of great importance?" and one has felt half inclined to do the same with certain brethren of the cloth. I know brethren who, from head to foot, in garb, tone, manner, necktie, and boots, are so utterly parsonic that no particle of manhood is visible. One young sprig of divinity must needs go through the streets in a gown, and another of the High Church order has recorded it in the newspapers with much complacency that he traversed Switzerland and Italy, wearing in all places his biretta; few boys would have been so proud of a fool's cap. None of us are likely to go as far as that in our apparel; but we may do the like by our mannerism. Some men appear to have a white cravat twisted round their souls, their manhood is throttled with that starched rag. Certain brethren maintain an air of superiority which they think impressive, but which is simply offensive, and eminently opposed to their pretensions as followers of the lowly Jesus. The proud Duke of Somerset intimated his commands to his servants by signs, not condescending to speak to such base beings; his children never sat down in his presence, and when he slept in the afternoon one of his daughters stood on each side of him during his august slumbers. When proud Somersets get into the ministry, they affect dignity in other ways almost equally absurd. "Stand by, I am holier than thou," is written across their foreheads.

A well-known minister was once rebuked by a sublime brother for his indulgence in a certain luxury, and the expense was made a great argument. "Well, well," he replied, "there may be something in that; but remember, I do not spend half so much upon my weakness as you do in starch." That is the article I am deprecating, that dreadful ministerial starch. If you have indulged in it, I

---

[1] Theodore Hook (1788–1841) was a prolific novelist, playwright, and composer.

The Minister's Ordinary Conversation

would earnestly advise you to "go and wash in Jordan seven times," and get it out of you, every particle of it. I am persuaded that one reason why our working-men so universally keep clear of ministers is because they abhor their artificial and unmanly ways. If they saw us, in the pulpit and out of it, acting like real men, and speaking naturally, like honest men, they would come around us. Baxter's remark still holds good: "The want of a familiar tone and expression is a great fault in most of our deliveries, and that which we should be very careful to amend."[2] The vice of the ministry is that ministers will parsonificate the gospel. We must have humanity along with our divinity if we would win the masses. Everybody can see through affectations, and people are not likely to be taken in by them. Fling away your stilts, brethren, and walk on your feet; doff your ecclesiasticism, and array yourselves in truth.

Always on duty
Still, a minister, wherever he is, is a minister, and should recollect that he is on duty. A policeman or a soldier may be off duty, but a minister never is. Even in our recreations we should still pursue the great object of our lives; for we are called to be diligent "in season and out of season." There is no position in which we may be placed but the Lord may come with the question, "What doest thou here, Elijah?" (1 Kgs. 19:9). and we ought to be able at once to answer, "I have something to do for thee even here, and I am trying to do it." The bow, of course, must be at times unstrung, or else it will lose its elasticity; but there is no need to cut the string. I am speaking at this time of the minister in times of relaxation; and I say that even then he should conduct himself as the ambassador of God, and seize opportunities of doing good. This will not mar his rest, but sanctify it. A minister should be like a

---

[2] Richard Baxter, *The Reformed Pastor* (London: The Religious Tract Society, 1862), 161.

certain chamber which I saw at Beaulieu, in the New Forest, in which a cobweb is never seen. It is a large lumber-room, and is never swept; yet no spider ever defiles it with the emblems of neglect. It is roofed with chestnut, and for some reason, I know not what, spiders will not come near that wood by the year together. The same thing was mentioned to me in the corridors of Winchester School: I was told, "No spiders ever come here." Our minds should be equally clear of idle habits.

On our public rests for porters in the city of London you may read the words, "Rest, but do not loiter;" and they contain advice worthy of our attention. I do not call the dolce far niente laziness; there is a sweet doing of nothing which is just the finest medicine in the world for a jaded mind. When the mind gets fatigued and out of order, to rest it is no more idleness than sleep is idleness; and no man is called lazy for sleeping the proper time. It is far better to be industriously asleep than lazily awake. Be ready to do good even in your resting times and in your leisure hours; and so be really a minister, and there will be no need for you to proclaim that you are so.

The Christian minister out of the pulpit should be a sociable man. He is not sent into the world to be a hermit, or a monk of La Trappe. It is not his vocation to stand on a pillar all day, above his fellow-men, like that hair-brained Simon Stylites[3] of olden time. You are not to warble from the top of a tree, like an invisible nightingale; but to be a man among men, saying to them, "I also am as you are in all that relates to man." Salt is of no use in the box; it must be rubbed into the meat; and our personal influence must penetrate and season society. Keep aloof from others, and how can you benefit them? Our Master went to a wedding, and ate bread with publicans and sinners, and yet was far more pure than

---

[3] Simon Stylites (c. 390–459) was a Syrian Christian hermit and proponent of extreme asceticism who famously lived upon a small platform atop a tall pillar for thirty-seven years.

The Minister's Ordinary Conversation

those sanctimonious Pharisees, whose glory was that they were separate from their fellow-men. Some ministers need to be told that they are of the same species as their hearers. It is a remarkable fact, but we may as well state it, that bishops, canons, archdeacons, prebendaries, rural deans, rectors, vicars, and even archbishops, are only men after all; and God has not railed off a holy corner of the earth to serve as a chancel for them, to abide therein by themselves.

A welcoming minister
It would not be amiss if there could be a revival of holy talk in the churchyard and the meeting-yard. I like to see the big yew-trees outside our ancient churches with seats all round them. They seem to say: "Sit down here, neighbour, and talk upon the sermon; here comes the pastor, he will join us, and we shall have a pleasant, holy chat." It is not every preacher we would care to talk with, but there are some whom one would give a fortune to converse with for an hour. I love a minister whose face invites me to make him my friend—a man upon whose doorstep you read, "Salve," "Welcome;" and feel that there is no need of that Pompeian warning, "Cave Canem," "Beware of the dog." Give me the man around whom the children come, like flies around a honey-pot; they are first-class judges of a good man. When Solomon was tried by the Queen of Sheba, as to his wisdom, the rabbis tell us that she brought some artificial flowers with her, beautifully made and delicately scented, so as to be facsimiles of real flowers. She asked Solomon to discover which were artificial and which were real. The wise man bade his servants open the window, and when the bees came in they flew at once to the natural flowers, and cared nothing for the artificial. So you will find that children have their instincts, and discover very speedily who is their friend, and depend upon it the children's friend is one who will be worth knowing. Have a good word to say to each and every member of

the family—the big boys, and the young ladies, and the little girls, and everybody. No one knows what a smile and a hearty sentence may do. A man who is to do much with men must love them, and feel at home with them. An individual who has no geniality about him had better be an undertaker, and bury the dead, for he will never succeed in influencing the living. I have met somewhere with the observation that to be a popular preacher one must have bowels. I fear that the observation was meant as a mild criticism upon the bulk to which certain brethren have attained, but there is truth in it. A man must have a great heart if he would have a great congregation. His heart should be as capacious as those noble harbours along our coast, which contain sea-room for a fleet. When a man has a large, loving heart, men go to him as ships to a haven, and feel at peace when they have anchored under the lee of his friendship. Such a man is hearty in private as well as in public; his blood is not cold and fishy, but he is warm as your own fireside. No pride and selfishness chill you when you approach him; he has his doors all open to receive you, and you are at home with him at once. Such men I would persuade you to be, every one of you.

The Christian minister should also be very cheerful. I don't believe in going about like certain monks whom I saw in Rome, who salute each other in sepulchral tones, and convey the pleasant information, "Brother, we must die;" to which lively salutation each lively brother of the order replies, "Yes, brother, we must die." I was glad to be assured upon such good authority that all these lazy fellows are about to die; upon the whole, it is about the best thing they can do; but till that event occurs, they might use some more comfortable form of salutation.

No doubt there are some people who will be impressed by the very solemn appearance of ministers. I have heard of one who felt convinced that there must be something in the Roman Catholic religion, from the extremely starved and pinched appearance of a

The Minister's Ordinary Conversation

certain ecclesiastic. "Look," said he, "how the man is worn to a skeleton by his daily fastings and nightly vigils! How he must mortify his flesh!" Now, the probabilities are that the emaciated priest was labouring under some internal disease, which he would have been heartily glad to be rid of, and it was not conquest of appetite, but failure in digestion, which had so reduced him; or, possibly a troubled conscience, which made him fret himself down to the light weights. Certainly, I have never met with a text which mentions prominence of bone as an evidence of grace. If so, "The Living Skeleton" should have been exhibited, not merely as a natural curiosity, but as the standard of virtue. Some of the biggest rogues in the world have been as mortified in appearance as if they had lived on locusts and wild honey. It is a very vulgar error to suppose that a melancholy countenance is the index of a gracious heart. I commend cheerfulness to all who would win souls; not levity and frothiness, but a genial, happy spirit. There are more flies caught with honey than with vinegar, and there will be more souls led to heaven by a man who wears heaven in his face than by one who bears Tartarus in his looks.

Young ministers, and, indeed, all others, when they are in company, should take care not to engross all the conversation. They are quite qualified to do so, no doubt; I mean from their capacity to instruct, and readiness of utterance; but they must remember that people do not care to be perpetually instructed; they like to take a turn in the conversation themselves. Nothing pleases some people so much as to let them talk, and it may be for their good to let them be pleased. I spent an hour one evening with a person who did me the honour to say that he found me a very charming companion, and most instructive in conversation, yet I do not hesitate to confess that I said scarcely anything at all, but allowed him to have the talk to himself. By exercising patience I gained his good opinion, and an opportunity to address him on other occasions. A man has no more right at table to talk all than to eat all. We are not to think ourselves Sir Oracle, before whom no dog must open his mouth. No; let all the company contribute of their stores, and they will think all the better of the godly words with which you try to season the discourse.

There are some companies into which you will go, especially when you are first settled, where everybody will be awed by the majesty of your presence, and people will be invited because the new minister is to be there. Such a position reminds me of the choicest statuary in the Vatican. A little room is screened off, a curtain is drawn, and lo, before you stands the great Apollo! If it be your trying lot to be the Apollo of the little party, put an end to the nonsense. If I were the Apollo, I should like to step right off the pedestal and shake hands all round, and you had better do the same; for sooner or later the fuss they make about you will come to an end, and the wisest course is to end it yourself. Hero-worship is a kind of idolatry, and must not be encouraged. Heroes do well when they, like the apostles at Lystra, are horrified at the honours done to them, and run in among the people crying, "Sirs, why do ye these things? We also are men of like passions with you" (Acts 14:15). Ministers will not have to do it long; for their foolish admirers are very apt to turn round upon them, and if they do not stone them nearly to death, they will go as far as they dare in unkindness and contempt.

While I say, "Do not talk all, and assume an importance which is mere imposture," still, do not be a dummy. People will form their estimate of you and your ministry by what they see of you in private as well as by your public deliverances. Many young men have ruined themselves in the pulpit by being indiscreet in the parlour, and have lost all hope of doing good by their stupidity or frivolity in company. Don't be an inanimate log. At Antwerp Fair, among many curiosities advertised by huge paintings and big drums, I observed a booth containing "a great wonder," to be seen for a penny a head; it was a petrified man. I did not expend the amount required for admission, for I had seen so many petrified men for nothing, both in and out of the pulpit—lifeless, careless, destitute of common sense, and altogether inert, though occupied with the weightiest business which man could undertake.

Intentionality in our conversation
Try to turn the conversation to profitable use. Be sociable and cheerful and all that, but labour to accomplish something. Why should you sow the wind, or plough a rock? Consider yourself, after all, as being very much responsible for the conversation which goes on where you are; for such is the esteem in which you will usually be held, that you will be the helmsman of the conversation. Therefore, steer it into a good channel. Do this without roughness or force. Keep the points of the line in good order, and the train will run on to your rails without a jerk. Be ready to seize opportunities adroitly, and lead on imperceptibly in the desired track. If your heart is in it and your wits are awake, this will be easy enough, especially if you breathe a prayer for guidance.

I shall never forget the manner in which a thirsty individual once begged of me upon Clapham Common. I saw him with a very large truck, in which he was carrying an extremely small parcel, and I wondered why he had not put the parcel into his pocket, and left the machine at home. I said, "It looks odd to see so large a truck for such a small load." He stopped, and looking me seriously in the face, he said, "Yes, sir, it is a very odd thing; but, do you know, I have met with an odder thing than that this very day. I've been about, working and sweating all this 'ere blessed day, and till now I haven't met a single gentleman that looked as if he'd give me a pint of beer, till I saw you." I considered that turn of the conversation very neatly managed, and we, with a far better subject upon our minds, ought to be equally able to introduce the topic upon which our heart is set. There was an ease in the man's manner which I envied, for I did not find it quite so simple a matter

Servants of Christ, Lovers of Men

to introduce my own topic to his notice; yet if I had been thinking as much about how I could do him good as he had upon how to obtain a drink, I feel sure I should have succeeded in reaching my point. If by any means we may save some, we must, like our Lord, talk at table to good purpose—yes, and on the margin of the well, and by the road, and on the sea-shore, and in the house, and in the field. To be a holy talker for Jesus might be almost as fruitful an office as to be a faithful preacher. Aim at excellence in both exercises, and if the Holy Spirit's aid be called in, you will attain your desire.

Here, perhaps, I may insert a canon, which nevertheless I believe to be quite needless, in reference to each one of the honourable brethren whom I am now addressing. Do not frequent rich men's tables to gain their countenance, and never make yourself a sort of general hanger-on at tea-parties and entertainments. Who are you that you should be dancing attendance upon this wealthy man and the other, when the Lord's poor, his sick people, and his wandering sheep require you? To sacrifice the study to the parlour is criminal. To be a tout for your church, and waylay people at their homes to draw them to fill your pews, is a degradation to which no man should submit. To see ministers of different sects fluttering round a wealthy man, like vultures round a dead camel, is sickening. Deliciously sarcastic was that famous letter "from an old and beloved minister to his dear son" upon his entrance into the ministry, the following extract from which hits our present point. It is said to have been copied from the Smellfungus Gazette, but I suspect our friend Paxton Hood[4] knows all about its authorship:

> Keep also a watchful eye on all likely persons, especially wealthy or influential, who may come to your town; call upon them, and attempt to win them over by the devotions

---

[4] Edwin Paxton Hood (1820–1885) was a Congregationalist minister and author.

The Minister's Ordinary Conversation

of the drawing-room to your cause. Thus you may most efficiently serve the Master's interests. People need looking after, and the result of a long experience goes to confirm my conviction, long cherished, that the power of the pulpit is trifling compared with the power of the parlour. We must imitate and sanctify, by the word of God and prayer, the exercises of the Jesuits. They succeeded not by the pulpit so much as by the parlour. In the parlour you can whisper—you can meet people on all their little personal private ideas. The pulpit is a very unpleasant place; of course it is the great power of God, and so on, but it is the parlour that tells, and a minister has not the same chance of success if he be a good preacher as if he is a perfect gentleman; nor in cultivated society has any man a legitimate prospect of success if he is not, whatever he may be, a gentleman. I have always admired Lord Shaftesbury's character of St. Paul in his "Characteristics"—that he was a fine gentleman. And I would say to you, be a gentleman. Not that I need to say so, but am persuaded that only in this way can we hope for the conversion of our growing, wealthy middle classes. We must show that our religion is the religion of good sense and good taste; that we disapprove of strong excitements and strong stimulants; and oh, my dear boy, if you would be useful, often in your closet make it a matter of earnest prayer that you may be proper. If I were asked what is your first duty, be proper; and your second, be proper; and your third, be proper.[5]

Those who remember a class of preachers who flourished fifty years ago will see the keenness of the satire in this extract. The evil is greatly mitigated now; in fact, I fear we may be drifting into another extreme.

---

[5] Edwin Paxton Hood, *Lamps, Pitchers, and Trumpets; Lectures Delivered to Students for the Ministry on the Vocation of the Preacher, Illustrated by Anecdotes, Biographical, Historical, and Elucidatory, of Every Order of Pulpit Eloquence, from the Great Preachers of All Ages* (London: Jackson, Walford, and Hodder, 1867), 580–581.

Servants of Christ, Lovers of Men

In all probability, sensible conversation will sometimes drift into controversy, and here many a good man runs upon a snag. The sensible minister will be particularly gentle in argument. He, above all men, should not make the mistake of fancying that there is force in temper, and power in speaking angrily. A heathen who stood in a crowd in Calcutta, listening to a missionary disputing with a Brahmin, said he knew which was right though he did not understand the language—he knew that he was in the wrong who lost his temper first. For the most part, that is a very accurate way of judging. Try to avoid debating with people. State your opinion and let them state theirs. If you see that a stick is crooked, and you want people to see how crooked it is, lay a straight rod down beside it; that will be quite enough. But if you are drawn into controversy, use very hard arguments and very soft words. Frequently you cannot convince a man by tugging at his reason, but you can persuade him by winning his affections. The other day I had the misery to need a pair of new boots, and though I bade the fellow make them as large as canoes, I had to labour fearfully to get them on. With a pair of boot-hooks I toiled like the men on board the vessel with Jonah, but all in vain. Just then my friend put in my way a little French chalk, and the work was done in a moment. Wonderfully coaxing was that French chalk. Gentlemen, always carry a little French chalk with you into society, a neat packet of Christian persuasiveness, and you will soon discover the virtues of it.

And lastly, with all his amiability, the minister should be firm for his principles, and bold to avow and defend them in all companies. When a fair opportunity occurs, or he has managed to create one, let him not be slow to make use of it. Strong in his principles, earnest in his tone, and affectionate in heart, let him speak out like a man and thank God for the privilege. There need be no reticence—there should be none. The maddest romances of spiritualists, the wildest dreams of utopian reformers, the silliest chit-

The Minister's Ordinary Conversation

chat of the town, and the vainest nonsense of the frivolous world, demand a hearing and get it. And shall not Christ be heard? Shall his message of love remain untold, for fear we should be charged with intrusion or accused of cant? Is religion to be tabooed—the best and noblest of all themes forbidden? If this be the rule of any society, we will not comply with it. If we cannot break it down, we will leave the society to itself, as men desert a house smitten with leprosy. We cannot consent to be gagged. There is no reason why we should be. We will go to no place where we cannot take our Master with us. While others take liberty to sin, we shall not renounce our liberty to rebuke and warn them.

Wisely used, our common conversation may be a potent means for good. Trains of thought may be started by a single sentence which may lead to the conversion of persons whom our sermons have never reached. The method of button-holing people, or bringing the truth before them individually, has been greatly successful: this is another subject, and can hardly come under the head of common conversation; but we will close by saying that it is to be hoped that we shall never, in our ordinary talk, any more than in the pulpit, be looked upon as nice sort of persons, whose business it is to make things agreeable all round, and who never by any possibility cause uneasiness to any one, however ungodly their lives may be. Such persons go in and out among the families of their hearers, and make merry with them, when they ought to be mourning over them. They sit down at their tables and feast at their ease, when they ought to be warning them to flee from the wrath to come. They are like that American alarum I have heard of, which was warranted not to wake you if you did not wish it to do so.

Be it ours to sow, not only on the honest and good soil, but on the rock and on the highway, and at the last great day to reap a glad harvest. May the bread which we cast upon the waters in odd times and strange occasions be found again after many days.

7
Earnestness

Introduction

The defining trait of Spurgeonic preaching was earnestness. It was the attribute of his preaching that was most distinctive and that most set him apart from the preachers of his day. It contributed as much as any other element to his popularity as a preacher, and it still gives his written sermons their enduring life and timeless appeal. Those who listened to him could tell, whatever else caught their attention, that his words came from the inmost part of his being. He spoke as a man who believed, who knew, he was in the presence of God and believed the fate of souls hung on his every word. His own consciousness of eternal realities was so imposing as to be irresistible. His earnestness about the things of God gripped the congregation and forced them to reckon with the Christ whom he would have them know.

As this lecture makes plain, Spurgeon believed earnestness was an essential element of true, Spirit-anointed preaching. He could not tolerate the rote rehearsal of doctrine in a detached and colorless manner. Such insipid and lackluster preaching did a discredit to the Bible and slighted the God who breathed out the Scriptures. Spurgeon believed the preacher's bearing, his tone of voice, and his whole demeanor should communicate a sense of earnestness and sobriety to the congregation. Everything about the preacher's deportment should indicate something of the gravity of the moment and of the message.

But it was not just the preacher's outward appearance that should grip the congregation and invite their serious attention. What ultimately communicated this sense of earnestness was the force of the truth preached. The holiness of God, the urgency of the gospel call, and the realities of heaven and hell demanded a certain measure of spiritual intensity from preacher and congregation alike. The preaching event was meant to precipitate an authentic encounter with the living God through his Word. To Spurgeon, it was simply impossible that such an event could be attended with anything less than a sense of gravity and seriousness.

In this lecture Spurgeon articulates the vital importance of earnestness in preaching and identifies the ways in which earnestness should be cultivated and maintained. Ultimately, earnestness is nurtured through an abiding communion with Christ and steadfast devotion to prayer and meditation on the Word. If ministers are to maintain their spiritual edge and vigor, they must always minister out of the overflow of genuine fellowship with God. However, it is not only communion with the Lord that gives birth to true earnestness. Spurgeon also believed a sympathetic presence among the people is critical to maintaining a sense of the gravity of eternal matters. When a minister lives daily among the souls for whom he will give an account, trivial things tend to fade into the background and the all-important task of presenting Christ's sheep mature in Him occupies center stage.

Earnestness

If I were asked—What in a Christian minister is the most essential quality for securing success in winning souls for Christ? I should reply, "earnestness," and if I were asked a second or a third time, I should not vary the answer, for personal observation drives me to the conclusion that, as a rule, real success is proportionate to the preacher's earnestness. Both great men and little men succeed if they are thoroughly alive unto God, and fail if they are not so. We know men of eminence who have gained a high reputation, who attract large audiences, and obtain much admiration, who nevertheless are very low in the scale as soul-winners; for all they do in that direction they might as well have been lecturers on anatomy, or political orators. At the same time we have seen their compeers in ability so useful in the business of conversion that evidently their acquirements and gifts have been no hindrance to them, but the reverse; for by the intense and devout use of their powers, and by the anointing of the Holy Spirit, they have turned many to righteousness. We have seen brethren of very scanty abilities who have been terrible drags upon a church, and have proved as inefficient in their spheres as blind men in an observatory; but on the other hand, men of equally small attainments are well known to us as mighty hunters before the Lord, by whose holy energy many hearts have been captured for the Saviour. I delight in M'Cheyne's remark, "It is not so much great talents that God blesses, as great likeness to Christ."[1] In many instances ministerial success is traceable almost entirely to an intense zeal, a

---

[1] Paraphrase from original text found in Andrew A. Bonar, *Memoir and Remains of the Rev. R. M. M'Cheyne: Minister of St. Peter's Church, Dundee* (London: Hamilton, Adams, & Co., and J. Nisbet & Co., 1845), 243.

consuming passion for souls, and an eager enthusiasm in the cause of God, and we believe that in every case, other things being equal, men prosper in the divine service in proportion as their hearts are blazing with holy love. "The God that answereth by fire, let him be God" (1 Kgs. 18:24), and the man who has the tongue of fire, let him be God's minister.

Earnestness in the pulpit

Brethren, you and I must, as preachers, be always earnest in reference to our pulpit work. Here we must labor to attain the very highest degree of excellence. Often have I said to my brethren that the pulpit is the Thermopylae of Christendom; there the fight will be lost or won. To us ministers the maintenance of our power in the pulpit should be our great concern, we must occupy that spiritual watch-tower with our hearts and minds awake and in full vigor. It will not avail us to be laborious pastors if we are not earnest preachers. We shall be forgiven a great many sins in the matter of pastoral visitation if the people's souls are really fed on the Sabbath-day; but fed they must be, and nothing else will make up for it. The failures of most ministers who drift down the stream may be traced to inefficiency in the pulpit. The chief business of a captain is to know how to handle his vessel, nothing can compensate for deficiency there, and so our pulpits must be our main care, or all will go awry. Dogs often fight because the supply of bones is scanty, and congregations frequently quarrel because they do not get sufficient spiritual meat to keep them happy and peaceful. The ostensible ground of dissatisfaction may be something else, but nine times out of ten deficiency in their rations is at the bottom of the mutinies which occur in our churches. Men, like all other animals, know when they are fed, and they usually feel good tempered after a meal; and so when our hearers come to the house of God, and obtain "food convenient for them," they forget a great many grievances in the joy of the festival, but if we send them

Earnestness

away hungry they will be in as irritable a mood as a bear robbed of her whelps.

Now, in order that we may be acceptable, we must be earnest when actually engaged in preaching. Cecil has well said that the spirit and manner of a preacher often effect more than his matter. To go into the pulpit with the listless air of those gentlemen who loll about, and lean upon the cushion as if they had at last reached a quiet resting place, is, I think, most censurable. To rise before the people to deal out commonplaces which have cost you nothing, as if anything would do for a sermon, is not merely derogatory to the dignity of our office, but is offensive in the sight of God. We must be earnest in the pulpit for our own sakes, for we shall not long be able to maintain our position as leaders in the church of God if we are dull. Moreover, for the sake of our church members, and converted people, we must be energetic, for if we are not zealous, neither will they be. It is not in the order of nature that rivers should run uphill, and it does not often happen that zeal rises from the pew to the pulpit. It is natural that it should flow down from us to our hearers; the pulpit must therefore stand at a high level of ardor, if we are, under God, to make and to keep our people fervent. Those who attend our ministry have a great deal to do during the week. Many of them have family trials, and heavy personal burdens to carry, and they frequently come into the assembly cold and listless, with thoughts wandering hither and thither; it is ours to take those thoughts and thrust them into the furnace of our own earnestness, melt them by holy contemplation and by intense appeal, and pour them out into the mould of the truth. A blacksmith can do nothing when his fire is out, and in this respect he is the type of a minister. If all the lights in the outside world are quenched, the lamp which burns in the sanctuary ought still to remain undimmed; for that fire no curfew must ever be rung. We must regard the people as the wood and the sacrifice, well wetted a second and a third time by the cares of the week, upon which, like the prophet, we must pray down the fire from heaven. A dull minister creates a dull audience. You cannot expect the office-bearers and the members of the church to travel by steam if their own chosen pastor still drives the old broad-wheeled wagon. We ought each one to be like that reformer who is described as "*Vividus vultus, vividi occuli, vividæ manus, denique omnia vivida,*" which I would rather freely render—"a countenance beaming with life, eyes and hands full of life, in fine, a vivid preacher, altogether alive."

> Thy soul must overflow, if thou
> Another's soul would reach,
> It needs the overflow of heart
> To give the lips full speech.[2]

The world also will suffer as well as the church if we are not fervent. We cannot expect a gospel devoid of earnestness to have any mighty effect upon the unconverted around us. One of the excuses most soporific to the conscience of an ungodly generation is that of half-heartedness in the preacher. If the sinner finds the preacher nodding while he talks of judgment to come, he concludes that the judgment is a thing which the preacher is dreaming about, and he resolves to regard it all as mere fiction. The whole outside world receives serious danger from the cold-hearted preacher, for it draws the same conclusion as the individual sinner: it perseveres in its own listlessness, it gives its strength to its own transient objects, and thinks itself wise for so doing. How can it be otherwise? If the prophet leaves his heart behind him when he professes to speak in the name of God, what can he expect but that the ungodly around him will persuade themselves that there is nothing in his message, and that his commission is a farce.

---

[2] Horatius Bonar, *Hymns of Faith and Hope* (London: James Nisbet and Co., 1867), 113.

Earnestness

Hear how Whitefield preached, and never dare to be lethargic again. Winter says of him that,

> sometimes he exceedingly wept, and was frequently so overcome, that for a few seconds you would suspect he never would recover; and when he did, nature required some little time to compose herself. I hardly ever knew him go through a sermon without weeping more or less. His voice was often interrupted by his affections; and I have heard him say in the pulpit, "You blame me for weeping; but how can I help it, when you will not weep for yourselves, although your own immortal souls are on the verge of destruction, and, for aught I know, you are hearing your last sermon, and may never more have an opportunity to have Christ offered to you?"[3]

Earnestness in the pulpit must be real. It is not to be mimicked. We have seen it counterfeited, but every person with a grain of sense could detect the imposition. To stamp the foot, to smite the desk, to perspire, to shout, to bawl, to quote the pathetic portions of other people's sermons, or to pour out voluntary tears from a watery eye will never make up for true agony of soul and real tenderness of spirit. The best piece of acting is but acting; those who only look at appearances may be pleased by it, but lovers of reality will be disgusted. What presumption! What hypocrisy it is by skilful management of the voice to mimic the passion which is the genuine work of the Holy Ghost. Let mere actors beware, lest they be found sinning against the Holy Spirit by their theatrical performances. We must be earnest in the pulpit because we are earnest everywhere; we must blaze in our discourses because we are continually on fire. Zeal which is stored up to be let off only on grand occasions is a gas which will one day destroy its proprietor.

---

[3] William Jay, *Memoirs of the Life and Character of the Late Reverend Cornelius Winter* (Bath: M. Gye, 1808), 27-28.

Nothing but truth may appear in the house of the Lord; all affectation is strange fire, and excites the indignation of the God of truth. Be earnest, and you will seem to be earnest. A burning heart will soon find for itself a flaming tongue. To sham earnestness is one of the most contemptible of dodges for courting popularity; let us abhor the very thought. Go and be listless in the pulpit if you are so in your heart. Be slow in speech, drawling in tone, and monotonous in voice, if so you can best express your soul; even that would be infinitely better than to make your ministry a masquerade and yourself an actor.

Earnestness at all times
But our zeal while in the act of preaching must be followed up by intense solicitude as to the after results; for if it be not so we shall have cause to question our sincerity. God will not send a harvest of souls to those who never watch or water the fields which they have sown. When the sermon is over we have only to let down the net which afterwards we are to draw to shore by prayer and watchfulness. Here, I think, I cannot do better than allow a far abler advocate to plead with you, and quote the words of Dr. Watts,

> Be very solicitous about the success of your labors in the pulpit. Water the seed sown, not only with public, but secret prayer. Plead with God importunately that he would not suffer you to labor in vain. But not like that foolish bird the ostrich, which lays her eggs in the dust and leaves them there, regardless whether they come to life or not (Job 39:14-17). God hath not given her understanding, but let not this folly be your character or practice; labor, and watch and pray, that your sermons and the fruit of your studies may become words of Divine life to souls.
>
> It is an observation of pious Mr. Baxter (which I have read somewhere in his works), that he has never known any considerable success from the brightest and noblest talents, nor from the most excellent kind of preaching, nor even

Earnestness

when the preachers themselves have been truly religious, if they have had a solicitous concern for the success of their ministrations. Let the awful and important thought of souls being saved by our preaching, or left to perish and to be condemned to hell through our negligence—I say, let this awful and tremendous thought dwell ever upon our spirits. We are made watchmen to the house of Israel, as Ezekiel was; and, if we give no warnings of approaching danger, the souls of multitudes may perish through our neglect; but the blood of souls will be terribly required at our hands (Ezek. 3:17, etc.).[4]

Such considerations should make us instant in season and out of season, and cause us at all times to be clad with zeal as with a cloak. We ought to be all alive, and always alive. A pillar of light and fire should be the preacher's fit emblem. Our ministry must be emphatic, or it will never effect these thoughtless times; and to this end our hearts must be habitually fervent, and our whole nature must be fired with an all-consuming passion for the glory of God and the good of men.

Impediments to ministerial earnestness

Now, my brethren, it is sadly true that holy earnestness, when we once obtain it, may be easily damped; as a matter of fact it is more frequently chilled in the loneliness of a village pastorate than amid the society of warmhearted Christian brethren. Adam,[5] the author of *Private Thoughts*, once observed that "a poor country parson, fighting against the devil in his parish, has nobler ideas than

---

[4] Isaac Watts, *The Works of the Reverend and Learned Isaac Watts, D. D. Containing, Besides His Sermons, and Essays on Miscellaneous Subjects, etc.* (London: J. Barfield, 1810), 31.

[5] Thomas Adam (1701–1784) was Anglican minister who served in Winteringham, Lincolnshire for nearly sixty years.

Alexander the Great ever had,"[6] and I will add, that he needs more than Alexander's ardor to enable him to continue victorious in his holy warfare. Sleepy Hollow and Dormer's Land will be too much for us unless we pray for daily quickening.

Yet town life has its dangers too, and zeal is apt to burn low through numerous engagements, like a fire which is scattered abroad instead of being raked together into a heap. Those incessant knocks at our door, and perpetual visits from idle persons, are so many buckets of cold water thrown upon our devout zeal. We must by some means secure uninterrupted meditation, or we shall lose power. London is a peculiarly trying sphere on this account.

Zeal also is more quickly checked after long years of continuance in the same service than when novelty gives a charm to our work. Mr. Wesley says, in his fifteenth volume of "Journals and Letters," "I know that, were I myself to preach one whole year in one place, I should preach both myself and most of my congregation asleep."[7] What then must it be to abide in the same pulpit for many years! In such a case it is not the pace that kills, but the length of the race. Our God is evermore the same, enduring for ever, and he alone can enable us to endure even to the end. He, who at the end of twenty years' ministry among the same people is more alive than ever, is a great debtor to the quickening Spirit.

Earnestness may be, and too often is, diminished by neglect of study. If we have not exercised ourselves in the word of God, we shall not preach with the fervor and grace of the man who has fed upon the truth he delivers, and is therefore strong and ardent. An Englishman's earnestness in battle depends, according to some authorities, upon his being well fed; he has no stomach for the

---

[6] Thomas Adam, *Private Thoughts on Religion and Other Subjects Connected With It, Extracted from the Diary of the Rev. Thomas Adam, etc.* (London: Ogles, Duncan, & Cochran, 1815), 262.

[7] John Wesley, *Works of the Rev. John Wesley, in Ten Volumes*, vol. 10 (New York: J. & J. Harper, 1827), 208.

Earnestness

fight if he is starved. If we are well nourished by sound gospel food we shall be vigorous and fervent. An old blunt commander at Cadiz is described by Selden[8] as thus addressing his soldiers, "What a shame will it be, you Englishmen, who feed upon good beef and beer, to let these rascally Spaniards beat you that eat nothing but oranges and lemons!"[9] His philosophy and mine agree: he expected courage and valor from those who were well nourished. Brethren, never neglect your spiritual meals or you will lack stamina and your spirits will sink. Live on the substantial doctrines of grace, and you will outlive and outwork those who delight in the pastry and syllabubs of "modern thought."

Zeal may, on the other hand, be damped by our studies. There is, no doubt, such a thing as feeding the brain at the expense of the heart, and many a man in his aspirations to be literary has rather qualified himself to write reviews than to preach sermons. A quaint evangelist was wont to say that Christ hung crucified beneath Greek, Latin, and Hebrew. It ought not to be so, but it has often happened that the student in college has gathered fuel, but lost the fire which is to kindle it. It will be to our everlasting disgrace if we bury our flame beneath the fagots which are intended to sustain it. If we degenerate into bookworms it will be to the old serpent's delight, and to our own misery.

True earnestness may be greatly lessened by levity in conversation, and especially by jesting with brother ministers, in whose company we often take greater liberties than we would like to do in society of other Christians. There are excellent reasons for our feeling at home with our brethren, but if this freedom be carried too far we shall soon feel that we have suffered damage through vanity of speech. Cheerfulness is one thing, and frivolity is another; he is a wise man who by a serious happiness of conversation

---

[8] John Selden (1584-1654) was an English philosopher, jurist, and legal scholar.
[9] John Selden, *The Table-Talk of John Selden, with a Biographical Preface and Notes by S. W. Singer, F. S. A.* 3rd edition (London: John Russell Smith, 1860), 229.

steers between the dark rocks of moroseness, and the quicksands of levity.

We shall often find ourselves in danger of being deteriorated in zeal by the cold Christian people with whom we come in contact. What terrible wet blankets some professors are! Their remarks after a sermon are enough to stagger you. You think that surely you have moved the very stones to feeling, but you painfully learn that these people are utterly unaffected. You have been burning and they are freezing; you have been pleading as for life or death and they have been calculating how many seconds the sermon occupied, and grudging you the odd five minutes beyond the usual hour, which your earnestness compelled you to occupy in pleading with men's souls. If these frost-bitten men should happen to be the officers of the church, from whom you naturally expect the warmest sympathy, the result is chilling to the last degree, and all the more so if you are young and inexperienced. It is as though an angel were confined in an iceberg. "Thou shalt not yoke the ox and the ass together" was a merciful precept, but when a laborious, ox-like minister comes to be yoked to a deacon who is not another ox, it becomes hard work to plough. Some crabbed professors have a great deal to answer for in this matter. One of them not so very long ago went up to an earnest young evangelist who had been doing his best, and said, "Young man, do you call that preaching?" He thought himself faithful, but he was cruel and uncourteous, and though the good brother survived the blow it was none the less brutal. Such offences against the Lord's little ones are, I hope, very rare, but they are very grievous, and tend to turn aside our hopeful youth.

Frequently the audience itself, as a whole, will damp your zeal. You can see by their very look and manner that the people are not appreciating your warm-hearted endeavors, and you feel discouraged. Those empty benches also are a serious trial, and if the place be large and the congregation small, the influence is seriously depressing; it is not every man who can bear to be "a voice crying in the wilderness." Disorder in the congregation also sadly afflicts sensitive speakers. The walking up the aisle of a woman with a pair of pattens, the squeak of a pair of new boots, the frequent fall of umbrellas and walking-sticks, the crying of infants, and especially the consistent lateness of half the assembly—all these tend to irritate the mind, take it off from its object, and diminish its ardor. We hardly like to confess that our hearts are so readily affected by such trifles, but it is so, and not at all to be wondered at. As pots of the most precious ointment are more often spoilt by dead flies than by dead camels, so insignificant matters will destroy earnestness more readily than greater annoyances. Under a great discouragement a man pulls himself together, and then throws himself upon his God, and receives divine strength, but under lesser depressions he may possibly worry, and the trifles will irritate and fester till serious consequences follow.

Maintaining physical vigor
Pardon my saying that the condition of your body must be attended to, especially in the matter of eating, for any measure of excess may injure your digestion and make you stupid when you should be fervent. From the memoir of Duncan Matheson[10] I cull an anecdote which is much to the point:

> In a certain place where evangelistic meetings were being held, the lay preachers, among whom was Mr. Matheson, were sumptuously entertained at the house of a Christian gentleman. After dinner they went to the meeting, not without some difference of opinion as to the best method of conducting the services of the evening. "The Spirit is grieved; he is not here at all, I feel it," said one of the younger, with a whine which somewhat contrasted with his previous

---

[10] Duncan Matheson (1824–1869) was a Scottish preacher and evangelist.

unbounded enjoyment of the luxuries of the table. "Nonsense," replied Matheson, who hated all whining and morbid spirituality; "Nothing of the sort. You have just eaten too much dinner, and you feel heavy."[11]

Duncan Matheson was right, and a little more of his common sense would be a great gain to some who are ultra-spiritual, and attribute all their moods of feeling to some supernatural cause when the real reason lies far nearer to hand. Has it not often happened that dyspepsia has been mistaken for backsliding, and a bad digestion has been set down as a hard heart? I say no more; a word to the wise is enough.

Many physical and mental causes may operate to create apparent lethargy where there is at heart intense earnestness. Upon some of us a disturbed night, a change in the weather, or an unkind remark, will produce the most lamentable effect. But those who complain of want of zeal are often the most zealous persons in the world, and a confession of want of life is itself an argument that life exists, and is not without vigor. Do not spare yourselves and become self-satisfied, but, on the other hand, do not slander yourselves and sink into despondency. Your own opinion of your state is not worth much. Ask the Lord to search you.

Long continued labor without visible success is another frequent damp upon zeal, though if rightly viewed it ought to be an incentive to sevenfold diligence. Quaint Thomas Fuller[12] observes that "herein God hath humbled many painstaking pastors, in making them to be clouds to rain, not over Arabia the happy, but over Arabia the desert and stony."[13] If non-success humbles us it is

---

[11] Jon Macpherson, *Life and Labours of Duncan Matheson, the Scottish Evangelist* (London: Morgan, Chase, and Scott, 1871), 232-233.

[12] Thomas Fuller (1608-1661) was an English Puritan and a prolific author and historian.

[13] Thomas Fuller, *The Holy State and the Profane State* (London: William Pickering, 1840), 66.

well, but if it discourages us, and especially if it leads us to think bitterly of more prosperous brethren, we ought to look about us with grave concern. It is possible that we have been faithful and have adopted wise methods, and are in our right place, and yet we have not struck the mark; we shall probably be heavily bowed down and feel scarcely able to continue the work; but if we pluck up courage and increase our earnestness we shall one day reap a rich harvest, which will more than repay us for all our waiting. "The husbandman waiteth for the precious fruits of the earth" (Jas. 5:7), and with a holy patience begotten of zeal we must wait on, and never doubt that the time to favor Zion will yet come.

Nor must it ever be forgotten that the flesh is weak and naturally inclined to slumber. We need a constant renewal of the divine impulse which first started us in the way of service. We are not as arrows, which find their way to the target by the sole agency of the force with which they started from the bow; nor as birds, which bear within themselves their own motive power. We must be borne onward, like ships at sea, by the constant power of the heavenly wind, or we shall make no headway. Preachers sent from God are not musical boxes which, being once wound up, will play through their set tunes, but they are trumpets which are utterly mute until the living breath causes them to give forth a certain sound. We read of some who are dumb dogs, given to slumber, and such would be the character of us all if the grace of God did not prevent. We have need to watch against a careless, indifferent spirit, and if we do not so we shall soon be as lukewarm as Laodicea itself.

Feed the flame: communion with Christ

Remembering then, dear brethren, that we must be in earnest, and that we cannot counterfeit earnestness, or find a substitute for it, and that it is very easy for us to lose it, let us consider for a while the ways and means for retaining all our fervor and gaining more.

If it is to continue, our earnestness must be kindled at an immortal flame, and I know of but one—the flame of the love of Christ, which many waters cannot quench. A spark from that celestial sun will be as undying as the source from whence it came. If we can get it, yea, if we have it, we shall still be full of enthusiasm, however long we may live, however greatly we may be tried, and however much for many reasons we may be discouraged. To continue fervent for life we must possess the fervor of heavenly life to begin with. Have we this fire? We must have the truth burnt into our souls, or it will not burn upon our lips. Do we understand this? The doctrines of grace must be part and parcel of ourselves, interwoven with the warp and woof of our being, and this can only be effected by the same hand which originally made the fabric. We shall never lose our love to Christ and our love to souls if the Lord has given them to us. The Holy Spirit makes zeal for God to be a permanent principle of life rather than a passion. Does the Holy Spirit rest upon us, or is our present fervor a mere human feeling? We ought upon this point to be seriously inquisitorial with our hearts, pressing home the question, Have we the holy fire which springs from a true call to the ministry? If not, why are we here? If a man can live without preaching, let him live without preaching. If a man can be content without being a soul-winner—I had almost said he had better not attempt the work, but I had rather say—let him seek to have the stone taken out of his heart, that he may feel for perishing men. Till then, as a minister, he may do positive mischief by occupying the place of one who might have succeeded in the blessed work in which he must be a failure.

 The fire of our earnestness must burn upon the hearth of faith in the truths which we preach, and faith in their power to bless mankind when the Spirit applies them to the heart. He who declares what may or what may not be true, and what he considers upon the whole to be as good as any other form of teaching, will of necessity make a very feeble preacher. How can he be zealous about that which he is not sure of? If he knows nothing of the inward power of the truth within his own heart, if he has never tasted and handled the good word of life, how can he be enthusiastic? But if the Holy Ghost has taught us in secret places, and made our soul to understand within itself the doctrine which we are to proclaim, then shall we speak evermore with the tongue of fire. Brother, do not begin to teach others till the Lord has taught you. It must be dreary work to parrot forth dogmas which have no interest for your heart, and carry no conviction to your understanding. I would prefer to pick oakum or turn a crank for my breakfast, like the paupers in the casual ward, rather than be the slave of a congregation and bring them spiritual meat of which I never taste myself. And then how dreadful the end of such a course must be! How fearful the account to be rendered at the last by one who publicly taught what he did not heartily believe, and perpetrated this detestable hypocrisy in the name of God!

Brethren, if the fire is brought from the right place to the right place, we have a good beginning, and the main elements of a glorious ending. Kindled by a live coal, borne to our lips from off the altar by the winged cherub, the fire has begun to feed upon our inmost spirit, and there it will burn though Satan himself should labor to stamp it out.

Yet the best flame in the world needs renewing. I know not whether immortal spirits, like the angels, drink on the wing, and feed on some superior manna prepared in heaven for them; but the probability is that no created being, though immortal, is quite free from the necessity to receive from without sustenance for its strength. Certainly the flame of zeal in the renewed heart, however divine, must be continually fed with fresh fuel. Even the lamps of the sanctuary needed oil. Feed the flame, my brother, feed it frequently; feed it with holy thought and contemplation, especially with thought about your work, your motives in pursuing it, the design of it, the helps that are waiting for you, and the grand results of it if the Lord be with you. Dwell much upon the love of God to sinners, and the death of Christ on their behalf, and the work of the Spirit upon men's hearts. Think of what must be wrought in men's hearts ere they can be saved. Remember, you are not sent to whiten tombs, but to open them, and this is a work which no man can perform unless, like the Lord Jesus at the grave of Lazarus, he groans in spirit, and even then he is powerless apart from the Holy Ghost. Meditate with deep solemnity upon the fate of the lost sinner, and, like Abraham, when you get up early to go to the place where you commune with God, cast an eye toward Sodom and see the smoke thereof going up like the smoke of a furnace. Shun all views of future punishment which would make it appear less terrible, and so take off the edge of your anxiety to save immortals from the quenchless flame. If men are indeed only a nobler kind of ape, and expire as the beasts, you may well enough let them die unpitied, but if their creation in the image of God involves immortality, and there is any fear that through their unbelief they will bring upon themselves endless woe, arouse yourselves to the agonies of the occasion, and be ashamed at the bare suspicion of unconcern. Think much also of the bliss of the sinner saved, and like holy Baxter derive rich arguments for earnestness from the "the saints' everlasting rest." Go to the heavenly hills and gather fuel there; pile on the glorious logs of the wood of Lebanon, and the fire will burn freely and yield a sweet perfume as each piece of choice cedar glows in the flame. There will be no fear of your being lethargic if you are continually familiar with eternal realities.

Above all, feed the flame with intimate fellowship with Christ. No man was ever cold in heart who lived with Jesus on such terms as John and Mary did of old, for he makes men's hearts burn within them. I never met with a half-hearted preacher who was much in communion with the Lord Jesus. The zeal of God's house ate up our Lord, and when we come into contact with him it begins to consume us also, and we feel that we cannot but speak the things which we have seen and heard in his company, nor can we help speaking of them with the fervor which comes out of actual acquaintance with them. Those of us who have been preaching for these five-and-twenty years sometimes feel that the same work, the same subject, the same people, and the same pulpit, are together apt to beget a feeling of monotony, and monotony may soon lead on to weariness. But then we call to mind another sameness, which becomes our complete deliverance; there is the same Saviour, and we may go to him in the same way as we did at the first, since he is "Jesus Christ the same yesterday, and today, and forever" (Heb. 13:8). In his presence we drink in the new wine and renew our youth. He is the fountain, forever flowing with the cool refreshing water of life, and in fellowship with him we find our souls quickened into perpetual energy. Beneath his smile our long accustomed work is always delightful, and wears a brighter charm than novelty could have conferred. We gather new manna for our people every morning, and as we go to distribute it we feel an anointing of fresh oil distilling upon us. "They that wait upon the Lord shall renew their strength; they shall mount up with wings as eagles; they shall run and not be weary; and they shall walk and not faint" (Isa. 40:31). Newly come from the presence of him that walketh among the golden candlesticks, we are ready to write or speak unto the churches in the power which he alone can give. Soldiers of Christ, you can only be worthy of your Captain by abiding in fellowship with him, and listening to his voice as Joshua did when he stood by Jordan, and inquired, "What saith my Lord unto his servant?" (Josh. 5:14).

Fan the flame: prayer and fresh service
Fan the flame as well as feed it. Fan it with much supplication. We cannot be too urgent with one another upon this point. No language can be too vehement with which to implore ministers to

pray. There is for our brethren and ourselves an absolute necessity for prayer. Necessity—I hardly like to talk of that, let me rather speak of the deliciousness of prayer—the wondrous sweetness and divine felicity which come to the soul that lives in the atmosphere of prayer. John Fox[14] said, "The time we spend with God in secret is the sweetest time, and the best improved. Therefore if thou lovest thy life, be in love with prayer."[15] The devout Mr. Hervey[16] resolved on the bed of sickness, "If God shall spare my life, I will read less and pray more."[17] John Cooke,[18] of Maidenhead, wrote, "The business, the pleasure, the honor, and advantage of prayer press on my spirit with increasing force every day."[19] A deceased pastor when drawing near his end, exclaimed, "I wish I had prayed more;" that wish many of us might utter. There should be special seasons for devotion, and it is well to maintain them with regularity, but the spirit of prayer is even better than the habit of prayer; to pray without ceasing is better than praying at intervals. It will be a happy circumstance if we can frequently bow the knee with devout brethren, and I think it ought to be a rule with us ministers never to separate without a word of prayer. Much more intercession would rise to heaven if we made a point of this, especially those of us who have been fellow-students. If it be possible, let prayer and praise sanctify each meeting of friend with friend. It is a refreshing practice to have a minute or two of supplication in the vestry before preaching if you can call

---

[14] John Fox (dates unknown; likely born in the early 1600s, and was known to be alive as late as 1676) was a Puritan minister in Gloucestershire.

[15] John Fox, *Time and the End of Time, in Two Discourses: The First on Redemption of Time, The Second on the Consideration of our Latter End* (London: Hamilton, Adams, & Co., 1855), 92.

[16] Here Spurgeon likely refers to James Hervey (1714-1758) who was an evangelical Anglican minister who was greatly influenced by John Wesley.

[17] John Cooke, *Memoirs and Select Remains of the Late Rev. John Cooke* (London: Hurst, Chance, and Co., 1828), 588.

[18] John Cooke (1760-1826) was an English Independent minister.

[19] Cooke, *Memoirs and Select Remains of the Late Rev. John Cooke*, 588.

Earnestness

in three or four warm-hearted deacons or other brethren. It always nerves me for the fight. But, for all that, to fan your earnestness to a vehement flame you should seek the spirit of continual prayer, so as to pray in the Holy Ghost, everywhere and always; in the study, in the vestry, and in the pulpit. It is well to be pleading evermore with God, when sitting down in the pulpit, when rising to give out the hymn, when reading the chapter, and while delivering the sermon; holding up one hand to God empty, in order to receive, and with the other hand dispensing to the people what the Lord bestows. Be in preaching like a conduit pipe between the everlasting and infinite supplies of heaven and the all but boundless needs of men, and to do this you must reach heaven, and keep up the communication without a break. Pray for the people while you preach to them. Speak with God for them while you are speaking with them for God. Only so can you expect to be continually in earnest. A man does not often rise from his knees unearnest; or, if he does, he had better return to prayer till the sacred flame descends upon his soul. Adam Clarke[20] once said, "Study yourself to death, and then pray yourself alive again."[21] It was a wise sentence. Do not attempt the first without the second; neither dream that the second can be honestly accomplished without the first. Work and pray, as well as watch and pray, but pray always.

Stir the fire also by frequent attempts at fresh service. Shake yourself out of routine by breaking away from the familiar fields of service and reclaiming virgin soil. I suggest to you, as a subordinate but very useful means of keeping the heart fresh, the frequent addition of new work to your usual engagements. I would say to brethren who are soon going away from the College, to settle in spheres where they will come into contact with but few superior

---

[20] Adam Clarke (1762–1832) was a prominent British Methodist minister and thrice President of the Methodist Conference (1806, 1814, 1822).

[21] Samuel Dunn, *The Life of Adam Clarke, LL. D., Author of a Commentary on the Old and New Testaments, Etc.* (London: William Tegg, 1863), 104.

minds, and perhaps will be almost alone in the higher walks of spirituality. Look well to yourselves that you do not become flat, stale, and unprofitable, and keep yourselves sweet by maintaining an enterprising spirit. You will have a good share of work to do, and few to help you in it, and the years will grind along heavily; watch against this, and use all means to prevent your becoming dull and sleepy, and among them use that which experience leads me to press upon you. I find it good for myself to have some new work always on hand. The old and usual enterprises must be kept up, but somewhat must be added to them. It should be with us as with the squatters upon our commons, the fence of our garden must roll outward a foot or two, and enclose a little more of the common every year. Never say "it is enough," nor accept the policy of "rest and be thankful." Do all you possibly can, and then do a little more. I do not know by what process the gentleman who advertises that he can make short people taller attempts the task, but I should imagine that if any result could be produced in the direction of adding a cubit to one's stature it would be by every morning reaching up as high as you possibly can on tiptoe, and, having done that, trying day by day to reach a little higher. This is certainly the way to grow mentally and spiritually—"reaching forth to that which is before." If the old should become just a little stale, add fresh endeavors to it, and the whole mass will be leavened anew. Try it and you will soon discover the virtue of breaking up fresh ground, invading new provinces of the enemy, and scaling fresh heights to set the banner of the Lord thereon. This is, of course, a secondary expedient to those of which we have already spoken, but still it is a very useful one, and may greatly benefit you. In a country town, say of two thousand inhabitants, you will, after a time, feel, "Well, now, I have done about all I can in this place." What then? There is a hamlet some four miles off, set about opening a room there. If one hamlet is occupied, make an excursion to another, and spy out the land, and set the relief of its spiritual destitution before you as an ambition. When the first place is supplied think of a second. It is your duty, it will also be your safeguard. Everybody knows what interest there is in fresh work. A gardener will become weary of his toil unless he is allowed to introduce new flowers into the hothouse, or to cut the beds upon the lawn in a novel shape. All monotonous work is unnatural and wearying to the mind, therefore it is wisdom to give variety to your labor.

Far more weighty is the advice, keep close to God, and keep close to your fellow-men whom you are seeking to bless. Abide under the shadow of the Almighty, dwell where Jesus manifests himself, and live in the power of the Holy Ghost. Your very life lies in this. Whitefield mentions a lad who was so vividly conscious of the presence of God that he would generally walk the roads with his hat off. How I wish we were always in such a mood. It would be no trouble to maintain earnestness then.

Be among the people
Take care, also, to be on most familiar terms with those whose souls are committed to your care. Stand in the stream and fish. Many preachers are utterly ignorant as to how the bulk of the people are living; they are at home among books, but quite at sea among men. What would you think of a botanist who seldom saw real flowers, or an astronomer who never spent a night with the stars? Would they be worthy of the name of men of science? Neither can a minister of the gospel be anything but a mere empiric unless he mingles with men, and studies character for himself. "Studies from the life,"—gentlemen, we must have plenty of these if we are to paint to the life in our sermons. Read men as well as books, and love men rather than opinions, or you will be inanimate preachers.

Get into close quarters with those who are in an anxious state. Watch their difficulties, their throes and pangs of conscience. It will help to make you earnest when you see their eagerness to find peace. On the other hand, when you see how little earnest the bulk of men remain, it may help to make you more zealous for their arousing. Rejoice with those who are finding the Saviour; this is a grand means of revival for your own soul. When you are enabled to bring a mourner to Jesus you will feel quite young again. It will be as oil to your bones to hear a weeping penitent exclaim, "I see it all now! I believe, and my burden is gone. I am saved." Sometimes the rapture of newborn souls will electrify you into apostolic intensity. Who could not preach after having seen souls converted? Be on the spot when grace at last captures the lost sheep, that by sharing in the Great Shepherd's rejoicings you may renew your youth. Be in at the death with sinners, and you will be repaid for the weary chase after them which it may be you have followed for months and years. Grasp them with firm hold of love, and say, "Yes, by the grace of God, I have really won these souls," and your enthusiasm will flame forth.

If you have to labor in a large town I should recommend you to familiarize yourself, wherever your place of worship may be, with the poverty, ignorance, and drunkenness of the place. Go if you can with a city missionary into the poorest quarter, and you will see that which will astonish you, and the actual sight of the disease will make you eager to reveal the remedy. There is enough of evil to be seen even in the best streets of our great cities, but there is an unutterable depth of horror in the condition of the slums. As a doctor walks the hospitals, so ought you to traverse the lanes and courts to behold the mischief which sin has wrought. It is enough to make a man weep tears of blood to gaze upon the desolation which sin has made in the earth. One day with a devoted missionary would be a fine termination to your College course, and a fit preparation for work in your own sphere. See the masses living in their sins, defiled with drinking and Sabbath-breaking, rioting and blaspheming; and see them dying sodden and hardened, or terrified and despairing. Surely this will rekindle expiring zeal if anything can do it. The world is full of grinding poverty, and crushing sorrow; shame and death are the portion of thousands, and it needs a great gospel to meet the dire necessities of men's souls. Verily it is so. Do you doubt it? Go and see for yourselves. Thus will you learn to preach a great salvation, and magnify the great Saviour, not with your mouth only, but with your heart; and thus will you be married to your work beyond all possibility of deserting it.

Deathbeds are grand schools for us. They are intended to act as tonics to brace us to our work. I have come down from the bedchambers of the dying, and thought that everybody was mad, and myself most of all. I have grudged the earnestness which men devoted to earthly things, and half said to myself, "Why was that man driving along so hastily? Why was that woman walking out in such finery?" Since they were all to die so soon, I thought nothing worth their doing but preparing to meet their God. To be often where men die will help us to teach them both to die and to live. M'Cheyne was wont to visit his sick or dying hearers on the Saturday afternoon, for, as he told Dr. James Hamilton,[22] "Before preaching he liked to look over the verge."[23]

Measure your work

I pray you, moreover, measure your work in the light of God. Are you God's servant or not? If you are, how can your heart be cold? Are you sent by a dying Saviour to proclaim his love and win the reward of his wounds, or are you not? If you are, how can you flag? Is the Spirit of God upon you? Has the Lord anointed you to preach glad tidings to the poor? If he has not, do not pretend it. If

---

[22] James Hamilton (1814–1867) was a Scottish minister and author who spent most of his ministerial career in London.

[23] James Hamilton, *Works of the Late Rev. James Hamilton, D. D. F. L. S. in Six Volumes*, vol. 4 (London: James Nisbet & Co., 1873), 81.

he has, go in this thy might, and the Lord shall be thy strength. Yours is not a trade, or a profession. Assuredly if you measure it by the tradesman's measure it is the poorest business on the face of the earth. Consider it as a profession; who would not prefer any other, so far as golden gains or worldly honors are concerned? But if it be a divine calling, and you a miracle-worker, dwelling in the supernatural, and working not for time but for eternity, then you belong to a nobler guild, and to a higher fraternity than any that spring of earth and deal with time. Look at it aright, and you will own that it is a grand thing to be as poor as your Lord, if, like him, you may make many rich; you will feel that it is a glorious thing to be as unknown and despised as were your Lord's first followers, because you are making him known, whom to know is life eternal. You will be satisfied to be anything or to be nothing, and the thought of self will not enter your mind, or only cross it to be scouted as a meanness not to be tolerated by a consecrated man. There is the point. Measure your work as it should be measured, and I am not afraid that your earnestness will be diminished. Gaze upon it by the light of the judgment day, and in view of the eternal rewards of faithfulness. Oh, brethren, the present joy of having saved a soul is overwhelmingly delightful; you have felt it, I trust, and know it now. To save a soul from going down to perdition brings to us a little heaven below, but what must it be at the day of judgment to meet spirits redeemed by Christ, who learned the news of their redemption from our lips! We look forward to a blissful heaven in communion with our Master, but we shall also know the added joy of meeting those loved ones whom we led to Jesus by our ministry. Let us endure every cross, and despise all shame, for the joy which Jesus sets before us of winning men for him.

One more thought may help to keep up our earnestness. Consider the great evil which will certainly come upon us and upon our hearers if we be negligent in our work. "They shall perish" — is not that a dreadful sentence? It is to me quite as awful as that

Earnestness

which follows it—"but their blood will I require at the watchman's hand" (Ezek. 33:6). How shall we describe the doom of an unfaithful minister? And every unearnest minister is unfaithful. I would infinitely prefer to be consigned to Tophet as a murderer of men's bodies than as a destroyer of men's souls; neither do I know of any condition in which a man can perish so fatally, so infinitely, as in that of the man who preaches a gospel which he does not believe, and assumes the office of pastor over a people whose good he does not intensely desire. Let us pray to be found faithful always, and ever. God grant that the Holy Spirit may make and keep us so.

8
The Blind Eye and the Deaf Ear

Introduction

Spurgeon had a wonderful gift for producing memorable images and metaphors to cement his points in the minds of his hearers. This gift is on full display in this lecture on what he calls "The Blind Eye and the Deaf Ear." The simple premise is that every minister should have one blind eye and one deaf ear to a number of things in his ministry that could otherwise distract or discourage him.

Spurgeon begins by encouraging the pastor to have a blind eye and deaf ear to conflict and controversy within the church that predated his ministry. Ministers should begin with a clean slate, and they should make this clear to their congregations. They will not be the arbiters of old petty grievances, but will instead work for peace and a cessation of hostilities between members past and present.

Ministers should also be blind and deaf in the matter of their salary, and the finances of the church in general. Though Spurgeon allows for exceptions to this rule, he recognizes that much can be forfeit in a man's reputation and his credibility with the congregation if he is overly involved in the setting of his own salary. Ministers should not be, either in fact or in appearance, obsessed with money matters.

The blind eye and deaf ear are valuable especially when it comes to gossip. A pastor's study must be where gossip goes to die. He should give no countenance to it. Furthermore, Spurgeon gives words of practical wisdom for how to quell gossip when it arises within a church.

Spurgeon also encourages ministers to avoid a suspicious spirit. If they are not careful, they can provoke trouble by their suspicion. This suspicion can come to expression in seeking out opinions of oneself at every turn, or inquiring always about what criticisms people have of the church. It can also affect the way a minister views the sheep if he suspects them always of nursing ill opinions of his ministry. Most often, such suspicions are unjustified and tend only to create anxiety and depression in pastors. Better to put suspicion to death and carry on with one's work.

Spurgeon again commends the use of the blind eye and deaf ear when it comes to listening to the comments of others about one's ministry. He essentially encourages pastors not to read their own press. This applies both in terms of criticism and praise. They should not be inordinately influenced by their critics or their fans, but should recognize that they will ultimately stand or fall before their Master. The Lord's approval should be all that matters.

Spurgeon further encourages pastors not to listen to false reports against themselves. Ministers should typically not answer false charges, lest they give countenance to frivolous accusations. However, Spurgeon adds the caveat that in the case of serious public charges, it may become necessary for the minister to defend himself. In such cases he should seek to clear his name by addressing the issue in as clear and straightforward a manner as possible, looking to the Lord to vindicate his integrity.

Finally, Spurgeon warns pastors against giving undue attention to other pastors and churches. Each man is responsible for his own flock and should not meddle in the affairs of other churches. Ministers would do best to keep their eyes and ears directed toward their own congregations.

This lecture is full of practical wisdom and is evergreen for ministers. Younger pastors in particular should pay heed to this lecture as they begin their ministries. Following Spurgeon's advice in this lecture may deliver a minister from a world of trouble.

The Blind Eye and the Deaf Ear

Having often said in this room that a minister ought to have one blind eye and one deaf ear, I have excited the curiosity of several brethren, who have requested an explanation; for it appears to them, as it does also to me, that the keener eyes and ears we have the better. Well, gentlemen, since the text is somewhat mysterious, you shall have the exegesis of it.

A part of my meaning is expressed in plain language by Solomon, in the book of Ecclesiastes (7:21): "Also take no heed unto all words that are spoken; lest thou hear thy servant curse thee." The margin says, "Give not thy heart to all words that are spoken;"—do not take them to heart or let them weigh with you, do not notice them, or act as if you heard them. You cannot stop people's tongues, and therefore the best thing is to stop your own ears and never mind what is spoken. There is a world of idle chit-chat abroad, and he who takes note of it will have enough to do. He will find that even those who live with him are not always singing his praises, and that when he has displeased his most faithful servants they have, in the heat of the moment, spoken fierce words which it would be better for him not to have heard. Who has not, under temporary irritation, said that of another which he has afterwards regretted? It is the part of the generous to treat passionate words as if they had never been uttered. When a man is in an angry mood it is wise to walk away from him, and leave off strife before it be meddled with, and if we are compelled to hear hasty language, we must endeavor to obliterate it from the memory, and say with David, "But I, as a deaf man, heard not. I was as a man that heareth not, and in whose mouth are no reproofs" (Ps. 38:13-14). Tacitus[1] describes a wise man as saying to one that railed at him, "You are lord of your tongue, but I am also master of my ears"—you may say what you please, but I will hear what I choose. We cannot shut our ears as we do our eyes, for we have no ear lids, and yet, as we read of him that "stoppeth his ears from hearing of blood" (Is. 33:15), it is, no doubt, possible to seal the portal of the ear so that nothing contraband shall enter. We would say of the general gossip of the village, and of the unadvised words of angry friends—do not hear them, or if you must hear them, do not lay them to heart, for you also have talked idly and angrily in your day, and would even now be in an awkward position if you were called to account for every word that you have spoken, even about your dearest friend. Thus Solomon argued as he closed the passage which we have quoted,—"For oftentimes also thine own heart knoweth that thou thyself likewise hast cursed others" (Eccl. 7:22).

A clean slate

In enlarging upon my text, let me say first, when you commence your ministry make up your mind to begin with a clean sheet. Be deaf and blind to the long standing differences which may survive in the church. As soon as you enter upon your pastorate you may be waited upon by persons who are anxious to secure your adhesion to their side in a family quarrel or church dispute; be deaf and blind to these people, and assure them that bygones must be bygones with you, and that as you have not inherited your predecessor's cupboard you do not mean to eat his cold meat. If any flagrant injustice has been done, be diligent to set it right, but if it be a mere feud, bid the quarrelsome party cease from it, and tell him once for all that you will have nothing to do with it. The answer of

---

[1] Tacitus (c. AD 56–120) was a Roman historian.

The Blind Eye and the Deaf Ear

Gallio will almost suit you: "If it were a matter of wrong or wicked lewdness, O ye Jews, reason would that I should bear with you: but if it be a question of words and names, and vain janglings, look ye to it; for I will be no judge of such matters" (Acts 18:14-15). When I came to New Park-street Chapel as a young man from the country, and was chosen pastor, I was speedily interviewed by a good man who had left the church, having, as he said, been "treated shamefully." He mentioned the names of half-a-dozen persons, all prominent members of the church, who had behaved in a very unchristian manner to him, he, poor innocent sufferer, having been a model of patience and holiness. I learned his character at once from what he said about others (a mode of judging which has never misled me), and I made up my mind how to act. I told him that the church had been in a sadly unsettled state, and that the only way out of the snarl was for every one to forget the past and begin again. He said that the lapse of years did not alter facts, and I replied that it would alter a man's view of them if in that time he had become a wiser and better man.

However, I added, that all the past had gone away with my predecessors, that he must follow them to their new spheres, and settle matters with them, for I would not touch the affair with a pair of tongs. He waxed somewhat warm, but I allowed him to radiate until he was cool again, and we shook hands and parted. He was a good man, but constructed upon an uncomfortable principle, so that he came across the path of others in a very awkward manner at times, and if I had gone into his narrative and examined his case, there would have been no end to the strife. I am quite certain that, for my own success, and for the prosperity of the church, I took the wisest course by applying my blind eye to all disputes which dated previously to my advent. It is the extreme of unwisdom for a young man fresh from college, or from another charge, to suffer himself to be earwigged by a clique, and to be bribed by kindness and flattery to become a partisan, and so to ruin himself with one-half of his people. Know nothing of parties and cliques, but be the pastor of all the flock, and care for all alike. Blessed are the peacemakers, and one sure way of peacemaking is to let the fire of contention alone. Neither fan it, nor stir it, nor add fuel to it, but let it go out of itself. Begin your ministry with one blind eye and one deaf ear.

Church finances
I should recommend the use of the same faculty, or want of faculty, with regard to finance in the matter of your own salary. There are some occasions, especially in raising a new church, when you may have no deacon who is qualified to manage that department, and, therefore, you may feel called upon to undertake it yourselves. In such a case you are not to be censured, you ought even to be commended. Many a time also the work would come to an end altogether if the preacher did not act as his own deacon, and find supplies both temporal and spiritual by his own exertions. To these exceptional cases I have nothing to say but that I admire the struggling worker and deeply sympathize with him, for he is overweighted, and is apt to be a less successful soldier for his Lord because he is entangled with the affairs of this life. In churches which are well established, and afford a decent maintenance, the minister will do well to supervise all things, but interfere with nothing. If deacons cannot be trusted they ought not to be deacons at all, but if they are worthy of their office they are worthy of our confidence. I know that instances occur in which they are sadly incompetent and yet they must be borne with, and in such a state of things the pastor must open the eye which otherwise would have remained blind. Rather than the management of church funds should become a scandal we must resolutely interfere, but if there is no urgent call for us to do so we had better believe in the division of labor, and let deacons do their own work. We have the same right as other officers to deal with financial matters if we please,

The Blind Eye and the Deaf Ear

but it will be our wisdom as much as possible to let them alone, if others will manage them for us. When the purse is bare, the wife sickly, and the children numerous, the preacher must speak if the church does not properly provide for him; but to be constantly bringing before the people requests for an increase of income is not wise. When a minister is poorly remunerated and he feels that he is worth more, and that the church could give him more, he ought kindly, boldly and firmly to communicate with the deacons first, and if they do not take it up he should then mention it to the brethren in a sensible, business-like way, not as craving a charity, but as putting it to their sense of honor, that the "laborer is worthy of his hire." Let him say outright what he thinks, for there is nothing to be ashamed of, but there would be much more cause for shame if he dishonored himself and the cause of God by plunging into debt. Let him therefore speak to the point in a proper spirit to the proper persons, and there end the matter, and not resort to secret complaining. Faith in God should tone down our concern about temporalities, and enable us to practice what we preach, namely, "Take no thought, saying, What shall we eat? or, What shall we drink; or, Wherewithal shall we be clothed? for your heavenly Father knoweth that ye have need of all these things" (Matt. 6:31–32). Some who have pretended to live by faith have had a very shrewd way of drawing out donations by turns of the indirect corkscrew, but you will either ask plainly, like men, or you will leave it to the Christian feeling of your people, and turn to the items and modes of church finance a blind eye and a deaf ear.

Dealing with gossip
The blind eye and the deaf ear will come in exceedingly well in connection with the gossips of the place. Every church, and, for the matter of that, every village and family, is plagued with certain Mrs. Grundys, who drink tea and talk vitriol. They are never quiet, but buzz around to the great annoyance of those who are devout and

practical. No one needs to look far for perpetual motion, he has only to watch their tongues. At tea-meetings, Dorcas meetings and other gatherings, they practise vivisection upon the characters of their neighbors, and of course they are eager to try their knives upon the minister, the minister's wife, the minister's children, the minister's wife's bonnet, the dress of the minister's daughter, and how many new ribbons she has worn for the last six months, and so on ad infinitum. There are also certain persons who are never so happy as when they are "grieved to the heart" to have to tell the minister that Mr. A. is a snake in the grass, that he is quite mistaken in thinking so well of Messrs. B. and C., and that they have heard quite "promiscuously" that Mr. D. and his wife are badly matched. Then follows a long string about Mrs. E, who says that she and Mrs. F. overheard Mrs. G. say to Mrs. H. that Mrs. J. should say that Mr. K. and Miss L. were going to move from the chapel and hear Mr. M., and all because of what old N. said to young O. about that Miss P. Never listen to such people. Do as Nelson[2] did when he put his blind eye to the telescope and declared that he did not see the signal, and therefore would go on with the battle. Let the creatures buzz, and do not even hear them, unless indeed they buzz so much concerning one person that the matter threatens to be serious; then it will be well to bring them to book and talk in sober earnestness to them. Assure them that you are obliged to have facts definitely before you, that your memory is not very tenacious, that you have many things to think of, that you are always afraid of making any mistake in such matters, and that if they would be good enough to write down what they have to say the case would be more fully before you, and you could give more time to its consideration. Mrs. Grundy will not do that; she

---

[2] Horatio Nelson (1758–1805) was a British Admiral in the Royal Navy, famous for his victories in the Napoleonic Wars.

The Blind Eye and the Deaf Ear

has a great objection to making clear and definite statements; she prefers talking at random.

I heartily wish that by any process we could put down gossip, but I suppose that it will never be done so long as the human race continues what it is, for James tells us that "every kind of beasts, and of birds, and of serpents, and of things in the sea, is tamed, and hath been tamed of mankind: but the tongue can no man tame; it is an unruly evil, full of deadly poison" (Jam. 3:7–8). What can't be cured must be endured, and the best way of enduring it is not to listen to it. Over one of our old castles a former owner has inscribed these lines—

They say.
What do they say?
Let them say.

Thin-skinned persons should learn this motto by heart. The talk of the village is never worthy of notice, and you should never take any interest in it except to mourn over the malice and heartlessness of which it is too often the indicator.

Mayow[3] in his "Plain Preaching" very forcibly says, "If you were to see a woman killing a farmer's ducks and geese, for the sake of having one of the feathers, you would see a person acting as we do when we speak evil of any one, for the sake of the pleasure we feel in evil speaking. For the pleasure we feel is not worth a single feather, and the pain we give is often greater than a man feels at the loss of his property."[4] Insert a remark of this kind now and then in a sermon, when there is no special gossip abroad, and it may be of some benefit to the more sensible: I quite despair of the rest.

---

[3] Robert Wynell Mayow (1810–1895) was a well-known Anglican minister.
[4] Robert Wynell Mayow, *Plain Preaching: or, Sermons for the Poor, and for People of All Ranks*, Second Edition (London: Baldwin, Cradock, and Joy, 1816), 173–174.

Above all, never join in tale-bearing yourself, and beg your wife to abstain from it also. Some men are too talkative by half, and remind me of the young man who was sent to Socrates[5] to learn oratory. On being introduced to the philosopher he talked so incessantly that Socrates asked for double fees. "Why charge me double?" said the young fellow. "Because," said the orator, "I must teach you two sciences: the one how to hold your tongue and the other how to speak."[6] The first science is the more difficult, but aim at proficiency in it, or you will suffer greatly, and create trouble without end.

The dangers of a suspicious spirit

Avoid with your whole soul that spirit of suspicion which sours some men's lives, *and to all things from which you might harshly draw an unkind inference turn a blind eye and a deaf ear*. Suspicion makes a man a torment to himself and a spy towards others. Once begins to suspect, and causes for distrust will multiply around you, and your very suspiciousness will create the major part of them. Many a friend has been transformed into an enemy by being suspected. Do not, therefore, look about you with the eyes of mistrust, nor listen as an eaves-dropper with the quick ear of fear. To go about the congregation ferreting out disaffection, like a gamekeeper after rabbits, is a mean employment and is generally rewarded most sorrowfully. Lord Bacon[7] wisely advises "the provident stay of inquiry of that which we would be loath to find."[8] When nothing is to be discovered which will help us to love others

---

[5] Socrates (c. 470–399 BC) was a famous Greek philosopher and the founder of the Western philosophical tradition.

[6] The origin of this anecdote is not clear, but it's possible Spurgeon first came across it in *The Child's Companion Juvenile Instructor* (London: Religious Tract Society, 1847), 199.

[7] Francis Bacon (1561-1626) was a famous English philosopher and Lord Chancellor of England. He is best known as the father of empiricism.

[8] Francis Bacon, *The Work of Francis Bacon*, vol. 1 (London: F. C. and J. Rivington, 1819), 193.

The Blind Eye and the Deaf Ear

we had better cease from the inquiry, for we may drag to light that which may be the commencement of years of contention. I am not, of course, referring to cases requiring discipline, which must be thoroughly investigated and boldly dealt with, but I have upon my mind mere personal matters where the main sufferer is yourself; here it is always best not to know, nor to wish to know, what is being said about you, either by friends or foes. Those who praise us are probably as much mistaken as those who abuse us, and the one may be regarded as a set off to the other, if indeed it be worth while taking any account at all of man's judgment. If we have the approbation of our God, certified by a placid conscience, we can afford to be indifferent to the opinions of our fellow-men, whether they commend or condemn. If we cannot reach this point we are babes and not men.

Some are childishly anxious to know their friend's opinion of them, and if it contain the smallest element of dissent or censure, they regard him as an enemy forthwith. Surely we are not popes, and do not wish our hearers to regard us as infallible! We have known men become quite enraged at a perfectly fair and reasonable remark, and regard an honest friend as an opponent who delighted to find fault; this misrepresentation on the one side has soon produced heat on the other, and strife has ensued. How much better is gentle forbearance! You must be able to bear criticism, or you are not fit to be at the head of a congregation; and you must let the critic go without reckoning him among your deadly foes, or you will prove yourself a mere weakling. It is wisest always to show double kindness where you have been severely handled by one who thought it his duty to do so, for he is probably an honest man and worth winning. He who in your early days hardly thinks you fit for the pastorate may yet become your firmest defender if he sees that you grow in grace, advance in qualification for the work; do not, therefore, regard him as a foe for truthfully expressing his doubts; does not your own heart confess that his fears were not altogether groundless? Turn your deaf ear to what you judge to be his harsh criticism, and endeavor to preach better.

Persons from love of change, from pique, from advance in their tastes, and other causes, may become uneasy under our ministry, and it is well for us to know nothing about it. Perceiving the danger, we must not betray our discovery, but bestir ourselves to improve our sermons, hoping that the good people will be better fed and forget their dissatisfaction. If they are truly gracious persons, the incipient evil will pass away, and no real discontent will arise, or if it does you must not provoke it by suspecting it.

Where I have known that there existed a measure of disaffection to myself, I have not recognized it, unless it has been forced upon me, but have, on the contrary, acted towards the opposing person with all the more courtesy and friendliness, and I have never heard any more of the matter. If I had treated the good man as an opponent, he would have done his best to take the part assigned him, and carry it out to his own credit. But I felt that he was a Christian man, and had a right to dislike me if he thought fit, and that if he did so I ought not to think unkindly of him; and therefore I treated him as one who was a friend to my Lord, if not to me, gave him some work to do which implied confidence in him, made him feel at home, and by degrees won him to be an attached friend as well as a fellow-worker. The best of people are sometimes out at elbows and say unkind things; we should be glad if our friends could quite forget what we said when we were peevish and irritable, and it will be Christlike to act towards others in this matter as we would wish them to do towards us. Never make a brother remember that he once uttered a hard speech in reference to yourself. If you see him in a happier mood, do not mention the former painful occasion. If he be a man of right spirit he will in future be unwilling to vex a pastor who has treated him so generously, and if he be a mere boor it is a pity to hold any argument with him, and therefore the past had better go by default.

The Blind Eye and the Deaf Ear

It would be better to be deceived a hundred times than to live a life of suspicion. It is intolerable. The miser who traverses his chamber at midnight and hears a burglar in every falling leaf is not more wretched than the minister who believes that plots are hatching against him, and that reports to his disadvantage are being spread. I remember a brother who believed that he was being poisoned, and was persuaded that even the seat he sat upon and the clothes he wore had by some subtle chemistry become saturated with death. His life was one perpetual scare, and such is the existence of a minister when he mistrusts all around him. Nor is suspicion merely a source of disquietude, it is a moral evil, and injures the character of the man who harbors it. Suspicion in kings creates tyranny, in husbands jealousy, and in ministers bitterness; such bitterness as in spirit dissolves all the ties of the pastoral relation, eating like a corrosive acid into the very soul of the office and making it a curse rather than a blessing. When once this terrible evil has curdled all the milk of human kindness in a man's bosom, he becomes more fit for the detective force than for the ministry; like a spider, he begins to cast out his lines, and fashions a web of tremulous threads, all of which lead up to himself and warn him of the least touch of even the tiniest midge. There he sits in the centre, a mass of sensation, all nerves and raw wounds, excitable and excited, a self-immolated martyr drawing the blazing fagots about him, and apparently anxious to be burned. The most faithful friend is unsafe under such conditions. The most careful avoidance of offence will not secure immunity from mistrust, but will probably be construed into cunning and cowardice. Society is almost as much in danger from a suspecting man as from a mad dog, for, he snaps on all sides without reason, and scatters right and left the foam of his madness. It is vain to reason with the victim of this folly, for with perverse ingenuity he turns every argument the wrong way, and makes your plea for confidence another reason for mistrust. It is sad that he cannot see the iniquity of his groundless censure of others, especially of those who have been his best friends and the firmest upholders of the cause of Christ.

> I would not wrong
> Virtue so tried by the least shade of doubt:
> Undue suspicion is more abject baseness
> Even than the guilt suspected.[9]

No one ought to be made an offender for a word; but, when suspicion rules, even silence becomes a crime. Brethren, shun this vice by renouncing the love of self. Judge it to be a small matter what men think or say of you, and care only for their treatment of your Lord. If you are naturally sensitive do not indulge the weakness, nor allow others to play upon it. Would it not be a great degradation of your office if you were to keep an army of spies in your pay to collect information as to all that your people said of you? And yet it amounts to this if you allow certain busybodies to bring you all the gossip of the place. Drive the creatures away. Abhor those mischief-making, tattling hand-maidens of strife. Those who will fetch will carry, and no doubt the gossips go from your house and report every observation which falls from your lips, with plenty of garnishing of their own. Remember that, as the receiver is as bad as the thief, so the hearer of scandal is a sharer in the guilt of it. If there were no listening ears, there would be no tale-bearing tongues. While you are a buyer of ill wares the demand will create the supply, and the factories of falsehood will be working full time. No one wishes to become a creator of lies, and yet he who hears slanders with pleasure and believes them with readiness will hatch many a brood into active life.

Solomon says "a whisperer separateth chief friends" (Prov. 16:28). Insinuations are thrown out, and jealousies aroused, till

---

[9] These lines appear to have their origin in Aaron Hill, *Merope: A Tragedy* (Dublin: S. Powell, 1749), 66–67.

The Blind Eye and the Deaf Ear

"mutual coolness ensues, and neither can understand why; each wonders what can possibly be the cause. Thus the firmest, the longest, the warmest, and most confiding attachments, the sources of life's sweetest joys, are broken up perhaps for ever."[10] This is work worthy of the arch-fiend himself, but it could never be done if men lived out of the atmosphere of suspicion. As it is the world is full of sorrow through this cause, a sorrow as sharp as it is superfluous. This is grievous indeed! Campbell[11] eloquently remarks, "The ruins of old friendships are a more melancholy spectacle to me than those of desolated palaces. They exhibit the heart which was once lighted up with joy all damp and deserted, and haunted by those birds of ill omen that nestle in ruins."[12] O suspicion, what desolations thou hast made in the earth!

Learn to disbelieve those who have no faith in their brethren. Suspect those who would lead you to suspect others. A resolute unbelief in all the scandalmongers will do much to repress their mischievous energies. Matthew Pool[13] in his Cripplegate Lecture says,

> Common fame hath lost its reputation long since, and I do not know anything which it hath done in our day to regain it; therefore it ought not to be credited. How few reports there are of any kind which, when they come to be examined, we do not find to be false! For my part, I reckon, if I believe one report in twenty, I make a very liberal allowance. Especially distrust reproaches and evil reports, because these spread fastest, as being grateful to most persons, who

---

[10] Ralph Wardlaw, *Lectures on the Book of Proverbs by the Rev. Ralph Wardlaw, D. D., Edited by His Son, the Rev. J. S. Wardlaw, A. M.*, vol. 2, 2nd ed. (London: A. Fullarton & Co., 1869), 109.

[11] Thomas Campbell (1777-1844) was a well-known Scottish poet.

[12] William Beattie, ed., *Life and Letters of Thomas Campbell*, vol. 3 (London: Edward Moxon, 1849), 412.

[13] It is likely Spurgeon is here referring to Matthew Poole (1624-1679) who was an English Nonconformist minister.

suppose their own reputation to be never so well grounded as when it is built upon the ruins of other men's.[14]

Because the persons who would render you mistrustful of your friends are a sorry set, and because suspicion is in itself a wretched and tormenting vice, resolve to turn towards the whole business your blind eye and your deaf ear.

Need I say a word or two about the wisdom of never hearing what was not meant for you. The eaves-dropper is a mean person, very little if any thing better than the common informer; and he who says he overheard may be considered to have heard over and above what he should have done.

Jeremy Taylor[15] wisely and justly observes, "Never listen at the door or window, for besides that it contains in it a danger and a snare, it is also invading my neighbor's privacy, and a laying that open, which he therefore encloses that it might not be open."[16] It is a well worn proverb that listeners seldom hear any good of themselves. Listening is a sort of larceny, but the goods stolen are never a pleasure to the thief. Information obtained by clandestine means must, in all but extreme cases, be more injury than benefit to a cause. The magistrate may judge it expedient to obtain evidence by such means, but I cannot imagine a case in which a minister should do so. Ours is a mission of grace and peace; we are not prosecutors who search out condemnatory evidence, but friends whose love would cover a multitude of offences. The peeping eyes of Canaan, the son of Ham, shall never be in our employ; we prefer the pious delicacy of Shem and Japhet, who went backward and covered the shame which the child of evil had published with glee.

---

[14] I was unable to locate the original source for this quote.

[15] Jeremy Taylor (1613–1667) was a well-known Anglican minister and author.

[16] Jeremy Taylor, *The Rule and Exercises of Holy Living with Prayers Containing the Whole Duty of a Christian* (London: William Pickering, 1847), 125.

The Blind Eye and the Deaf Ear

Don't believe your own press

To opinions and remarks about yourself turn also as a general rule the blind eye and the deaf ear. Public men must expect public criticism, and as the public cannot be regarded as infallible, public men may expect to be criticised in a way which is neither fair nor pleasant. To all honest and just remarks we are bound to give due measure of heed, but to the bitter verdict of prejudice, the frivolous faultfinding of men of fashion, the stupid utterances of the ignorant, and the fierce denunciations of opponents, we may very safely turn a deaf ear. We cannot expect those to approve of us whom we condemn by our testimony against their favorite sins; their commendation would show that we had missed our mark. We naturally look to be approved by our own people, the members of our churches, and the adherents of our congregations, and when they make observations which show that they are not very great admirers, we may be tempted to discouragement if not to anger: herein lies a snare. When I was about to leave my village charge for London, one of the old men prayed that I might be "delivered from the bleating of the sheep." For the life of me I could not imagine what he meant, but the riddle is plain now, and I have learned to offer the prayer myself. Too much consideration of what is said by our people, whether it be in praise or in depreciation, is not good for us. If we dwell on high with "that great Shepherd of the sheep," we shall care little for all the confused bleatings around us, but if we become "carnal, and walk as men," we shall have little rest if we listen to this, that, and the other which every poor sheep may bleat about us. Perhaps it is quite true that you were uncommonly dull last Sabbath morning, but there was no need that Mrs. Clack should come and tell you that Deacon Jones thought so. It is more than probable that having been out in the country all the previous week, your preaching was very like milk and water, but there can be no necessity for your going round among the people to discover whether they noticed it or not. Is it not enough that your conscience is uneasy upon the point? Endeavor to improve for the future, but do not want to hear all that every Jack, Tom, and Mary may have to say about it. On the other hand, you were on the high horse in your last sermon, and finished with quite a flourish of trumpets, and you feel considerable anxiety to know what impression you produced. Repress your curiosity: it will do you no good to inquire. If the people should happen to agree with your verdict, it will only feed your pitiful vanity, and if they think otherwise your fishing for their praise will injure you in their esteem. In any case it is all about yourself, and this is a poor theme to be anxious about; play the man, and do not demean yourself by seeking compliments like little children when dressed in new clothes, who say, "See my pretty frock." Have you not by this time discovered that flattery is as injurious as it is pleasant? It softens the mind and makes you more sensitive to slander. In proportion as praise pleases you censure will pain you. Besides, it is a crime to be taken off from your great object of glorifying the Lord Jesus by petty considerations as to your little self, and, if there were no other reason, this ought to weigh much with you. Pride is a deadly sin, and will grow without your borrowing the parish water-cart to quicken it. Forget expressions which feed your vanity, and if you find yourself relishing the unwholesome morsels confess the sin with deep humiliation. Payson[17] showed that he was strong in the Lord when he wrote to his mother,

> You must not, certainly, my dear mother, say one word which even looks like an intimation that you think me advancing in grace. I cannot bear it. All the people here, whether friends or enemies, conspire to ruin me. Satan and my own heart, of course, will lend a hand; and if you join too, I fear all the cold water which Christ can throw upon my pride will not prevent its breaking out into a destructive

---

[17] Edward Payson (1783–1827) was an American Congregationalist minister.

The Blind Eye and the Deaf Ear

flame. As certainly as anybody flatters and caresses me my heavenly Father has to whip me: and an unspeakable mercy it is that he condescends to do it. I can, it is true, easily muster a hundred reasons why I should not be proud, but pride will not mind reason, nor anything else but a good drubbing. Even at this moment I feel it tingling in my fingers' ends, and seeking to guide my pen.[18]

Knowing something myself of those secret whippings which our good Father administers to his servants when he sees them unduly exalted, I heartily add my own solemn warnings against your pampering the flesh by listening to the praises of the kindest friends you have. They are injudicious, and you must beware of them.

A sensible friend who will unsparingly criticise you from week to week will be a far greater blessing to you than a thousand undiscriminating admirers if you have sense enough to bear his treatment, and grace enough to be thankful for it. When I was preaching at the Surrey Gardens, an unknown censor of great ability used to send me a weekly list of my mispronunciations and other slips of speech. He never signed his name, and that was my only cause of complaint against him, for he left me in a debt which I could not acknowledge. I take this opportunity of confessing my obligations to him, for with genial temper, and an evident desire to benefit me, he marked down most relentlessly everything which he supposed me to have said incorrectly. Concerning some of these corrections he was in error himself, but for the most part he was right, and his remarks enabled me to perceive and avoid many mistakes. I looked for his weekly memoranda with much interest, and I trust I am all the better for them. If I had repeated a sentence two or three Sundays before, he would say, "See same expression in such a sermon," mentioning number and page. He remarked on one

---

[18] Edward Payson, *Memoir, Select Thoughts and Sermons of the late Rev. Edward Payson*, vol. 1 (Portland: Hyde & Lord, 1849), 207.

occasion that I too often quoted the line, "Nothing in my hands I bring,"[19] and, he added, "we are sufficiently informed of the vacuity of your hands." He demanded my authority for calling a man covechus; and so on. Possibly some young men might have been discouraged, if not irritated, by such severe criticisms, but they would have been very foolish, for in resenting such correction they would have been throwing away a valuable aid to progress. No money can purchase outspoken honest judgment, and when we can get it for nothing let us utilize it to the fullest extent. The worst of it is that of those who offer their judgments few are qualified to form them, and we shall be pestered with foolish, impertinent remarks, unless we turn to them all the blind eye and the deaf ear.

False reports
In the case of false reports against yourself, for the most part use the deaf ear. Unfortunately liars are not yet extinct, and, like Richard Baxter and John Bunyan, you may be accused of crimes which your soul abhors. Be not staggered thereby, for this trial has befallen the very best of men, and even your Lord did not escape the envenomed tongue of falsehood. In almost all cases it is the wisest course to let such things die a natural death. A great lie, if unnoticed, is like a big fish out of water, it dashes and plunges and beats itself to death in a short time. To answer it is to supply it with its element, and help it to a longer life. Falsehoods usually carry their own refutation somewhere about them, and sting themselves to death. Some lies especially have a peculiar smell, which betrays their rottenness to every honest nose. If you are disturbed by them the object of their invention is partly answered, but your silent endurance disappoints malice and gives you a partial victory, which God in his care of you will soon turn into a complete deliverance.

---

[19] Augustus M. Toplady, "Rock of Ages" in *"Our Own Hymn-book": A Collection of Psalms and Hymns for Public, Social, and Private Worship,* ed. C. H. Spurgeon (London: Passmore and Alabaster, 1866), #552.

The Blind Eye and the Deaf Ear

Your blameless life will be your best defence, and those who have seen it will not allow you to be condemned so readily as your slanderers expect. Only abstain from fighting your own battles, and in nine cases out of ten your accusers will gain nothing by their malevolence but chagrin for themselves and contempt from others. To prosecute the slanderer is very seldom wise. I remember a beloved servant of Christ who in his youth was very sensitive, and, being falsely accused, proceeded against the person at law. An apology was offered, it withdrew every iota of the charge, and was most ample, but the good man insisted upon its being printed in the newspapers, and the result convinced him of his own unwisdom. Multitudes, who would otherwise have never heard of the libel, asked what it meant, and made comments thereon, generally concluding with the sage remark that he must have done something imprudent to provoke such an accusation. He was heard to say that so long as he lived he would never resort to such a method again, for he felt that the public apology had done him more harm than the slander itself. Standing as we do in a position which makes us choice targets for the devil and his allies, our best course is to defend our innocence by our silence and leave our reputation with God. Yet there are exceptions to this general rule. When distinct, definite, public charges are made against a man he is bound to answer them, and answer them in the clearest and most open manner. To decline all investigation is in such a case practically to plead guilty, and whatever may be the mode of putting it, the general public ordinarily regard a refusal to reply as a proof of guilt. Under mere worry and annoyance it is by far the best to be altogether passive, but when the matter assumes more serious proportions, and our accuser defies us to a defence, we are bound to meet his charges with honest statements of fact. In every instance counsel should be sought of the Lord as to how to deal with slanderous tongues, and in the issue innocence will be vindicated and falsehood convicted.

Some ministers have been broken in spirit, driven from their position, and even injured in character by taking notice of village scandal. I know a fine young man, for whom I predicted a career of usefulness, who fell into great trouble because he at first allowed it to be a trouble and then worked hard to make it so. He came to me and complained that he had a great grievance; and so it was a grievance, but from beginning to end it was all about what some half-dozen women had said about his procedure after the death of his wife. It was originally too small a thing to deal with — a Mrs. Q. had said that she should not wonder if the minister married the servant then living in his house; another represented her as saying that he ought to marry her, and then a third, with a malicious ingenuity, found a deeper meaning in the words, and construed them into a charge. Worst of all, the dear sensitive preacher must needs trace the matter out and accuse a score or two of people of spreading libels against him, and even threaten some of them with legal proceedings. If he could have prayed over it in secret, or even have whistled over it, no harm would have come of the tittle-tattle; but this dear brother could not treat the slander wisely, for he had not what I earnestly recommend to you, namely, a blind eye and a deaf ear.

Other churches and their pastors

Once more, my brethren, the blind eye and the deaf ear will be useful to you *in relation to other churches and their pastors*. I am always delighted when a brother in meddling with other people's business burns his fingers. Why did he not attend to his own concerns and not episcopize in another's diocese? I am frequently requested by members of churches to meddle in their home disputes; but unless they come to me with authority, officially

The Blind Eye and the Deaf Ear

appointing me to be umpire, I decline. Alexander Cruden[20] gave himself the name of "the Corrector," and I have never envied him the title. It would need a peculiar inspiration to enable a man to settle all the controversies of our churches, and as a rule those who are least qualified are the most eager to attempt it. For the most part interference, however well intentioned, is a failure. Internal dissensions in our churches are very like quarrels between man and wife: when the case comes to such a pass that they must fight it out, the interposing party will be the victim of their common fury. No one but Mr. Verdant Green[21] will interfere in a domestic battle, for the man of course resents it, and the lady, though suffering from many a blow, will say, "You leave my husband alone; he has a right to beat me if he likes." However great the mutual animosity of conjugal combatants, it seems to be forgotten in resentment against intruders; and so, amongst the very independent denomination of Baptists, the person outside the church who interferes in any manner is sure to get the worst of it. Do not consider yourself to be the bishop of all the neighboring churches, but be satisfied with looking after Lystra, or Derbe, or Thessalonica, or whichever church may have been allotted to your care, and leave Philippi and Ephesus in the hands of their own pastors. Do not encourage disaffected persons in finding fault with their minister, or in bringing you news of evils in other congregations. When you meet your brother ministers do not be in a hurry to advise them; they know their duty quite as well as you know yours, and your judgment upon their course of action is probably founded upon partial information supplied from prejudiced sources. Do not grieve your neighbors by your meddlesomeness.

---

[20] Alexander Cruden (1699–1770) was a Scottish author who wrote a concordance to the Bible. He was also a proofreader and publisher who took to himself the nickname "the Corrector."

[21] Cuthbert Bede, *The Adventures of Mr. Verdant Green, An Oxford Freshman* (London: Nathaniel Cooke, 1853).

Servants of Christ, Lovers of Men

We have all enough to do at home, and it is prudent to keep out of all disputes which do not belong to us. We are recommended by one of the world's proverbs to wash our dirty linen at home, and I will add another line to it, and advise that we do not call on our neighbors while their linen is in the suds. This is due to our friends, and will best promote peace. "He that passeth by and meddleth with strife belonging not to him, is like one that taketh a dog by the ears" (Prov. 26:17)—he is very apt to be bitten, and few will pity him. Bridges[22] wisely observes that "Our blessed Master has read us a lesson of godly wisdom. He healed the contentions in his own family, but when called to meddle with strife belonging not to him, he gave answer—'Who made me a judge or a divider over you?'"[23] Self-constituted judges win but little respect; if they were more fit to censure they would be less inclined to do so.

Many a trifling difference within a church has been fanned into a great flame by ministers outside who had no idea of the mischief they were causing. They gave verdicts upon *ex parte* statements, and so egged on opposing persons who felt safe when they could say that the neighboring ministers quite agreed with them. My counsel is that we join the "Know-nothings," and never say a word upon a matter till we have heard both sides; and, moreover, that we do our best to avoid hearing either one side or the other if the matter does not concern us.

Is not this a sufficient explanation of my declaration that I have one blind eye and one deaf ear, and that they are the best eye and ear I have?

---

[22] Charles Bridges (1794–1869) was an evangelical Anglican minister best known for his classic book of pastoral theology titled, *The Christian Ministry*.

[23] Charles Bridges, *An Exposition of the Book of Proverbs* (New York: Robert Carter & Brothers, 1850), 421.

9
Forward!

Introduction

The address below was first delivered at one of the annual college conference gatherings and was published in *An All-Round Ministry*. It also appeared in the second volume of *Lectures to My Students* under the title "The Necessity of Ministerial Progress,"[1] though it was originally a conference address and not a lecture. Spurgeon's central argument is that pastors must not allow themselves to stagnate but must always be advancing and progressing in their gifts, qualifications, and ministerial labors. In this way, Spurgeon echoes the words of the Apostle Paul to Timothy, "Do not neglect the gift you have, which was given you by prophecy when the council of elders laid their hands on you. Practice these things, immerse yourself in them, so that all may see your progress" (1 Tim. 4:14–15).

Spurgeon identifies six areas in which ministers must endeavor to continually grow and progress. The first area for needed growth is in what he calls *mental acquirements*. He encourages ministers to seek to constantly grow in knowledge and intellectual ability. This inevitably includes a heavy dose of self-education, especially in the realm of theology. However, no subject is to be neglected, and Spurgeon encourages pastors to study science, geology, and history, among a host of other subjects.

Second, Spurgeon calls pastors to progress in *oratorical qualifications*. All pastors can grow as preachers. Spurgeon particularly encourages ministers to grow in clarity and cogency in their

---

[1] C. H. Spurgeon, *Lectures to My Students*, Second Series (London: Passmore and Alabaster, 1881), 23–38.

preaching. Every preacher can be clearer, and the thoughts and arguments of the preacher can always be more robust and muscular. Spurgeon also encourages ministers to labor to be as natural as possible in their preaching so as to remove distraction and enhance one's persuasiveness in the pulpit.

Spurgeon calls ministers, thirdly, to *grow in moral qualities*. He first identifies various vices to put off and mortify, such as self-importance, anger, and levity. He then invites ministers to pursue moral virtues such as integrity, honesty, and courage that adorn a man's ministry and tend to increase his effectiveness. Spurgeon believed a man's usefulness would rarely outstrip the strength of his character, and therefore moral virtue should be cultivated with the utmost devotion.

The fourth area in which ministers should always endeavor to *grow is in spiritual qualifications*. Here Spurgeon has in mind a kind of spiritual knowledge of oneself and of Christ, leading to holiness of life. Those who grow in spiritual qualifications are those who are continually becoming more like Christ and are growing in spiritual-mindedness.

Fifthly, Spurgeon urges pastors *to go forward in actual work*. In an oft-quoted passage, Spurgeon says,

> Brethren, do something; do something, do something. While Committees waste their time over resolutions, do something. While Societies and Unions are making constitutions, let us win souls. Too often we discuss, and discuss, and discuss, while Satan only laughs in his sleeve. It is time we had done planning, and sought something to plan. I pray you, be men of action all of you. Get to work, and quit yourselves like men.

Spurgeon calls ministers to give themselves to diligent labor for Christ, and to go forward in serving him with all their might.

Forward!

Finally, Spurgeon calls ministers *to go forward in their sphere of labor*. Here he encourages pastors to consider whether or not they should go to pioneer missions contexts to preach the gospel. Spurgeon provides a window into how he himself evaluated this very question, though he ultimately decided to remain in London for practical and strategic purposes. However, he is not shy at all about encouraging pastors to consider whether or not they should go to frontier missions settings to make Christ known where he has not yet been preached.

Forward!

Brethren, the substance of my address, this morning, will be found in the words of God to His servant Moses, "Speak unto the children of Israel, that they go forward" (Exod. 14:15). "Forward" is the watchword of our Conference, let it ring through your ranks. Onward, ye elect of God! Victory is before you; your very safety lies in that direction. To retreat is to perish. You have most of you read the story of the boy in an American village who climbed the wall of the famous Natural Bridge, and cut his name in the rock above the initials of his fellows, and then became suddenly aware of the impossibility of descending. Voices shouted, "Do not look down, try and reach the top." His only hope was to go right up, up, up, till he landed on the top. Upward was terrible, but downward was destruction. Now, we, dear brethren, are all of us in a like condition. By the help of God, we have cut our way to positions of usefulness, and to descend is death. To us, forward means upward, and therefore forward and upward let us go. While we prayed, this morning, we committed ourselves beyond all recall. We did that most heartily when we first preached the gospel, and publicly declared, "I am my Lord's, and He is mine." We put our hand to the plough then; thank God, we have not looked back yet, and we must never do so. The only course open to us is to plough right on to the end of the furrow, and never think of leaving the field till the Master shall call us home. But this morning you committed yourselves again to the Lord's work. You did not deliberate, or consult with flesh and blood, but you plunged right in, renouncing all for Jesus, and except ye be reprobates, ye have enlisted for life in His service. You are the branded servants of Christ, bearing in your bodies His mark. You have now no liberty to serve another, you are the sworn soldiers of the Crucified. Forward is your only way; you are shut up to it. You have no armour for your backs, and whatever dangers lie in front, there are ten thousand times as many behind. It is onward or nothing, nay, onward or dishonour; onward or death.

We were compared, last night, in the eloquent address of our friend Mr. Gange,[1] to the little army of Sir Garnet Wolseley marching to Coomassie, and the parallel was very beautifully worked out in all respects. Fellow-soldiers, we are few, and we have a desperate fight in the bush before us, therefore it is needful that every man should be made the most of, and nerved to his highest point of strength. It is desirable that you should be the picked men of the church, yea, of the entire universe, for such the age demands, therefore it is as to yourselves that I am most concerned that you should go forward. You must go forward in personal attainments, growing in gifts and in grace, in fitness for the work of God, and conformity to the image of Jesus. The points I shall speak upon begin at the bottom, and ascend.

Forward in mental acquirements
First, dear brethren, I think it necessary to say to myself and to you that we must go forward in our mental acquirements.

It will never do for us to continually present ourselves to God at our worst. We are not worth His having at our best; but, at any rate, let not the offering be maimed and blemished by our idleness. "Thou shalt love the Lord thy God with all thy heart" (Matt. 22:37) is, perhaps, more easy to comply with than to love Him with all our mind, yet we must give Him our mind as well as our affections, and that mind should be well furnished, that we may not offer Him an empty casket. Our ministry demands mind. I

---

[1] E. G. Gange was a student of the Pastors' College and pastor of Broadmead Chapel, Bristol from 1869–1893.

Forward!

shall not insist upon that phrase which is so frequently heard nowadays, "the enlightenment of the age." Still, it is quite certain that there is a great educational advance among all classes, and that there will be much more of it. The time is past when ungrammatical speech sufficed for a preacher. Even in a country village, where, according to tradition, "nobody knows nothing," the schoolmaster is now abroad, and want of education will hinder usefulness more than it once did. For, when the speaker wishes his audience to remember the gospel, they, on the other hand, will remember his ungrammatical expressions, and will repeat them as a theme of jest, when we could have wished they had rehearsed the gospel of Jesus Christ one to another in solemn earnest.

Dear brethren, we must cultivate ourselves to the highest possible point, and do this, first, by gathering in knowledge that we may fill the barn; then, by acquiring discrimination that we may winnow the heap; and, lastly, by a firm retentiveness of mind, which lays up the winnowed grain in the storehouse. The three points may not be equally important, but they are necessary to a complete man.

We must, I say, first, make great efforts to acquire information, especially of a Biblical kind. We must not confine ourselves to one topic of study, or we shall not exercise our whole mental manhood. God made the world for man, and made man with a mind intended to occupy and use all the world. He is the tenant, and nature is for a while his house. Why should he shut himself out of any of its rooms? Why refuse to taste any of the cleansed meats the great Father has put upon the table? Still, our main business is to study the Scriptures. The smith's main business is to shoe horses. Let him see that he knows how to do it, for should he be able to belt an angel with a girdle of gold, he will fail as a smith if he cannot make and fix a horseshoe. It is a small matter that you should be able to write the most brilliant poetry,—as possibly you could,—unless you can preach a good and telling sermon, which will have the effect of comforting saints and convincing sinners. Study the Bible, dear brethren, through and through, with all helps that you can possibly obtain. Remember that the appliances now within the reach of ordinary Christians are much more extensive than they were in our father's days, and therefore you must be greater Biblical scholars if you would keep in front of your hearers. Intermeddle with all knowledge, but, above all things, meditate day and night in the law of the Lord.

    Be well instructed in theology, and do not regard the sneers of those who rail at it because they are ignorant of it. Many preachers are not theologians, and hence the mistakes which they make. It cannot do any hurt to the most lively evangelist to be also a sound theologian, and it may often be the means of saving him from gross blunders. Nowadays, we hear men tear a single sentence of Scripture from its connection, and cry, "Eureka! Eureka!" as if they had found a new truth, and yet they have not discovered a diamond, but only a piece of broken glass. Had they been able to compare spiritual things with spiritual, had they understood the analogy of the faith, and had they been acquainted with the holy learning of the great Bible students of past ages, they would not have been quite so fast in vaunting their marvellous knowledge. Let us be thoroughly well acquainted with the great doctrines of the Word of God, and let us be mighty in expounding the Scriptures. I am sure that no preaching will last so long, or build up a church so well, as the expository. To renounce altogether the hortatory discourse for the expository, would be running to a preposterous extreme, but I cannot too earnestly assure you that, if your ministries are to be lastingly useful, you must be expositors. For this purpose, you must understand the Word yourselves, and be able so to comment upon it that the people may be built up by the Word. Be masters of your Bibles, brethren. Whatever other works you have not searched, be at home with the writings of the

Forward!

prophets and apostles. "Let the Word of God dwell in you richly" (Col. 3:16).

Having given that the precedence, neglect no field of knowledge. The presence of Jesus on the earth has sanctified the whole realm of nature, and what He has cleansed, call not you common. All that your Father has made is yours, and you should learn from it. You may read a naturalist's journal, or a traveller's narrative of his voyages, and find profit in it. Yes, and even an old herbal, or a manual of alchemy may, like Samson's dead lion, yield you honey. There are pearls in oyster shells, and sweet fruits on thorny boughs. The paths of true science, especially natural history and botany, drop fatness. Geology, so far as it is fact, and not fiction, is full of treasures. History—wonderful are the visions which it makes to pass before you—is eminently instructive; indeed, every portion of God's dominion in nature teems with precious teachings. Intermeddle with all knowledge, according as you have the time, the opportunity, and the peculiar faculty; and do not hesitate to do so because of any apprehension that you will educate yourselves up to too high a point. When grace abounds, learning will not puff you up, or injure your simplicity in the gospel. Serve God with such education as you have, and thank Him for blowing through you if you are a ram's horn, but if there be a possibility of your becoming a silver trumpet, choose it rather.

I said that, next, we must learn always to discriminate between things that differ; and at this particular time, this point needs insisting on very emphatically. Many run after novelties, charmed with every new thing; learn to judge between truth and its counterfeits, and you will not be led astray. Others adhere to old teachings, like limpets stick to the rock, and yet these may only be ancient errors, wherefore, "prove all things," and "hold fast that which is good." The use of the sieve and the winnowing fan, is much to be commended. A man who has asked the Lord to give him clear eyes, by which he shall see the truth, and discern its bearings, and who, by reason of the constant exercise of his faculties, has obtained an accurate judgment, is one fit to be a leader of the Lord's host, but all ministers are not thus qualified. It is painful to observe how many embrace anything it if be but earnestly brought before them. They swallow the medicine of every spiritual quack who has enough of brazen assurance to appear to be sincere. I say to you, as Paul wrote to the Corinthians, "Brethren, be not children in understanding" (1 Cor. 14:20). Test everything that claims your faith. Ask the Holy Spirit to give you the faculty of discerning between good and evil, so shall you conduct your flocks far from poisonous meadows, and lead them into safe pasturage.

But then, if you have the power to acquire knowledge, and also to discriminate, seek next for ability to retain and hold firmly what you have learned. Alas! In these times, certain men glory in being weathercocks. They hold fast nothing. They have, in fact, nothing worth the holding. They believed yesterday, but not that which they believe to-day, nor that which they will believe to-morrow, and he would be a greater prophet than Isaiah who should be able to tell what they will believe when next the moon doth fill her horns, for they are constantly changing, and seem to have been born under that said moon, and to partake of her changing moods. These men may be as honest as they claim to be, but of what use are they? Like good trees oftentimes transplanted, they may be of a noble nature, but they bring forth nothing. Their strength goes out in rooting and re-rooting, they have no sap to spare for fruit. Be sure you have the truth, and then be sure you hold it. Be ready for fresh truth, if it be truth, but be very chary how you subscribe to the belief that a better light has been found than that of the sun. Those who hawk new truth about the street, as the boys do a new edition of the evening paper, are usually no better than they should be. The fair maid of truth does not paint her cheeks and tire her head, like Jezebel, following every new philosophic

Forward!

fashion. She is content with her own native beauty, and in her aspect she is the same yesterday, and today, and forever.

When men change often, they generally need to be changed in the most emphatic sense. Our "modern thought" gentry are doing incalculable mischief to the souls of men. Immortal souls are being damned, yet these men are spinning theories. Hell gapes wide, and with her open mouth swallows up myriads, yet those who should spread the tidings of salvation are "pursuing fresh lines of thought." Highly cultured soul-murderers will find their boasted "culture" to be no excuse in the day of judgment. For God's sake, let us know how men are to be saved, and get to the work. To be for ever deliberating as to the proper mode of making bread while a nation dies of famine, is detestable trifling. It is time we knew what to teach, or else renounced our office. "Ever learning, and never able to come to the knowledge of the truth," is the motto of the worst rather than of the best of men. Are they to be our model? "I shape my creed every week," was the confession of one of these divines to me. Whereunto shall I liken such unsettled ones? Are they not like those birds which frequent the Golden Horn, and are to be seen from Constantinople, of which it is said that they are always on the wing, and never rest? No one ever saw them alight on the water or on the land, they are for ever poised in mid-air. The natives call them "lost souls"—seeking rest and finding none; and, methinks, men who have no personal rest in the truth, if they are not themselves unsaved, are, at least, very unlikely to be the means of saving others. He who has no assured truth to tell must not wonder if his hearers set small store by what he says. We must know the truth, understand it, and hold it with firm grip, or we cannot be of service to the sons of men. Brethren, I charge you, seek to know, and, knowing, to discriminate; having discriminated, I charge you to "hold fast that which is good." Keep in constant operation the three processes of filling the barn, winnowing the grain, and storing it in granaries, so shall you mentally "go forward."

Forward in oratorical qualifications

We also need to go forward in oratorical qualifications.

I am beginning at the bottom, but all these matters are important, for it is a pity that even the feet of this image should be of clay. Nothing is trifling which can be of any service to our grand design. Only for want of a nail the horse lost its shoe, and so became unfit for the battle; that shoe was only a trifling rim of iron which smote the ground, and yet the neck clothed with thunder was of no avail when the shoe was gone. A man may be irretrievably ruined for spiritual usefulness, not because he fails either in character or spirit, but because he breaks down mentally or oratorically; and, therefore, I again remark that we must improve in utterances.

It is not every one of us who can speak as some can do, and even these men cannot speak up to their own ideal. If there be any brother here who thinks he can preach as well as he should, I would advise him to leave off altogether. If he did so, he would be acting as wisely as the great painter who broke his palette, and, turning to his wife, said, "My painting days are over, for I have satisfied myself, and therefore I am sure my power is gone." Whatever other perfection may be attainable, I am certain that he who thinks he has gained perfection in oratory mistakes volubility for eloquence, and verbiage for argument. Whatever you may know, you cannot be truly efficient ministers if you are not "apt to teach." You are probably all acquainted with ministers who have mistaken their calling, and evidently have no gifts for preaching; make sure that none think the same of you. There are brethren in the ministry whose speech is intolerable. Either they dun you to death, or else they send you to sleep. No chloral can ever equal their discourse in sleep-giving properties. No human being,

Forward!

unless gifted with infinite patience, could long endure to listen to them, and nature does well to give the victim deliverance through sleep. I heard one say the other day that a certain preacher had no more gifts for the ministry than an oyster, and in my own judgment this was a slander on the oyster, for that worthy bivalve shows great discretion in his openings, and he also knows when to close. If some men were sentenced to hear their own sermons, it would be a righteous judgment upon them, but they would soon cry out with Cain, "My punishment is greater than I can bear" (Gen. 4:13). Let us not fall under the same condemnation through any faults in our preaching which we can remedy.

Brethren, we should cultivate a clear style. When a man does not make me understand what he means, it is because he does not himself know what he means. An average hearer, who is unable to follow the course of thought of the preacher, ought not to worry himself, but to blame the preacher, whose business it is to make the matter clear. If you look down into a well, if it be empty, it will appear to be very deep, but if there be water in it, you will see its brightness. I believe that many "deep" preachers are simply so because they are like dry wells with nothing whatever in them, except decaying leaves, a few stones, and perhaps a dead cat or two. If there be living water in your preaching, it may be very deep, but the light of the truth will give clearness to it. At any rate, labour to be plain, so that the truths you teach may be easily received by your hearers.

We must cultivate a cogent as well as a clear style; we must be forceful. Some imagine that this consists in speaking loudly, but I can assure them they are in error. Nonsense does not improve by being bellowed. God does not require us to shout as if we were speaking to three millions when we are only addressing three hundred. Let us be forcible by reason of the excellence of our matter, and the energy of spirit which we throw into the delivery of it. In a word, let our speaking be natural and living. I hope we have forsworn the tricks of professional orators, the strain after effect, the studied climax, the prearranged pause, the theatrical strut, the mouthing of words, and I know not what besides, which you may see in certain pompous divines who still survive upon the face of the earth. May such preachers become extinct animals ere long, and may a living, natural, simple way of talking out the gospel be learned by us all, for I am persuaded that such a style is one which God is likely to bless.

Among many other things, we must cultivate persuasiveness. Some of our brethren have great influence over men, and yet others with greater gifts are devoid of it. These last do not appear to get near to the people, they cannot grip them, and make them feel. There are preachers who, in their sermons, seem to take their hearers one by one by the buttonhole, and drive the truth right into their souls, while others generalize so much, and are withal so cold, that one would think they were speaking to dwellers in some remote planet, whose affairs did not much concern them. Learn the art of pleading with men. You will do this well if you often see the Lord. If I remember rightly, the old classic story tells us that, when a soldier was about to kill Darius, his son, who had been dumb from his childhood, suddenly cried out in surprise, "Know you not that he is the king?" His silent tongue was unloosed by love to his father, and well may ours also find earnest speech when the Lord is seen by us crucified for sin. If there be any speech in us, this will arouse it. The knowledge of "the terror of the Lord" should also bestir us to persuade men. We cannot do other than plead with them to be reconciled to God. Brethren, mark those who woo sinners to Jesus, find out their secret, and never rest till you obtain the same power. If you find them very simple and homely, yet if you see them really useful, say to yourself, "That method will do for me;" but if, on the other hand, you listen to a preacher who is much admired, and on enquiry you find that no souls are savingly converted under his ministry, say to

Forward!

yourself, "This style is not the thing for me, for I am not seeking to be great, but to be really useful."

Let your oratory, therefore, constantly improve in clearness, cogency, naturalness, and persuasiveness. Try, dear brethren, to get such a style of speaking that you suit yourselves to your audiences. Much lies in that. The preacher, who should address an educated congregation in the language which he would use in speaking to a company of costermongers, would prove himself a fool, and, on the other hand, he who goes down amongst miners and colliers, with technical theological terms and drawing-room phrases, acts like an idiot. The confusion of tongues at Babel was more thorough than we imagine. It did not merely give different languages to great nations, but it made the speech of each class to vary from that of others. A fellow of Billingsgate cannot understand a fellow of Brasenose. Now, as the costermonger cannot learn the language of the College, let the collegian learn the language of the costermonger. "We use the language of the market," said Whitefield, and this was much to his honour, yet, when he stood in the drawing-room of the Countess of Huntingdon,[2] and his speech entranced the infidel noblemen whom she brought to hear him, he adopted another style. His language was equally plain in each case, because it was equally familiar to his audience; but he did not use the *ipsissima verba*, else his speech would have lost its plainness in the one case or the other, and would either have been slang to the nobility or Greek to the crowd. In our modes of speech, we should aim at being "all things to all men" (1 Cor. 9:22). He is the greatest master of oratory who is able to address any class of people in a manner suitable to their condition, and likely to touch their hearts.

---

[2] Selina Hastings, Countess of Huntingdon (1707-1791) was a wealthy patroness and supporter of the Methodist revivals in England and Wales.

Brethren, let none excel us in power of speech. Let none surpass us in the mastery of our mother-tongue. Beloved fellow-soldiers, our tongues are the swords which God has given us to use for Him, even as it is said of our Lord, "Out of His mouth went a sharp two-edged sword" (Rev. 1:16). Let these swords be sharp. Cultivate your powers of speech, and be amongst the foremost in the land for utterance. I do not exhort you to this because you are remarkably deficient; far from it, for everybody says to me, "We know your College men by their plain, bold speech." This leads me to believe that you have the gift largely in you, and I beseech you to take pains to perfect it.

Forward in moral qualities
Brethren, we must be even more earnest to go forward in moral qualities.

Let the points I shall mention here come home to those who shall require them, but I assure you I have no special persons among you in my mind's eye. We desire to rise to the highest style of ministry, but even if we obtain the mental and oratorical qualifications I have mentioned, we shall fail, unless we also possess high moral qualities. There are evils which we must shake off, as Paul shook the viper from his hand, and there are virtues which we must gain at any cost. Self-indulgence has slain its thousands. Let us tremble lest we perish by the hands of this Delilah. Let us have every passion and habit under due restraint. If we are not masters of ourselves, we are not fit to be leaders in the Church of Christ.

We must also put away all notion of self-importance. God will not bless the man who thinks himself great. To glory even in the work of God the Holy Spirit in yourself, is to tread dangerously near to self-adulation. "Let another man praise thee, and not thine own mouth" (Prov. 27:2), and be very glad when that other has sense enough to hold his tongue.

Forward!

We must also have our tempers well under restraint. A vigorous temper is not altogether an evil. Men who are as easy as an old shoe are generally of as little worth. I would not say to you, "Dear brethren, have a temper," but I do say, "If you have one, control it carefully." I thank God when I see a minister have temper enough to be indignant at wrong, and to be firm for the right. Still, temper is an edged tool, and often cuts the man who handles it. "Gentle, and easy to be entreated," preferring to bear evil rather than inflict it, this is to be our spirit. If any brother here naturally boils over too soon, let him mind that, when he does do so, he scalds nobody but the devil, and then let him boil away as fast as he likes.

We must—some of us especially must—conquer our tendency to levity. A great distinction exists between holy cheerfulness, which is a virtue, and that general levity, which is a vice. There is a levity which has not enough heart to laugh, but trifles with everything; it is flippant, hollow, unreal. A hearty laugh is no more levity than a hearty cry. I speak of that religious veneering which is pretentious, but thin, superficial, insincere about the weightiest matters. Godliness is no jest, nor is it a mere form. Beware of being actors. Never give earnest men the impression that you do not mean what you say, and are mere professionals. To be burning at the lip, and freezing at the soul, is a mark of reprobation. God deliver us from being either superfine or superficial. May we never be the butterflies of the garden of God!

At the same time, we should avoid everything like the ferocity of bigotry. There are religious people about, who, I have no doubt, were born of a woman, but they appear to have been suckled by a wolf. I have done them no dishonour by that comparison, for were not Romulus and Remus, the founders of the city of Rome, nourished in that fashion? Some warlike men of this order have had power to found dynasties of thought, but human kindness and brotherly love consort better with the Kingdom of Christ. We are not to be always going about the world searching out heresies, like terrier dogs sniffing for rats, and to be always so confident of our own infallibility that we erect ecclesiastical stakes at which to roast all who differ from us, not, 'tis true, with faggots of wood, but with those coals of juniper, which consist of strong prejudice and cruel suspicion.

In addition to all this, there are mannerisms, and moods, and ways, which I cannot now describe, against which we must struggle, for little faults may often be the source of failure, and to get rid of them may be the secret of success. Count nothing little which makes you even a little more useful. Cleanse out from the temple of your soul the seats of them that sell doves as well as the traffickers in sheep and oxen.

And, dear brethren, we must acquire certain moral faculties and habits, as well as put aside their opposites. He will never do much for God who has not integrity of spirit. If we be guided by policy, if there be any mode of action for us but that which is straightforward, we shall make shipwreck before long. Resolve, dear brethren, that you can be poor, that you can be despised, that you can lose life itself, but that you cannot do a crooked thing. For you, let the only policy be honesty.

May you also possess the grand moral characteristic of courage. By this, I do not mean impertinence, impudence, or self-conceit, but real courage to do and say calmly the right thing, and to go straight on at all hazards, though there should be none to give you a good word. I am astonished at the number of Christians who are afraid to speak the truth to their brethren. I thank God that I can say this,—there is no member of my church, no officer of the church, and no man in the world, to whom I am afraid to say before his face what I would say behind his back. Under God, I owe my position in my own church to the absence of all policy, and the habit of always saying what I mean. The plan of making things pleasant all round is a perilous as well as a wicked one. If you say one thing to one man, and another to another, they will one day compare notes, and find you out, and then you will be despised. The man of two faces will sooner or later be the object of contempt, and justly so. Now, above all things, avoid that. If you have anything that you feel you ought to say about a man, let the measure of what you say be this, "How much dare I say to his face?" We must not allow ourselves a word more than that in censure of any man living. If that be your rule, your courage will save you from a thousand difficulties, and win you lasting respect.

Having the integrity and the courage, dear brethren, may you be gifted with an unconquerable zeal! Zeal—what is it? How shall I describe it? Possess it, and you will know what it is. Be consumed with love for Christ, and let the flame burn continuously; not flaming up at public meetings, and dying out in the routine work of every day. We need indomitable perseverance, dogged zeal, and a combination of sacred obstinacy, self-denial, holy gentleness, and invincible courage.

Excel also in one power, which is both mental and moral, namely, the power of concentrating all your forces upon the work to which you are called. Collect your thoughts, rally all your faculties, mass your energies, focus your capacities. Turn all the springs of your soul into one channel, causing it to flow onward in an undivided stream. Some men lack this quality. They scatter themselves, and therefore fail. Mass your battalions, and hurl them upon the enemy. Do not try to be great at this, and great at that—to be "everything by starts, and nothing long," but suffer your entire nature to be led in captivity by Jesus Christ, and lay everything at His dear feet who bled and died for you.

Forward in spiritual qualifications
Above all these things, we need to go forward in spiritual qualifications, the graces which must be wrought in us by the Holy Spirit

Himself. This is the main matter, I am sure. Other things are precious, but this is priceless.

We need, first, to know ourselves. The preacher should be well acquainted with the science of the heart, the philosophy of inward experience. There are two schools of experience, and neither is content to learn from the other. Let us be willing, however, to learn from both. The one school speaks of the child of God as one who knows the deep depravity of his heart, who understands the loathsomeness of his nature, and daily feels that in his flesh there dwelleth no good thing. "That man has not the life of God in his soul," say the men of this school, "who does not know and feel this, and feel it by bitter and painful experience from day to day." It is in vain to talk to them about liberty, and joy in the Holy Ghost; they will not have it. Yet let us learn from these one-sided brethren. They know much that should be known, and woe to that minister who ignores their set of truths! Martin Luther used to say that temptation is the best teacher for a minister. There is truth on that side of the question.

Believers of another school dwell much—and rightly and blessedly so—upon the glorious work of the Spirit of God. They believe in the Spirit of God as a cleansing power, sweeping the Augean stable of the soul, and making it into a temple for God. But frequently they talk as if they had ceased to sin, or to be annoyed by temptation. They glory as if the battle were already fought, and the victory won. Yet let us also learn what we can from these brethren. All the truth they can teach us, let us know. Let us become familiar with the hilltops of salvation, and the glory that shines thereon—the Hermons and the Tabors, where we may be transfigured with our Lord. Do not be afraid of ever growing too holy, or of being too full of the Holy Spirit.

I would have you wise on all sides, and able to deal with man both in his conflicts and in his joys, as one who is familiar with both experiences. Know where Adam left you; know where the

Forward!

Spirit of God has placed you. Do not know either of these things so exclusively as to forget the other. I believe that, if any men are likely to cry, "O wretched man that I am! who shall deliver me from the body of this death?" (Rom. 7:24), it will always be the ministers of the gospel, because we need to be tempted in all points, so that we may be able to comfort others. In a railway carriage, last week, I saw a poor man with his leg placed upon the seat. An official happening to see him in that posture, remarked, "Those cushions were not made for you to put your dirty boots on." As soon as the guard was gone, the man put up his leg again, and said to me, "He never broke his leg in two places, I am sure, or he would not be so sharp with me." When I have heard brethren, who have lived at ease, enjoying good incomes, condemning others who are much tried, because they could not rejoice in their fashion, I have felt that they knew nothing of the broken bones which others have to carry throughout the whole of their pilgrimage.

Brethren, know man, in Christ, and out of Christ. Study him at his best, and study him at his worst. Know his anatomy, his secrets, and his passions. You cannot gain this knowledge from books; you must have personal acquaintance with men if you are to help them in their varied spiritual experience. God alone can give you that wisdom which you will need in dealing wisely with them, but He will give it to you in answer to believing prayer.

Among spiritual acquirements, it is beyond all other things needful to know Him who is the sure remedy for all human diseases. Know Jesus. Sit at His feet. Consider His nature, His work, His sufferings, His glory. Rejoice in His presence. Commune with Him from day to day. To know Christ is to understand the most excellent of all sciences. You cannot fail to be wise if you commune with Incarnate Wisdom. You cannot lack strength if you have constant fellowship with God. Let this be your desire,

I would commune with Thee, my God;
E'en to Thy seat I come;
I leave my joys, I leave my sins,
And seek in Thee my home.³

Dwell in God, brethren; not sometimes go to Him, but abide in Him. They say in Italy that, where the sun does not enter, the physician must. Where Jesus does not shine, the soul is sick. Bask in His beams, and you shall be vigorous in the service of your Lord.

Last Sunday night, I had a text which mastered me: "No man knoweth the Son, but the Father" (Matt. 11:27). I told the people that poor sinners, who had gone to Jesus, and trusted Him, thought they knew Him, but that they knew only a little of Him. Saints of sixty years' experience, who have walked with Him every day, think they know Him, but they are only beginning to know Him yet. The perfect spirits before the throne, who have been for five thousand years perpetually adoring Him, perhaps think they know Him, but they do not to the full. "No man knoweth the Son, but the Father." He is so glorious, that only the infinite God has full knowledge of Him, therefore there will be no limit to our study, or narrowness in our line of thought, if we make our Lord the great object of all our thoughts and researches.

So, brethren, as the outcome of this knowledge, if we are to be strong men, we must be conformed to our Lord. Oh, to be like Him! Blessed be that cross on which we shall suffer, if we suffer for being made like unto the Lord Jesus. If we obtain conformity to Christ, we shall have a wondrous unction upon our ministry, and without that, what is a ministry worth? In a word, we must labour for holiness of character. What is holiness? Is it not wholeness of character? A balanced condition in which there is neither

---

³ George Burden Bubier, "Sweet Communion" in *"Our Own Hymn-book": A Collection of Psalms and Hymns for Public, Social, and Private Worship,* ed. C. H. Spurgeon (London: Passmore and Alabaster, 1866), #764.

Forward!

lack nor redundance. It is not morality, that is a cold, lifeless statue; holiness is life. You must have holiness, and, dear brethren, if you should fail in mental qualifications (though I hope you will not), and if you should have a slender measure of the oratorical faculty (though I trust you will not), yet, depend upon it, a holy life is, in itself, a wonderful power, and will make up for many deficiencies. It is, in fact, the best sermon the best man can ever deliver. Let us resolve that all the purity which can be had we will have, that all the sanctity which can be reached we will obtain, and that all the likeness to Christ that is possible in this world of sin shall certainly be in us through the effectual working of the Spirit of God. The Lord lift us all, as a College, right up to a higher platform, and He shall have the glory!

Forward in actual work
I have not finished my message, for I have further to say, go forward in actual work.

After all, we shall be known by what we have done, more than by what we have said. Like the apostles, I hope our memorial will be our acts. There are good brethren in the world who are impractical. The grand doctrine of the Second Advent makes them stand with open mouths, peering into the skies, so that I am ready to say, "Ye men of Plymouth, why stand ye here gazing up into Heaven?" The fact that Jesus Christ is to come again, is not a reason for star-gazing, but for working in the power of the Holy Ghost. Be not so taken up with speculations as to prefer a Bible-reading over an obscure passage in the Revelation to teaching in a Ragged-school or discoursing to the poor concerning Jesus. We must have done with daydreams, and get to work. I believe in eggs, but we must get chickens out of them. I do not mind how big your egg is, it may be an ostrich's egg if you like, but if there is nothing in it, pray clear away the shell. If something comes of your speculations, God bless them, and even if you should go a little further than I think it wise to venture in that direction, still, if you are thereby made more useful, God be praised for it!

We want facts—deeds done, souls saved. It is all very well to write essays, but what souls have you been the means of saving from going down to hell? Your excellent management of your school interests me, but how many children have been brought into the church by it? We are glad to hear of those special meetings, but how many have really been born to God in them? Are saints edified? Are sinners converted? To swing to and fro on a five-barred gate, is not progress, yet some seem to think that it is. I see them in a kind of perpetual Elysium, humming over to themselves and their friends, "We are very comfortable." God save us from living in comfort while sinners are sinking into hell! In travelling along the mountain roads in Switzerland, you will continually see marks of the boring-rod, and in every minister's life there should be traces of stern labour. Brethren, do something; do something, do something. While Committees waste their time over resolutions, do something. While Societies and Unions are making constitutions, let us win souls. Too often we discuss, and discuss, and discuss, while Satan only laughs in his sleeve. It is time we had done planning, and sought something to plan. I pray you, be men of action all of you. Get to work, and quit yourselves like men. Old Suwarrow's idea of war is mine: "Forward and strike! No theory! Attack! Form column! Fix bayonets, and charge right into the very centre of the enemy." Our one aim is to save sinners, and this we are not merely to talk about, but to effect in the power of God.

Forward in one's sphere of action
Lastly, and here I am going to deliver a message which weighs upon me, go forward in the matter of the choice of your sphere of action.

Forward!

I plead this day for those who cannot plead for themselves, namely, the great outlying masses of the heathen world. Our existing pulpits are tolerably well supplied, but we need men who will build on new foundations. Who will do this? Are we, as a company of faithful men, clear in our consciences about the heathen? Millions have never heard the Name of Jesus. Hundreds of millions have seen a missionary only once in their lives, and know nothing of our King. Shall we let them perish? Can we go to our beds and sleep, while China, India, Japan, and other nations are being damned? Are we clear of their blood? Have they no claim upon us? We ought to put it on this footing—not, "Can I prove that I ought to go?" but, "Can I prove that I ought not to go?" When a man can honestly prove that he ought not to go, then he is clear, but not else. What answer do you give, my brethren? I put it to you man by man. I am not raising a question among you which I have not honestly put to myself. I have felt that, if some of our leading ministers would go forth, it would have a grand effect in stimulating the churches, and I have honestly asked myself whether I ought to go. After balancing the whole thing, I feel bound to keep my place, and I think the judgment of most Christians would confirm my decision, but I hope I would readily, and willingly, and cheerfully, go abroad if I did not feel that I ought to remain at home. Brethren, put yourselves through the same process. We must have the heathen converted. God has myriads of His elect among them, we must go and search for them somehow or other. Many difficulties are now removed, all lands are open to us, and distance is almost annihilated. True, we have not the Pentecostal gift of tongues, but languages are now readily acquired, while the art of printing is a full equivalent for the lost gift. The dangers incident to missions ought not to keep any true man back, even if they were very great, but they are now reduced to a minimum. There are hundreds of places where the cross of Christ is unknown, to which we can go without risk. Who will go?

Servants of Christ, Lovers of Men

The men who ought to go are young brethren of good abilities who have not yet taken upon themselves family cares. Each student entering the College should consider this matter, and surrender himself to the work unless there are conclusive reasons for his not doing so. It is a fact that, even for the Colonies, it is very difficult to find men, for I have had openings in Australia which I have been obliged to decline. It ought not to be so. Surely there is some self-sacrifice among us yet, and some among us who are willing to be exiled for Jesus. The mission languishes for want of men. If the men were forthcoming, the liberality of the Church would supply their needs; and, in fact, the liberality of the Church has provided the supply, and yet there are not the men to go. I shall never feel, brethren, that we, as a band of men, have done our duty until we see our comrades fighting for Jesus in every land in the van of the conflict. I believe that, if God moves you to go, you will be among the best of missionaries, because you will make the preaching of the gospel the great feature of your work, and that is God's sure way of power.

I wish that our churches would imitate that of Pastor Harms, in Germany,[4] where every member was consecrated to God in deed and of a truth. The farmers gave the produce of their lands, the workingmen their labour. One gave a large house to be used as a missionary college, and Pastor Harms obtained money for a ship which he fitted out, to make voyages to Africa, and then he sent missionaries, and little companies of his people with them, to form Christian communities among the Bushmen. When will our churches be equally self-denying and energetic? Look at the Moravians, how every man or woman becomes a missionary, and how much they do for the Lord in consequence. Let us catch their spirit. Is it a right spirit? Then it is right for us to have it. It is not

---

[4] Louis Harms (1808–65) was a German Lutheran revivalist pastor who ministered in the village of Hermannsburg, Germany.

Forward!

enough for us to say, "Those Moravians are very wonderful people." We ought to be wonderful people, too. Christ did not purchase the Moravians any more completely than He purchased us. They are under no more obligation to make sacrifices than we are. Why then this backwardness? When we read of heroic men who gave up all for Jesus, we are not merely to admire, but to imitate them. Who will imitate them now? Come to the point? Are there not some among you willing to consecrate yourselves to the Lord? "Forward" is the watchword today! Are there no bold spirits to lead the van? Pray all of you that, during this Pentecost, the Spirit may say, "Separate Me Barnabas and Saul for the work whereunto I have called them" (Acts 13:2).

Brethren, on wings of love mount upward, and fly forward. Amen.

10
A New Departure

Introduction

The most remarkable thing about Spurgeon's ministry is not that he was able to draw such large crowds, but that he was able to keep them for nearly four decades. He moved to London in 1854, and served the same church until his death in 1892. The membership of the Metropolitan Tabernacle grew in almost every year of Spurgeon's pastorate, and twice the building had to be enlarged to accommodate the massive crowds that came to hear him preach. He preached Sunday morning and Sunday evening, and often multiple times during the week as well. His published sermons now total nearly 4,000. He was chiefly responsible to lead the church's officers and to oversee the church's many ministries. He also was an avid writer and produced nearly 150 books, publishing more words in English than any Christian in the history of the English language.

When one considers Spurgeon's career, it is simply astounding that he was able to give himself for so many years to such a broad array of endeavors. Christian George writes, "Spurgeon constantly switched hats among pastor, president, editor, author, and traveling evangelist."[1] Spurgeon himself once wrote,

> No one living knows the toil and care I have to bear ... I have to look after the Orphanage, have charge of a church with four thousand members, sometimes there are marriages and

---

[1] Christian T. George, "A Man of His Time" in C. H. Spurgeon *The Lost Sermons of C. H. Spurgeon: His Earliest Outlines and Sermons Between 1851 and 1854*, Edited with Introduction and Notes by Christian George, vol. 1, (Nashville, TN: B&H Academic, 2016), 13.

burials to be undertaken, there is the weekly sermon to be revised, The Sword and the Trowel to be edited, and besides all that, a weekly average of five hundred letters to be answered. This, however, is only half my duty, for there are innumerable churches established by friends, with the affairs of which I am closely connected, to say nothing of the cases of difficulty which are constantly being referred to me.[2]

Spurgeon's life was an explosion of activity and his ministerial output was simply prodigious. In August 1881, he gave an account of a typical week,

> Here is a specimen week in which we did no more than ordinarily ... Five sermons, three prayer-meetings, chair at two public meetings, speech at a third, one communion, one College afternoon of two hours' lecturing. Some of these occupied far more time in preparation than in the actual doing of them. We are thankful to be able to work. Oh that we could accomplish far more![3]

Though Spurgeon entered in upon his work with unusual fervor and devotion, he nonetheless knew what it was like to feel run down and burned out. He understood the vicissitudes and challenges of life and ministry. He was well acquainted with the experience of feeling spiritually and emotionally depleted through overexertion in pastoral work. Thus, he understood the need for revival and renewal in the ministry. This lecture explores the reasons why such renewal is needed and how it can be experienced.

---

[2] Iain Murray ed., *Autobiography Volume 2: The Full Harvest (1860–1892)* (Carlisle, PA: Banner of Truth, 1973), 192.

[3] C. H. Spurgeon, ed., *The Sword and the Trowel* (London: Passmore and Alabaster, August, 1881): 418.

A New Departure

Beloved fellow-servants of Christ, our work requires us to be in the best possible condition of heart. When we are at our best, we are feeble enough. We would not, therefore, fall below our highest point. As instruments, we owe all our power for usefulness to the divine hand, but, since tools should always be kept in order, we would have our spirit free from rust, and our mind sharp of point and keen of edge to answer at once to the Master's will. It is because I fear we do not always keep up to the mark that the subject for this morning's address shall be "A New Departure" or, in other words, a renewal, a revival, a starting afresh, a return to our first love, even the love of our espousals, when first our soul was wedded to our Redeemer's work.

The subject is exceedingly needful to us all, because the process of running down is such a very easy one. Upon that topic, let me speak for a few minutes. To run down, requires no care or effort. It can be accomplished without a wish. It can come to pass, in a measure, in opposition to our wish. We can decline and decay without so much as being conscious of it, and all the more easily because we fancy that we are rich and increased in goods. By a law which asks no help from us, we gravitate to a lower level. Do not wind up the weights, and the wheels will soon cease to move, and the old clock on the stairs will remain motionless, useless, silent, dead, like a coffin set on end. To keep a farm in good order, needs constant labour and watchfulness, but to let the land get out of heart till it would starve a lark, is a very simple matter, which can be accomplished by any sluggard; simply let it alone, or take crop after crop from it, and give it neither manure nor rest, and you will change fruitful fields into barrenness, and turn a garden into a desert. It is just so with ourselves. Only do not wind up your soul with daily prayer, and you will soon run down. Only neglect the culture of the heart, and thorns and briers will grow uninvited. Neglect your inner life, and your whole being will deteriorate.

I do not know, my brethren, that we can expect to see energy continuous at its full in any one of us. I suspect that he who burns like a seraph knows moments in which the flame somewhat abates. As the sun itself is not at all times alike powerful, so the man who, like the shining light, shineth more and more unto the perfect day, is not uniformly bright, nor always at his noon. Nature does not hold the sea for ever at flood; ebbs intervene, and the ocean pauses a while ere it returns again to the fulness of its strength. The vegetable world has its winter, and enjoys a long sleep beneath its bed of snow. It is not wasted time, that ebb or that winter. Flood and summer owe much to ebb and frost. I suspect that, because we are in affinity with nature, we, too, shall have our changes, and shall not abide at one elevation. No man's life is all climax. Let us not despond if, just now, our spirit is at a low ebb. The tide of life will roll up as before, and even reach a higher point. When we stand leafless and apparently lifeless, our soul having become like a tree in winter, let us not dream that the axe will cut us down, for our substance is in us though we have lost our leaves, and before long the time of the singing of birds will come, we shall feel the genial warmth of returning spring, and our lives shall again be covered with blossoms, and laden with fruit.

It will not be wonderful if there should be lulls and pauses in our spiritual work, for we see the like in the affairs of men. The most eager after worldly objects, who can by no means be accused of a want of earnestness in their endeavours, are yet conscious that, by a sort of law, dull times will come, wherein business necessarily flags. It is not the tradesman's fault that, sometimes, trade must be pushed, and that after pushing it remains as dull as ever. It seems to be the rule that there should be years of great prosperity, and then years of decline. The lean kine still devour the fat kine. If men were not what they are, there might be a perpetuity of equable progress, but it is evident that we have not reached that point yet.

In religious affairs, history shows us that churches have their palmy days, and then again their times of drought. The universal church has been thus circumstanced. It has had its Pentecosts, its reformations, its revivals, and between these there have been sorrowful pauses, in which there was much more cause for lamentation than for rejoicing, and the Miserere was more suitable than the Hallelujah. I should not, therefore, wish any brother to condemn himself if he is not conscious just now of possessing all the vivacity of his youth—he may find it return before our meetings close. I would have the husbandman long for spring, and yet not despair because of the present cold. So would I have a man lament every degree of decline, and yet not despond. If any man walk in darkness, and see no light, let him trust in God, and look to Him for brighter days.

Some causes of decline
Still, taking all this into account, and allowing all margin and discount, I fear that many of us do not maintain our proper elevation, but sink below par. Many things tend that way, and it may do us good to think of them. A degree of running down in spirit may be purely physical, and arise out of the evaporation of our youthful vigour. Some of you enjoy all the force of your early manhood; you are fleet of foot as the roes of the field, and swift of movement as birds on the wing, but others of us wear a tinge of grey in our locks, and middle life has sobered us. Our eye has not yet waxed dim, nor has our natural force abated, but yet the flash and flame of our youth have departed, and from the style of our speech and the manner of our action men miss that morning dew which was the glory of life's young hours. Older men are apt to ridicule young

fellows for being too zealous. Let them not retaliate, but cautiously abstain from ever charging the elder brethren with excess of fervour. Surely, malice itself would not dare to invent such a libel.

For my own part, I would have remained a young man if I could, for I fear I am by no means improved by keeping. Oh, that I could again possess the elasticity of spirit, the dash, the courage, the hopefulness of days gone by! My days of flying are changed to those of running, and my running is toning down to a yet steadier pace. It is somewhat cheering that the Scriptures seem to indicate that this is progress, for such is the order which it prescribes for saints: "They shall mount up with wings as eagles," away they go, out of sight. In your first sermons—how you mounted up! Your first evangelistic efforts—what flights they were! After that, you slackened and yet improved your pace, but it grew more steady, and perhaps more slow, as it is written, "They shall run, and not be weary; and they shall walk, and not faint" (Isa. 40:31). God grant that we may not faint, and if our running days are over, may we walk with God as Enoch did, till the Lord shall take us home!

Another cause which frequently conduces to the abatement of vigour is the possible cessation of early success. I do not mean that it is always so, but, usually, when a man goes to a new field, there are many unreaped portions, and he gathers a large harvest, which he does not find afterwards because there is less to reap. If you have a narrow pond, you cannot keep on catching as many fish as you did at first, because there are not so many fish remaining. In London, we are, as it were, in an ocean, and we may spread our nets as often as we please, but in a small town or village, a man may soon have done all his direct converting work if the Lord greatly blesses him, and if, after a time, more souls are not saved, it may be because few unconverted persons attend his ministry. God may have given the brother all those whom He intended to bless by him in that place, and it may be wise for him to fish in other waters. I have read of a lighthouse-keeper who puts a rope

A New Departure

round the lighthouse, and then to this cord he attaches a number of lines and hooks. These are all under water at high tide, and at favourable times the fish bite, and when the tide goes down, the lighthouse is festooned with fish of all kinds. There they hang, and the successful fisherman has nothing to do but to gather the spoils. Thus it was with us at first; we baited our hooks, and we drew in the fish without stint. But perhaps, later on, the lighthouse-keeper peers out from his tower, and he cannot see, for the fog is dense, the storm-cloud has settled down around his light, and the wind rages furiously. He is obliged to keep every door and window closed, or he could not live, and then he thinks it hard to be a lighthouse-keeper, and wishes himself ashore. We also are, at times, in a similar condition. We are asked, "Watchman! What of the night?" And the answer is, "No morning cometh, but the night thickens, and the darkness grows denser." We do not every day draw the net to land full of great fishes, but we experience dreary intervals of fruitless toil, and then it is no wonder that a man's spirit faints within him.

The natural wear and tear of an active life also tend to our running down. Some of our people think that we have little or nothing to do but to stand in the pulpit, and pour out a flood of words two or three times a week, but they ought to know that, if we did not spend much time in diligent study, they would get poverty-stricken sermons. I have heard of a brother who trusts in the Lord, and does not study, but I have also heard that his people do not trust in him. In fact, I am informed that they wish him to go elsewhere with his inspired discourses, for they say that, when he did study, his talk was poor enough, but now that he gives them that which comes first to his lips, it is altogether unbearable. If any man will preach as he should preach, his work will take more out of him than any other labour under heaven. If you and I attend to our work and calling, even among a few people, it will certainly produce a friction of soul and a wear of heart which will tell upon the strongest. I speak as one who knows by experience what it is to be utterly exhausted in the Master's service. No matter how willing we may be in spirit, the flesh is weak, and He who made a tender apology for His sleeping servants in the garden knows our frame, and remembers that we are dust. We need that the Master should say to us, every now and then, "Come ye yourselves apart into a desert place, and rest a while" (Mark 6:31), and He does say so, for He is not a hard taskmaster, and whoever may use the lash, and cause the weary steed to die in harness, our gentle Lord doth not so.

Besides this, we are very apt to run down through our duty becoming routine work, by reason of its monotony. Unless we are careful, we shall be likely to say to ourselves, "Monday evening here again, I must give an address at the prayer-meeting. Thursday evening, and I have to preach, although I have not yet a topic! Sunday morning, Sunday evening; I have to preach again! Yes, preach again! Then there are all those extra engagements; it is for ever preach, preach, preach! I am always preaching. What a weariness it is!" Preaching ought to be a joy, and yet it may become a task. Constant preaching should be constant enjoyment, and yet, when the brain is tired, pleasure flies. Like the sick boy in the prophet's day, we are ready to cry, "My head! my head!" We ask, "How can we keep up our freshness?" It is hard to produce so much with such scant leisure for reading. It is almost as bad as making bricks without straw. Nothing can maintain us in the freshness of our beginnings but the daily anointing of the Spirit.

I do not wonder that some brethren run down through want of association with others of warm heart and of kindred spirit. I will give you another lighthouse illustration; a gentleman, who called to see the keepers of a lone light, said to one of them, "I suppose, after all, you fellows are quite happy in this tower?" "We might be happy," replied the man, "if we had a chat with one another; but my mate and I have not exchanged a word with each other for

A New Departure

a month." If you are banished to a country place, where you have no superior or even equal mind to converse with, no intellectual or spiritual friend near at hand, I can feel for you. "Iron sharpeneth iron; so a man sharpeneth the countenance of his friend" (Prov. 27:17), and when that sharpening is missed, it is no marvel that the mind grows dull. We cannot live alone, brethren, and yet a dreadful solitude as to our higher cares is one of our sorest trials. Oh, for a twin spirit to converse with! The worst of it is that, if we have few to refresh us with their conversation, we have many to vex us with their chatter, and when we would fain be uplifted to noble themes, we find ourselves dragged down by the dreary gossip of a hamlet. What wonder if, with such surroundings, we lose force, and run down!

Yet, dear brethren, none of these things furnish us with an excuse for falling into a low state, and it may possibly be true that our mental decline is the result of our weak spiritual condition. It may be that we have left our first love, that we have wandered away from the simplicity of our faith, that we have backslidden in heart, and grieved the Holy Spirit, so that our God walks contrary to us because we walk contrary to Him. Perhaps the rain is withheld because prayer has been restrained, and the heavenly wind has ceased to blow because we have been too indolent to spread the sail. Has there been no unbelief to hinder the blessing? We often talk of unbelief as if it were an affliction to be pitied instead of a crime to be condemned. For us to give the lie to Him who has unveiled the secrets of His heart to us, and almost, I was about to say, gone out of His way to bless us in an extraordinary and unusual manner, must pain the great Father's heart. Perhaps we feel less love to Jesus than we once did, less zeal in doing His work, and less anguish for the souls of others. If so, it is no wonder that we enjoy less of the presence of God, and are soon cast down. If the root is not strong, how can the branches flourish?

May not self-indulgence have mixed with unbelief? Have we made provision for the flesh? Have we lost the intimacy with Jesus which we once enjoyed? Have we violated the consecration with which we started? If so, the blue mould will settle on the unsound place. Selfishness will mar our strength, and destroy our usefulness. I will not suppose that this is the case with any of you, or, at least, I will only suppose it, and let it remain a supposition.

The ill effects of decline

It is a dreadful fact that, sometimes, these runnings down end in a catastrophe. After secret backsliding comes a sin which is publicly reported, and men cry, "Shame!" Yet it is not that one sin, but the general state of the man's heart which is the saddest part of it. No man becomes bad all at once. True, the single lightning flash slew its victim, but the bolt had not fallen if there had been no previous gathering of the elements into the condition of storm. The overt scandal is only the development of what was in the man— the root of the evil lies deeper still. When we hear of a man who has ruined his character by a surprising act of folly, we may surmise, as a rule, that this mischief was but one sulphurous jet from a soil charged with volcanic fire, or, to change the figure, one roaring lion from a den of wild beasts. As you would, on your bended knees, cry day and night that no moral catastrophe may occur to you, beware of the sin which leads to it, beware of the backsliding which culminates in it; for if we have not the cause, the effect will not follow. The Lord will preserve us if, day by day, we cry unto Him to cleanse our way.

There is an evil under the sun which is as terrible as an open catastrophe—indeed, it works greater ill to the church in the long run—and that is, when a man's ministry is eaten through and through with spiritual dry rot.

I heard an old Indian describe the way in which furniture may be devoured by the white ants. The ants will come into the house,

A New Departure

and eat up everything, and yet, to all appearance, nothing is touched. The bookcases stand just where they did, and the trunks and everything else remain exactly as they were; at least, it is so to the eye, but directly they are touched, they all crumble to pieces, for the ants have eaten the substance out of them. In the same way, some men still remain in the ministry, and yet the soul of their ministry has gone. They have a name to live, yet they are dead. What can be worse than this condition? One might almost sooner have an explosion, and have done with it, than see men continuing to maintain the form of religion after vital godliness has gone, scattering death all around them, and yet maintaining what is called a respectable position. God save us from this last as much as from that first! If I am a rotten bough, let me be cut off, but to hang upon the tree, all verdant with parasitical lichen and moss, is deplorable. A respectable ministry, devoid of spiritual life, is little better than respectable damnation, from which may God deliver us.

When men drift into this condition, they generally adopt some expedient to hide it. Conscience suggests that there is something or other wrong, and the deceitful heart labours to conceal or palliate this fact. Some do this by amusing themselves with hobbies instead of preaching the gospel. They cannot do the Lord's work, so they try to do their own. They have not honesty enough to confess that they have lost gospel power, so they ride a hobby, and it is a very mild form of evil when they raise some side issue, which has no other fault about it than that it diverts them from the main point. Many are these playthings. I have no time to mention more than one.

I have known certain brethren give themselves solely to expound prophecy. Now, a man full of the life of God may expound prophecy as much as he likes, but there are some who, having lost their love of the gospel, try to win back what little popularity they once had by taking up with guesses at the future. They may be quite sure that, if they cannot profit men by bringing them to the manger and the cross, they will make a complete failure of it if they handle the seals and the vials. Did you ever notice, in Calvin's Commentaries, that there is no exposition of the Book of Revelation? Why not? He said, "I have not expounded that Book because I do not understand it."[1] When I hear a man say, "I have found much in Matthew which does not belong to the Church, I have outgrown much of the Romans and Galatians, and I cannot enjoy the Psalms, for they do not rise to the perfection of my experience; I want something more elevated and spiritual, more abstruse and wonderful," I conclude that this brother is spinning his last hank, and spending his last pennyworth of sense.

I have been amused by observing the manner in which speculators have been taken in when they have left the old ship of the gospel to become prophets. The beast of the Revelation was reported to be Napoleon I,[2] and then the creature suddenly reappeared in his nephew, Napoleon III.[3] By-and-by, the deadly wound was healed, and the Prince Imperial wore the dreadful honours of the prophetic book, but the prince is now dead, and it will be needful for the seers to invent a new theory. There is no fear but what they will do it before long, and, meanwhile, "our Israelitish origin" will do to fill up the time. In the story of Sindbad the Sailor, it is said that, as they sailed along, they saw an island, and at the sight thereof they greatly rejoiced. The crew left the ship, and feasted on the island, and were going to take possession of it in the name of the king, when suddenly it began to quiver and to plunge, and finally it went down altogether, for it was a whale's back, and not an island at all! I have known brethren disport themselves upon the back of some novel speculation, when suddenly

---

[1] I was unable to find this quote in Calvin.
[2] Napoleon Bonaparte (1769–1821) was a French military genius and political leader who came to prominence during the French Revolution. He occupied the position of Emperor of the French from 1804 to 1814 and again in 1815.
[3] Napoleon III (1808–1873) served as President of France from 1848 to 1852 and then as Emperor of the French from 1852 to 1870.

A New Departure

the facts of history have gone against them, and the whole thing has gone down very like a whale. I have mentioned one of the more harmless hobbies, but some have taken to fancies which have bred greater mischief. Speculation is an index of the spiritual poverty of the man who surrenders himself to it. His flour has all been used, so he tries plaster of Paris. He has no more gold or silver, so he coins the baser metals. He cannot prophesy after the measure of faith, so he exercises his immeasurable imagination. His own experience does not serve him with topics for his ministry, and therefore he takes airy flights into regions of which he knows nothing.

Far worse is it when a man so runs down in heart and spirit that he has no principles left, and believes nothing at all. He is a Baptist, but he would very cheerfully minister to a Paedo-baptist church. He is a Calvinist, but he is not narrow, and will promise to offend no one. He holds certain views, but "a view to the pastorate" is the chief of them, and in that view the salary is the charm. He boasts of possessing large-heartedness, and receptivity of spirit, and all that sort of thing. He has dry rot in his soul! That is the truth of the case, and he tries to cover it up with this nonsense! Such persons remind me of an advertisement of a school in France; its concluding paragraph was to this effect, "The pupils will be taught any religion which may be selected by their parents." It is abominable when ministers as good as say that any religion will be taught which may be selected by the deacons. "Pray inform me whether the church likes a high-toned Calvinism, or prefers Arminianism." It is with such as it was with the showman who exhibited the battle of Waterloo, and in answer to the question, "Which is Wellington, and which is Napoleon?" replied, "Whichever you please, my little dears; you pays your money, and you takes your choice." These broad-churchmen are prepared to supply any article for which there is a demand. This is a terrible condition of things, but men do not generally rest there; in the lowest depth, there is still a lower deep.

When the heart has got out of order, and the spiritual life has run down, men soon fall into actual doctrinal error, not so much because their head is wrong, for many of them have not erred very much there, but because their heart is in an ill condition. We should never have known that some men had brains at all if they had not addled them. Such departers from the faith usually fall by little and little. They begin by saying very little concerning grace. They serve out homoeopathic doses of gospel. It is marvellous what a very small globule of the gospel will save a soul, and it is a great mercy that it is so, or few would be saved. These snatches of gospel, and the preacher who gives them, remind us of the famous dog of the Nile, of whom the ancients said that he was so afraid of the crocodiles that he drank of the river in a great hurry, and was away from it directly. These intellectual gentry are so afraid of the critical crocodiles that the moment they touch the living water of the gospel they are away again. Their doubts are stronger than their beliefs. The worst of it is that they not only give us very little gospel, but they give us much that is not the gospel. In this they are like mosquitoes, of whom I have often said that I do not mind their taking a little of my blood, but it is the poison which they put into me which is my great cause of quarrel with them. That a man should rob me of the gospel, is bad enough, but that he should impregnate me with his poisonous doctrine, is intolerable.

When men lose all love to the gospel, they try to make up for the loss of its attractions by sparkling inventions of their own. They imitate life by the artificial flash of culture, reminding me of the saline crystals which cover the salt deserts. There is a lifeless plain, in the heart of Persia, so sterile and accursed that even saline plants do not thrive, "but the salt itself, as if in bitter mockery, fashions its crystals in the form of stems and stalks, and covers the steppe with a carpet of unique vegetation, glittering and glistening

A New Departure

like an enchanted prairie in the dazzling light of the Eastern sun." Woe be unto the poor congregations who behold this substitute for life, this saline efflorescence of dainty errors and fascinating inventions. Alas, whatever a man may now propound, he will find learned personages to support him in it.

Fontenelle[4] used to say that, if he could only get six philosophers to write in its favour, people could be made to believe that the sun is not the source of light and heat, and I think there is a great deal of truth in the remark. We are told, "Well, he is a very learned man, he is a Fellow of Brazenface College, and he has written a book in which he upsets the old dogmas." If a learned man writes any nonsense, of course it will have a run, and there is no opinion so insane but, if it has the patronage of so-called scientific men, it will be believed in certain quarters. I have myself watched the labours of novelists in theology, and have tried to get what I could out of their books, but I have been struck with the remarkably poor results of their lucubrations. I have stood by the shore at Mentone, and seen fishermen with miles of line, and a vast net buoyed up by great tubs, visible far out at sea. A dozen men are hauling at one rope, and as many more are pulling in another, drawing this great net to land. Pull away! Ahoy! Pull away at the ropes, and bring the fish to land. I believe that, on one occasion, I did see them produce a fish not so long as my little finger, but that was a rather successful occasion!

Our German friends have diligently made vast nets with which they have enclosed the sea of thought, and upon drawing them out, what a noise there has been, and what a sensation, and what a trembling and a fainting among the old ladies of Christendom, but when we have seen their mighty catch, it has not been the tenth part of a sardine! The next philosopher who came along, has

---

[4] Bernard Le Bovier de Fontenelle (1657–1757) was a French scientist, mathematician, and author.

fitted on his spectacles with due gravity, after wiping them most solemnly, and then he has put his critical fork into this small fish, and, holding it up to be admired of all, he has discoursed upon its species, till another philosopher equally wise has declared that it was rotten, and pitched it back into the deeps. This kind of game is continually going on, and many young ministers have been fools enough to give up the apostolic fishery to join in this stupid waste of mental effort. What have they ever done, these doubters, since the world began? What will they do? What can they do? All that they can do now is to wriggle into our churches, and hiss from pulpits which were once filled by the orthodox. They cannot build places of worship of their own—they could not build a mousetrap. As a rule, there is not power enough in their teaching to gather a congregation, or to keep one when it is gathered. All the vitality, force, and energy they possess are spent, cuckoo-like, in laying their eggs in the nests which we take the trouble to fashion, for they cannot build their own.

God forbid that we should ever try to cover our decline of heart by the invention of our self-conceit! I hope that, when our ministry begins to lose power, we shall be driven to our knees, and to our God, that He may quicken us again by His good Spirit.

The need for renewal
Perhaps I have spoken at too great length upon the former part of my subject. I now propose to dwell upon the necessity of renewing grace. If any of us have come down from the heights, it is time that we returned to them again. If we have fallen from our first love, it is most needful that we should at once renew the ardour of our youth. If we have gone down even in a small degree, it behooves us to ask for help to get back what we have lost.

This is necessary on account of our own happiness, for I appeal to any brother who declines in heart, and grows weak in faith, and doubtful in spirit, whether he is not unhappy. Do you not derive

A New Departure

the purest joy and the most solid satisfaction from walking with God? Indeed, those who are "called to be saints" are doomed to be unhappy apart from Christ. It is a doom which destiny has fixed upon you that, if you depart from Christ, you must depart into hell, for it is hell for you to depart from Christ. If, therefore, in any measure, you have roamed away from Christ, mind that you fly home again to Him at once.

Last year, when sojourning in the South of France, I went for a mountain ride to the foot of Castiglione, an old, half-deserted town. It was clear and bright at the time, and while the friends who were with me went up the hill to survey the place, I remained a little lower down. I soon observed that the clouds were coming from the other side of the mountains, and in a few minutes I was in a fog, chilled to the bone. I could just see Mentone under the bottom of the clouds, and I said to my man-servant, "Get the horses in, for I must get down again into the sun at once." Soon, the fog was all round me, and I hastened to descend until I reached the sunlight again. You must feel like that, my brethren. If you are caught in a mist, and a chill is upon you, you must hurry back to Christ. You may joyfully repose in Him, and find every blessing and comfort surrounding you, but if you have climbed into high notions, and entered upon the cold regions of speculation, you must hasten down again. You must say of the old gospel, "I can see the blessed spot of my repose, and I will get back to it at once." This is wise advice for those who are conscious of lost comfort through leaving the good old way.

We cannot afford, I am sure, to be in a state of running down, for we were never too much alive. Our shortcomings, at our best, are quite sufficient to warn us against what we should be if we were worse. I can imagine some men losing a part of their courage, and yet remaining brave; but if any of mine were to evaporate, I should be a coward indeed. There would have been power in Calvin even if half the steadfastness of his mind had gone, for he was a man of mighty faith; but if I were to lose any measure of my faith, I should be a sorry unbeliever, for I have not a grain of faith to spare.

Dear brethren, have we ever reached our right condition as compared with our early ideal of what we hoped to be? Do you recollect when you first entered the College or the ministry? Do you remember what a high standard you set up for yourself? You did well to fix the mark high, for, if you aim at the moon, you will shoot higher than if you fired at a bush. You did well to have a high standard, but you do not well to fall short of it, and, yet, who does not fall short even of his own ideal? Do you not wish to hide your head when you contrast yourself with your Lord? He saved others, and therefore could not save Himself, but we are keen to guard ourselves and our reputations, and often act as if we thought self-preservation the highest law of nature. Our Lord endured great contradiction of sinners against Himself, while we are provoked if we are thwarted in any degree. He loved His sheep, and followed them when they went astray, but we have far too little pity even upon those who gather at our call. We are far, far, far below the true glory of the well-beloved, and even fall short of our poor ideal of Him. Neither in private in His prayers, nor in public in His life, or His ministry, or His teaching, do we approximate to Him so nearly as we should, and yet, to fall short of likeness to Him, ought to make us blush and weep. We cannot afford, therefore, to run down.

Indeed, if we do not compare ourselves with our Master, but only with our brother-ministers (for certain of them have done right noble work for Jesus), we shall come to the same conclusion. Some of our brethren have held on under fearful discouragements, serving the Lord faithfully; others have won souls for Christ, to whom the winning of one soul has cost more self-denial than the winning of hundreds has cost certain of us. I could sit with delight at the feet of such consecrated brethren as I am now thinking of, and look up to them, and glorify God in them. Such have been found among men of inferior abilities, slender powers, and small attainments, but how they have worked, and how they have prayed, and how God has blessed them! It may be that, with ten times their ability and opportunity, we have not done anything like as much as they have. Do we not mourn over this? Can we afford to decline?

The need for restoration
Beloved brethren, we cannot afford to remain in any state lower than the very best, for, if so, our work will not be well done. Time was when we preached with all our might. When we began to preach, what preaching it was for zeal and life! In looking back, it must increase our self-humiliation if we perceive that, in our younger days, we were more real and intense than we are now. We preach much better, so the critics say; and we know that there is more thought and more accuracy in our sermons, and that we use better elocution than we did in our young days; but where are the tears of our early ministry? Where is the heart-break of those first sermons in our first sphere? Where is the passion, where is the self-annihilation that we often felt when we poured out our very life with every syllable we spoke? Now, sometimes, we go into the pulpit resolved that we will do as we did then, just as Samson went out to shake himself as he had done aforetime. He had snapped the cords and bands before, and he was going to do the same again, but the Lord had departed from him, and he was weak as another man. Brethren, what if the Lord should depart from us? Alas for us, and for our work!

Nothing can be done if the Holy Spirit be withdrawn, indeed, nothing truly good will be attempted. I have marvelled at the way in which certain persons avoid preaching the gospel when they profess to be doing it. They get a text which you think must cut into the conscience, and they contrive to speak so as neither to arouse the careless nor distress the self-confident. They play with the sword of the Spirit as if they were mountebanks at a show, instead of thrusting the two-edged sword into the hearts of men, as soldiers do in actual combat. The Emperor Gallienus,[5] when a man hurled a javelin many times at a bull without hitting him, and the people hissed him, called the performer to his seat, and placed a wreath on his head, saying, "You are most clever to be able to miss so large a mark so many times." What shall we twine into a crown for those ministers who never strike the heart, never convince men of sin, never drive a Pharisee out of his own righteousness, never influence the guilty so that he casts himself as a lost sinner at the feet of Jesus? He may expect one day to be crowned with shame for such a crime. Meanwhile, twine the deadly nightshade about his brows. Be it ours to be like the left-handed men of Benjamin who "could sling stones at an hair breadth, and not miss" (Judg. 20:16). We cannot reach to this unless the life of God be in us and abound.

A man ought to take care of himself, merely as a man, for the sake of himself and his household, but much more should a man, who is a minister, take care of himself for the sake of those who are committed to his charge. A captain in the South Seas was observed to go beyond the usual point for turning into the harbour, taking a longer but a safer course. On someone remarking to him that he was too careful, he replied, "I have so many souls on board, I cannot afford to run any risk." How many souls there are on board of some of our vessels! How many souls—ay, notwithstanding that the doctrine is unfashionable, I repeat it—how many souls, not of creatures which will die out like cats and dogs, but of priceless, immortal beings, are committed to our charge. Since, upon our ministry, under God, hang everlasting things—life and

---

[5] Emperor Gallienus (218-268 AD) was Emperor of Rome from 253 AD until his death.

A New Departure

death, Heaven and hell—what manner of persons ought we to be? How careful we ought to be as to our inner health! How anxious to be always at our very best! If I were a surgeon, and I had to operate upon a patient, I should not like to touch either the knife or his flesh if I felt bilious, or if my hand was quivering. I would not like to be in any but the calmest, coolest, most forceful condition, at the moment in which the difference of a hair's breadth might touch a vital chord, and end a precious life. God help all soul-physicians to be always at their best!

I believe the headway of God's cause in the world depends upon our being in prime condition. We are come to the kingdom for such a time as this. As much as ever Simon Menno[6] was raised up to preach believers' baptism in Holland, and keep the lamp burning for God there, and as surely as ever, in our own land, such men as Hansard Knollys, and Kiffin, and Keach,[7] and the like, were bold to stand the brunt of the battle for the Lord, so I believe that you are intended to be in lineal succession defenders of the purest form of gospel truth. We have it in charge to pass on to the next age the everlasting gospel which our venerable sires have handed down to us. As Neander[8] said, there is a future for the Baptists. There is a future for any church which has faithfully kept the ordinances of God, and is resolved in all things to be obedient to its covenant Head. We have neither prestige, nor wealth, nor the state at our back, but we have something better than all these.

When a Spartan was asked what were the boundaries of his country, he replied, "The limits of Sparta are marked by the

---

[6] Menno Simons (1496-1561) was a prominent Anabaptist leader.

[7] Hansard Knollys, (1599-1691), William Kiffin (1616-1701), and Benjamin Keach (1640-1704) were all prominent Particular Baptist ministers in London in the seventeenth century and were each original signatories of the Second London Baptist Confession of 1689. Benjamin Keach was also one of Spurgeon's predecessors, pastoring the church at Horsleydown, Southwark (which after a few name changes became the Metropolitan Tabernacle) for thirty-six years from 1668-1704.

[8] August Neander (1791-1850) was a well-known German church historian.

points of our spears." The limit of our church is also determined by the points of our spears, but our weapons are not carnal. Wherever we go, we preach Christ crucified, and His word of solemn proclamation, "He that believeth and is baptized shall be saved" (Mark 16:16). The enquirer turned, and said to the Spartan, "You have no walls to Sparta." "No," he replied, "the walls of Sparta are the breasts of her sons." We have no defences for our churches, either in Acts of Parliament or enforced creeds, but the regenerated hearts and consecrated spirits of men, who resolve to live and die in the service of King Jesus, have hitherto sufficed, in the hands of the Spirit, to preserve us from grievous heresy. I see no beginning to this business, this battle of truth commenced so long ago; and I see no end to it, except the coming of the Master and the eternal victory. Yet some trembling persons say we ought to stop, and let the young men already in College learn a trade, and forego the ministry, lest England should become over-ministered, and they add that there is no use in preparing men for the foreign fields, for the Missionary Society is in debt, and its expenses must be curtailed. God bless the Missionary Society! But the condition of a society is not the limit of our personal endeavour; besides, the society will soon throw off its burden. If you, my brethren, are worthy of your calling, you will be bravely independent, and not hang too much upon the help of others. Sparta could not have been defended by a race of timid creatures armed with pointless spears, neither can young men of timorous spirit do great things for God. You must be braced to heroism, brethren, if you are to meet the demands of the hour. May God make the feeblest among you as David, and the house of David as God! (Zech. 12:8).

The need for revival
I have a proposal to make before I come to my conclusion, and it is this: let this be the time of renewal to each one of us. Let us each seek for a personal revival by the Divine Spirit.

A New Departure

We shall see that it is a fit time if we take an outlook upon our own nation. Politically, we have come back to a condition in which there will be a respect for righteousness, justice, and truth, rather than for self-assertion, and national gain, and conquest. We shall, I trust, no longer be steered by a false idea of British interests, and the policy which comes of it, but by the great principles of right, justice, and humanity. This is all I want to see: parties, as such, are nothing to us, nor individual statesmen, except so far as they represent right principles. We are for those who are on the side of justice, peace, and love. And now, instead of lying still year after year, and making no progress—no laws amended, no home legislation attended to, but time wasted upon glittering foreign adventures—something will be done that is worth doing.

At this period, also, our schools are educating the people, and I thank God for that. Though education will not save men, it may be a means to that end, for when all our peasants can read their Bibles, we may surely hope that God will bless His own Word. It will be a grand thing for all our agricultural labourers, by going to the New Testament for themselves, to escape from receiving their religion at second-hand. Godly people must take care to supply them with good books, and so feed the new appetite with healthy food. All light is good, and we, who most of all prize the light of revelation, are on the side of all kinds of true light. God is raising up the people, and I think our time is come to avail ourselves of their advance, and as our one business is to preach Jesus Christ, the more we keep to our work the better, for true religion is the strength of a nation, and the foundation of all right government.

Whatsoever things are honest, true, kind, humane, and moral, may reckon on our aid. We are on the side of temperance, and therefore on the side of the limitation of the abominable traffic which is ruining our country, and we are opposed to all that licenses vice among men, or allows cruelty to animals. We are up to the hilt advocates of peace, and we earnestly war against war. I wish that Christian men would insist more and more on the unrighteousness of war, believing that Christianity means no sword, no cannon, no bloodshed, and that, if a nation is driven to fight in its own defence, Christianity stands by to weep and to intervene as soon as possible, and not to join in the cruel shouts which celebrate an enemy's slaughter. Let us always be on the side of right. Today, then, my brethren, I beg you to join with me in seeking renewal. Now is the time for a man to buckle on his harness, and bestir himself.

Surely our holy fellowship at this happy hour should help us all to rise to a higher level. The sight of many of our brethren is cheering and stimulating. When I remember concerning some their holiness, their depth of piety, their perseverance, I feel comforted in the belief that, if the Lord has strengthened others, He has yet a blessing in reserve for us also. Let this Feast of Tabernacles be the time for renewing our vows of consecration unto the Lord our God.

The need for repentance
Let us begin it with repentance for all our mistakes and shortcomings. Let each one do this for himself. You remember how the ancient giant fought with Hercules, and the hero could not overcome him, because every time he fell he touched his mother earth, and received new strength. Let us, too, fall upon our faces, that we may rise invigorated. Let us go back to our first simple faith, and recover our lost strength. Men who have been sore sick have cried, "Take me back to my native air, and I shall soon be well. Among the buttercups and daisies of the meadows, in which I used to play when I was a child, and near the brook where I caught the minnows, I shall soon revive." Ah! it does our soul good to get back to our days of child-like faith, when we sang,

A New Departure

> Just as I am,—without one plea
> But that Thy blood was shed for me,
> And that Thou bidd'st me come to Thee,
> O Lamb of God, I come.⁹

This will help you to renew your youth. It seems an easy way, but it is the only way.

The need for recommission
Next, let us renew our consecration. I do not invite any of you literally to stain the door-post of the College with your blood, but I ask you to think upon that Israelitish slave whose time had run out, but who chose to remain in service because he loved his master and his master's children, and therefore he put his ear against the post of the door, and they bored it through with an awl. May the Lord bore the ear of each of us, that we may be His servants for ever! We love our Master, do we not, brethren? We love our Master's work, and we love our Master's servants and His children, and for His sake we will serve them all, for better or worse, till death doth part us from this lower service. Oh, to get back to the old moorings! I would like for us to preach our old sermons. I do not mean the same sermons, but with the same force as when we began to,

> Tell to sinners round,
> What a dear Saviour we had found.¹⁰

People said, "That dear young man does not know very much, but he loves Jesus Christ, and he talks about nothing else." I would

---

⁹ Charlotte Elliot, "Just As I Am" in *"Our Own Hymn-book": A Collection of Psalms and Hymns for Public, Social, and Private Worship*, ed. C. H. Spurgeon (London: Passmore and Alabaster, 1866), #546.
¹⁰ John Cennick, "The Way" in *"Our Own Hymn-book"*, ed. C. H. Spurgeon, #408.

Servants of Christ, Lovers of Men

like to preach again as I did at first, only a great deal better. I intensely believed and meant every word I spoke. I do so now, but doubts will arise now which never vexed me then. I would like to be a child again before the Lord, and to keep so, for I am sure that questions and doubts are a sad loss to any man.

Return, my brethren, to your earliest Bible readings, when you were wont to let the promise lie under your tongue as a dainty morsel. Ah! This Book, as I turn it over, wakes up many a memory. Its pages glow with a light which I cannot describe, for they are set with stars which in my many hours of gloom have been the light of my soul. I did not then read this divine volume to find a text, but to hear my Lord speak to my own heart. I was not then as Martha, cumbered with much serving, but as Lazarus, who sat at the table with Jesus.

God grant us also a revival of the first aims of our spiritual career. Then, we thought nothing of pleasing men, but only aimed at pleasing God and winning souls. We were rash enough to care for nothing but the fulfilment of our mission. Is it so now? We can preach now, can we not? We feel that we are proficient in our art. It might be better if we did not feel quite so well equipped. I find it better to go to the pulpit in prayerful weakness than in self-reliant strength. When I groan out, "What a fool I am!" and come down, after the sermon, ashamed of my poor attempt, I am sure it is better with me than when I am pleased with my performance. Are any of us such babies as to feel like that? What a sense of responsibility we had in our first services. Do we retain that solemnity of spirit? We then prayed about the choice of every hymn, and the manner of reading the Scriptures. We did nothing carelessly, for a heavy anxiety pressed upon us. I always read the Scripture carefully at home, and tried to understand it before I read it to the people, and I thus formed a habit from which I have never swerved, but it is not so with all. Some say, "I have been about all the day, and I have to preach tonight, but I can manage." Yes, but

A New Departure

it will not please God for us to offer Him that which costs us nothing. Others have a stock of sermons, and I have heard that, just before the time for entering the pulpit, they turn over their precious manuscripts, pick out a likely one, and without further preparation read it as God's message to the people. The Lord deliver us from a state of mind in which we dare to put on the table of shewbread the first loaf which comes to hand! No, let us serve the Lord with growing carefulness and reverence.

It would be well for many to get back to their first prayers and watchfulness, and all else that is good.

A recovery is possible

Can it be done? Brother, it can be done. You can have all the life you had, and more, by the blessing of the Holy Spirit. You can be as intense as you ever were. I have seen old horses turned out to grass, and come back fresh and vigorous. I know a pasture wherein, if a worn-out steed doth graze, it shall come back to be harnessed to the gospel chariot with strength renewed. Let us remember those hallowed spots where Jesus has met with us in former days, where, or ever we were aware, our soul was made "like the chariots of Amminadib" (Song of Sg. 6:12). Lord, renew Thy former mercies, and we shall rise, like the phoenix, from our ashes!

It may cost you a great deal to be set right again. John Bunyan speaks of the pilgrim who lost his roll, and had to go back for it, so that he travelled three times over the road, and then found the sun setting ere he reached his lodging. But cost us whatever it may, we must get right with God. I read a dream, the other day, which was the means of a man's conversion. He thought that he was going with his friend into one of the Eastern towns, and as he was about to enter, the portcullis above the gate began to fall. As it descended, he stooped, but it fell so fast that he could not get through, stooping, kneeling, crouching, or even lying down. He felt that he must enter, so he made a desperate effort. He had on a very fine laced vest, and he pulled that off, but the portcullis still descended, till he found that the only thing he could do was to strip himself, and then, close to the earth, and grazed by the gravel, he crept through. When he was safely inside the gate, a shining one covered him from head to foot with glittering garments. It may be that, in order to get right with God, we shall have to part with that fine vest, that splendid theory, that love of popularity, that rhetorical flourishing; but, oh! if we once get through that gate, and God covers us with the robe of acceptance in the Beloved, it will well repay us for anything that the struggle may cost us.

I am sorry to say that I am made of such ill stuff that my Lord has to chasten me often and sorely. I am like a quill pen that will not write unless it be often nibbed, and therefore I have felt the sharp knife many times, and yet I shall not regret my pains and crosses so long as my Lord will write with me on men's hearts. That is the cause of many ministers' afflictions; they are necessary to our work. You have heard the fable of the raven that wished to drink, but the pitcher had so little water in it that he could not reach it, and therefore he took stone after stone, and dropped them into the vessel until the water rose to the brim, and he could drink. There is so little grace, in some men, that they need many sicknesses, bereavements, and other afflictions to make their graces available for usefulness. If, however, we receive grace enough to bear fruit without continual pruning, so much the better.

It is expected of us, brethren, that from this time we rise to a higher point. It is the Lord's due, if we think of what He has done for us. Some of my comrades in arms, now before me, have gone through battles as hard as any men may wish to fight, and after such success as they have had, they must never say die. After what the Lord has done for us, we must never strike our flag, nor turn

A New Departure

our backs in the day of battle. Sir Francis Drake,[11] when it was feared that he would be wrecked in the Thames, said, "What! have I been round the world, and am I now to be drowned in a ditch? Not I." So say I to you, brethren, you have done business in stormy waters, and will you sink in a village pond? We shall not be worse treated than we have been. We are now in fine fighting trim, for we are hardened by former blows. A great pugilist at Rome was so battered, his nose, eyes, and face were so disfigured, that he was always ready to fight, because he said, "I cannot look worse than I do." Personally, I am in much the same plight. Men cannot say anything worse of me than they have said. I have been belied from head to foot, and misrepresented to the last degree. My good looks are gone, and none can damage me much now.

Some of you have had more to batter you than you are ever likely to endure again. You have had trial and tribulation and affliction as heavy as you can have them, and after having stood in the lists so long, surely you are not going to yield, and slink away like cowards? God forbid it! God forbid it! God grant, on the contrary, that the elder ones among you may have the pleasure, not only of winning battles for Christ, but of seeing others, who have been saved under your instrumentality, trained to fight for Jesus better than you yourselves have fought! The other day, I read a story, and with that I will conclude, desiring that I may, in spiritual things, have the same joy myself, and that it may be the lot of you all. Diagoras the Rhodian[12] had, in his time, won many wreaths at the Olympian games. He had two boys, and he brought them up to the same profession. The day came when his own force abated, and he was no longer able to strive for masteries in his own person; but he went up to the Olympian games with his two sons. He saw

---

[11] Sir Francis Drake (1540-1596) was an English explorer who famously circumnavigated the world in a single expedition.

[12] Diagoras of Rhodes was a famous Greek boxer who competed in the Olympic games in the fifth century BC.

the blows they gave and received, and rejoiced when he discovered that they were both victorious. A Lacedaemonian said to him, "You may die now, Diagoras," meaning that the old man might be content to die, because he had, in his own person, and in that of his sons, obtained the highest honours. The old man seemed to feel that it was even so, for when his two sons came, and shouldered their father, and carried him through the arena amid the ringing cheers of the great assembly, the old man, flushed with excitement, died under the eyes of the assembled Greeks. It would have been a wiser thing to have lived, for he had a third son, who became more renowned than the other two, but he passed away on a wave of victory. O brethren, may you have spiritual children who shall win battles for the Lord, and may you live to see them doing it. Then may you say, with old Simeon, "Lord, now lettest Thou Thy servant depart in peace, according to Thy Word" (Luke 2:29).

In the Name of the Ever-blessed, we this day again set up our banners. Our watchword is "Victory." We mean to win for the grand old cause of Puritanism, Protestantism, Calvinism—all poor names which the world has given to our great and glorious faith—the doctrine of Paul the apostle, the gospel of our Lord and Saviour Jesus Christ. We can both strike, and bear the strokes which are returned. Through Divine grace, we have given to us both energy and patience. We can work, and we can wait. May the Divine life in us put forth its mightiest force, and make us strong to the utmost of human possibility, and then we shall gain the victory, and give all the glory of it to our omnipotent Leader. The Lord be with you, beloved! Amen.

Scripture Index

Old Testament

Genesis
- 4:13 215
- 27:20 75
- 42:36 128

Exodus
- 13:21 33
- 14:15 207
- 16:15 99
- 27:20 77
- 28:33 34
- 28:34 34

Leviticus
- 21:17–20 33

Numbers
- 13:33 124

Joshua
- 5:14 170

Judges
- 6:14 83
- 20:16 250

1 Samuel
- 2:17 34
- 30:6 128

1 Kings
- 18:24 154
- 19:9 139

Job
- 1:2 28
- 39:14–17 158

Psalms
- 38:13–14 182
- 121:1 74

Proverbs
- 16:28 192
- 26:17 202
- 27:2 218
- 27:17 239

Ecclesiastes
- 7:21 181
- 7:22 182

Song of Solomon
- 6:12 257

Isaiah
- 6:8 42
- 14:10 20
- 33:15 182
- 40:31 .... 169, 236
- 41:15 124
- 52:11 34
- 58:1 64
- 62:6 45

Jeremiah
- 1:4–10 43
- 3:15 45
- 13:17 80
- 15:19 45
- 23:4 45
- 23:21–22 56
- 23:32 42

Ezekiel
- 2:1–3 43
- 3:1–4 43
- 3:17 159
- 33:6 177

Daniel
 12:3 21

Zechariah
 4:6 130
 12:8 252

Scripture Index

New Testament

Matthew
- 2:9 33
- 5:4 118
- 6:29 99
- 6:31–32 185
- 11:27 224
- 22:37 208

Mark
- 3:13 46
- 6:31 .... 125, 238
- 16:16 252

Luke
- 2:29 260

John
- 3:7 17

Acts
- 5:31 128
- 6:4 72
- 9:15 45
- 13:2 229
- 14:15 144
- 18:14–15 183
- 20:28 45

Romans
- 7:24 223

1 Corinthians
- 1:1 44
- 4:1 44
- 9:11 41
- 9:22 217
- 14:20 212
- 14:34 41

2 Corinthians
- 1:3–4 129
- 2:15 45
- 2:16 119
- 4:1 42
- 5:18 44
- 5:19 44
- 5:20 44
- 6:3 36
- 6:3–10 69

Galatians
- 1:1 45

Ephesians
- 4:11 45

Colossians
- 3:16 211

1 Thessalonians
- 5:17 74

2 Thessalonians
- 1:7 53
- 1:8 53

1 Timothy
- 2:12 41
- 3:1-7 12
- 3:2–7 54
- 4:7 105
- 4:14–15 203
- 5:18 41

2 Timothy
- 2:1 53
- 2:4 41
- 2:21 45

Titus
- 1:5-9 12
- 1:6–9 54
- 1:7 44

Hebrews
- 8:10 97

13:8 169
James
  3:7–8 187
  5:7 165
1 Peter
  5:2 41

2 Peter
  1:10 17
Revelation
  1:16 218
  2:1 44
  22:17 41

www.ingramcontent.com/pod-product-compliance
Lightning Source LLC
Chambersburg PA
CBHW020441110526
44587CB00038B/772